Basil T. A. Evetts, Ernest Babelon

Manual of Oriental Antiquities

Including the architecture, sculpture and industrial arts of Chaldaea, Assyria, Persia,

Syria, Judaea, Phoenicia and Carthage

Basil T. A. Evetts, Ernest Babelon

Manual of Oriental Antiquities
Including the architecture, sculpture and industrial arts of Chaldaea, Assyria, Persia, Syria, Judaea, Phoenicia and Carthage

ISBN/EAN: 9783337227180

Printed in Europe, USA, Canada, Australia, Japan

Cover: Foto ©Andreas Hilbeck / pixelio.de

More available books at **www.hansebooks.com**

MANUAL

OF

ORIENTAL ANTIQUITIES

INCLUDING THE

Architecture, Sculpture, and Industrial Arts

OF

CHALDÆA, ASSYRIA, PERSIA, SYRIA, JUDÆA,
PHŒNICIA, AND CARTHAGE.

BY

ERNEST BABELON,

Librarian of the Department of Medals and Antiques in the
Bibliothèque Nationale, Paris.

TRANSLATED AND ENLARGED BY

B. T. A. EVETTS, M.A.,

Of the Department of Egyptian and Assyrian Antiquities, British Museum.

With Two Hundred and Forty-one Illustrations.

NEW YORK: G. P. PUTNAM'S SONS.
LONDON: H. GREVEL & CO.
1889.

PREFACE.

THE domain which we are about to tra-
verse in this little work embraces all
the civilisations of the ancient East except
that of Egypt. It includes the Chaldæans,
the Assyrians, the Persians before Alexander,
the Hittites of Syria, Cappadocia, and Asia
Minor, the Jews, the Phœnicians, and even
Cyprus, ending with the Carthaginians and
their colonies. So vast a field, which, in the
monumental work of MM. G. Perrot and
C. Chipiez, occupies four volumes, can only
be explored here in a summary manner, and
the author claims no more than to have
written a modest abridgment. It must not be
supposed, however, in spite of the diversity
and remoteness from one another of the
peoples that we have just enumerated, that
the subject lacks cohesion and unity. If
the reader will have the goodness to follow
us to the conclusion, he will be, on the con-

b

trary, struck by the perfect homogeneity of the book and the connection of all its parts. The picture, so to speak, contains many figures, but all concur in a common action, and the spectator grasps, at the first glance, the harmony of the composition.

For, in these old Eastern civilisations which held sway over the world before Greece and Rome, only two streams of artistic influence are really to be traced—that which rises in Egypt and that which issues from Assyria. Often they took a parallel course, side by side, sharing like brothers the empire of the arts; sometimes they opposed or obstinately excluded one another; or else they joined forces, mingled closely with one another, and united their original capacities in a common fund. But if these varying conditions produced in certain countries a local and indigenous art which is neither purely Egyptian nor purely Assyrian, we can always decompose its elements and make a chemical analysis of it, so to speak; and, when we have restored to Egypt that which properly belongs to her, and to Assyria all that has been borrowed from her, we perceive that nothing remains at the bottom of the crucible. Thus it may be said that, properly speaking, there is no Persian art, or Hittite art, or Jewish art, or Phœnician or Carthaginian art; everywhere we find the forms of Egypt or those of Assyria grouped, mixed, perhaps altered, in proportions which vary according to time, environment, and political conditions.

Leaving Egypt on one side, it is the Asiatic, or, more strictly, the Chaldæo-Assyrian stream that we have undertaken to study exclusively. We see it at its source, almost on the site of that Garden of Eden where Genesis and the Chaldæan legends place the ancestors of mankind; we follow it into Assyria, and observe its progress and transformations. Before long it overflows and passes on all sides beyond the limits of the basin of the Tigris and Euphrates; on one side, in Persia, it invades the palaces of Susa and Persepolis; on the other side, among the Hittites, the Aramæan populations of Syria, and the Jews, it spreads and divides into many rivulets, until it arrives at the frontier of Egypt and the heart of Asia Minor. Far from losing itself in the waves of the Mediterranean, it reaches all the shores of that great lake, Cyprus,

Sicily, Africa, Spain ; even passing beyond the
Pillars of Hercules.

It seemed to us, then, that it would be a
work of interest to draw a picture of Chaldæo-
Assyrian art not only in its native country
where it develops at its ease, but in its
many ramifications among the neighbouring
nations where it comes into collision with its
rival and is interpreted by foreigners, until the
day when Greece snatches the torch of the arts
from the failing hand of the East.   This Asiatic
art, as we shall see, has no cause to be ashamed
by the side of the Egyptian art.   Chaldæa
possesses a genius as spontaneous as that of
Egypt, and the valley of the Euphrates is not
less fertile than that of the Nile.   The ambi-
tions of her architects and sculptors were as
high and noble as those of the artists who
flourished at the court of the Pharaohs, and the
staged towers were the equals of the Pyramids.
Both nations pursued an ideal which contains a part of the truth, for in making a
building colossal and imposing by its size,
they thought that they attained to supreme
greatness and perfection.   The Greeks, through
their greater refinement, did not fall into these

excesses. But who will ever be able to say how much the powerful originality of the Hellenic genius borrowed from the imperfect models furnished by Egypt and Assyria? Who will ever be able to define with clearness and precision the kind of influence which Chaldæo-Assyrian art, in particular, imported by the ships of Phœnicia into all maritime countries, had on the origin of art in that younger civilisation of which Athens was the centre?

The ancient peoples of Asia, which form a compact group from the point of view of the history and development of the arts, are also akin in the complete destruction which has overtaken their architectural monuments. As if by a providential chastisement, from the table-land of Iran to the Pillars of Hercules, at Susa, at Babylon, at Nineveh, as at Jerusalem, Tyre, Carthage, and Gades, nothing is left of those temples, palaces, and towers which threw a challenge in the face of Heaven, and which wore out so many generations of slaves in the building of them. While the Pyramids still rise opposite to the Parthenon, and our astonishment is still excited by the imposing ruins of Egypt, Greece and Rome, nothing remains of the grand monuments which were the pride of the capitals of Asia. Everywhere we have to dig into the bowels of the earth and uncover the base of crumbled walls. Everything is reduced to dust like the image with the feet of clay, and a shroud of ashes covers that world the material culture of which is to be brought to life again, as far as possible, in the following pages.

In the present English edition, M. Babelon's work has been somewhat enlarged, and occasionally revised. Mr. Le Page Renouf has kindly looked through the proofs.

TABLE OF CONTENTS.

CHAPTER I.

CHALDÆAN ART.

CHAPTER II.

ASSYRIAN ARCHITECTURE.

CHAPTER III.

ASSYRIAN SCULPTURE AND PAINTING.

CHAPTER IV.

THE INDUSTRIAL ARTS IN ASSYRIA.

CONTENTS.

CHAPTER V.

PERSIAN ART.

CHAPTER VI.

THE HITTITES.

CHAPTER VII.

JEWISH ART.

CHAPTER VIII.

THE ART OF PHŒNICIA AND CYPRUS.

LIST OF ILLUSTRATIONS.

ERRATA.

Page 5, *for* "between every thirtieth course," *read* "at every," etc.

„ 31, *for* "Amathonte," *read* "Amathus."

ORIENTAL ANTIQUITIES.

CHAPTER I.

CHALDÆAN ART.

THE extensive region of Western Asia to which the Greeks gave the name of Mesopotamia was already, at the period which lies farthest back among the memories of mankind, the centre of a mighty civilisation rivalling that of Egypt, and disputing with the latter the glory of having formed the cradle of the arts in the ancient East. Babylon and Nineveh were by turns, according to the course of political events, the intellectual hearth at which the bold and original genius was kindled, which marks the artistic productions of Chaldæa and Assyria, and the reflection of which is shown in the monuments of Persia, Judæa, Phœnicia, and Carthage, the island of Cyprus, and the Hittite races. Yet it is neither in the capital of Chaldæa nor in that of Assyria that the oldest traces have hitherto been found of this great civilisation, extinct now for twenty-four centuries; it is not among the ruins of these famous cities that we can hear, as it were, an echo of the first wailings of the genius of plastic art, observe its groping efforts, touch with our finger its rudest attempts. In the country, formerly so fertile, called Lower Chaldæa, where, according to the popular tradition preserved by Berosus, the fish-god Oannes taught men in the beginning "all that serves to soften life," the traveller comes, almost at every step, upon artificial mounds known as *tells*, con-cealing under a veil of dust the remains of cities which yield in point of antiquity neither to Babylon nor Nineveh ; and it is there that modern archæologists have had the good fortune to disinter ruins far more ancient than those of the palaces of Sargon, Assur-bânipal, or Nebuchadnezzar.   Though a number of tumuli remain unexplored, and, as we may conjecture, future excavations will afford much new matter for science, nevertheless a brilliant light has already been thrown by numerous and important discoveries on the oriental origin of art and on the degree of material culture reached by the nation which founded Babel and the other Chaldæan towns of Genesis.   The ruins of Abu Habbah, identified with the two Sipparas (Sephar-vaim, that of the god Samas and that of the goddess Anunit), have yielded to our curiosity several monu-ments of the highest interest ; those of Abu Shahrein (Eridu), Senkereh (Larsa), Mugheir (Ur, the native city of Abraham), the great necropolis of Warka (Uruk, the Erech of the Bible), are sites which have all furnished already an important harvest of remains belonging to the most distant ages, incomplete as their exploration has been.   But the extensive and methodical excavations   undertaken   from   1877   to   1881   by   M. E. de Sarzec at Tello (Tell Loh) have enriched the Louvre with a collection of monuments unique in the museums of Europe, and enable us to give, at the present time, an exact and precise account of the character of Chaldæan architecture and sculpture long before Nineveh and Babylon had succeeded in imposing their supremacy upon these regions. Tello, fifteen hours north of Mugheir, twelve hours east of Warka, seems to represent the ancient Sirpurla.* Its ruins, which cover a space of four miles and a quarter, consist of a series of mounds at a short distance from the course of an ancient canal dug by the hand of man, the Shatt el Hai, which starts from the Euphrates and flows into the Tigris twelve hours below Bagdad. The principal tell contained the substructures of a palace which was, two or three thousand years before our era, the dwelling of a prince named, according to Assyriologists, Gudea. Hither we must especially transport ourselves, as well as to the mounds of Mugheir, Warka, and Abu Shahrein, where the English explorers Loftus and Taylor made some excavations with good results. The narrative of these excavations and the monuments which they have yielded to our museums, will help us to determine the peculiar features of an essentially self-made art, born spontaneously on the soil where it flourished, and apparently in no degree borrowed from its neighbours.

I. ARCHITECTURE.

One of the fundamental characters of Chaldæo-Assyrian architecture is the exclusive use of bricks as the constructive material. This is required by the very nature of the soil of Mesopotamia, in which

---

* The authority of a syllabary and a bilingual text enables us to correct the pronunciation of this name to Lagas. See Pinches in *Babylonian and Oriental Record*, vol. iii., p. 24. [Translator's note.]

building-stone and wood suitable for carpenters' work
are entirely wanting, while the clay is thick, adhesive,
and peculiarly adapted for fashioning in the mould and
baking in the kiln. Accordingly, while the modern
inhabitants of the country continue to make bricks,
their manufacture is already recorded in the biblical
reminiscences of the Tower of Babel: " Go to," say
the men who would build a tower that should reach
to Heaven, "let us make brick and burn them
throughly : and they had brick for stone and slime
had they for mortar."* The prophet Nahum informs
us of the method of brick-making : " Draw thee waters,"
he says, ". . . go into clay, and tread the mortar, make
strong the brick-kiln."† There were two kinds of
bricks. The unbaked brick is a square of whitish clay,
mixed with fine straw and simply dried in the sun
when it comes out of the mould ; it was generally from
8 in. to 1 ft. square by 4 in. thick. The month in
which the heat of summer first becomes intolerable in
these regions, namely the month of Sivan (May-June)
was called "the brick month," or that in which the
clay cakes were submitted to the action of the sun.
To judge by what is done in Egypt at the present day,
one workman could by himself make from one thousand
to fifteen hundred bricks a day. The baked brick was
subjected to the action of fire in proper kilns, like those of
our modern brickyards; it acquired, through the baking,
a reddish colour, and was less sensible than the crude
brick to the decomposing action of damp ; it was also
more limited in its dimensions, in order that the heat
might penetrate the internal substance of the mass,

* Genesis xi. 3. † Nahum iii. 14.

without danger of calcination on the surface. On one side of every brick, baked or unbaked, the name and official titles of the reigning prince were stamped by means of a matrix or a die used as a seal; thus, at Tello most-of the bricks were marked with the name of Gudea, and at Babylon bricks of Nebuchadnezzar are found by hundreds of thousands.

While describing the construction of the fortifications at Babylon, Hero-dotus shows the process followed by the Chaldæans in building a wall: "As they dug the moat, they made bricks of the earth taken out of the trench, and when they had made a certain number of bricks they baked them in kilns. Then, using boiling bitumen as

Fig. 1.—Brick from Tello (Louvre).

mortar, and inserting mats of woven reeds between every thirtieth course of bricks, they built first the borders of the moat, and next the wall itself in the same way."* Mesopotamia possesses abundant wells of bitumen, notably at Hit and at Kalah Shergat; as for the tall reeds which still grow in abundance in the marshes of Lower Chaldæa, their employment in building had the effect of giving more solidity and cohesion to the courses of bricks. For walls less

* Herodotus i. 179.

carefully constructed, or for partition-walls in the interior of the houses, a simple mortar of clay was used instead of bitumen. In great structures, such as Birs Nimroud at Babylon, the bricks are bound together by mortar made of lime, solid enough to stand all tests. The ruins of Mugheir have revealed the use of a mixture of ashes and lime, which is still employed by the natives, and called by them *sharir*.

The necessarily limited size of bricks baked in kilns or dried in the sun must have helped to bring about a speedier disintegration of the structures, and have been a serious obstacle to the erection of walls of a height to be compared, for instance, with that of the Egyptian temples. At certain seasons of the year in Mesopotamia the rain falls in torrents, and, filtering through walls in bad repair, would soon open cracks and bring about the ruin of the structure. In these lowlands furrowed with watercourses, the crude brick of the foundations often on this account ran the risk of returning to its condition of clayey mud without consistency. Greek tradition relates that the Medes and Chaldæans saw a part of the walls of Nineveh fall of themselves, when they prolonged a blockade which forced the besieged to admit the waters of the Tigris during many weeks into the moats beneath the ramparts. The cuneiform inscriptions themselves, while the empire founded by Nebuchadnezzar was flourishing, often point out temples and palaces falling to ruin, which the kings strive without ceasing to repair or rebuild.

The old sanctuaries of primitive Chaldæa, E-saggil, E-zida, the Temple of the Great Light, E-parra, E-anna,

E-ulbar, and others consecrated to Sin, to Samas, to
Nana, to Bel Marduk, to Nebo, are restored at great
expense by Nabonidus, the last King of Babylon, who
sets himself the task of recalling in his inscriptions
the material difficulties of this work worthy of a pious
antiquarian. Let no one be surprised after this at the
striking contrast between the ruins of Mesopotamia,
and those of Egypt as we now see them. In the
valley of the Nile building-stone abounds, and the
architect has only to make his choice among the various
qualities of material. Accordingly he hews out gigantic
monoliths, erects imposingly majestic pylons, rears to
an aerial height forests of pillars which seem to uphold
the sky, plants in the middle of the desert those
massive Pyramids which will defy to the end of time
even the most determined of Vandals. On the banks
of the Tigris and Euphrates, on the contrary, there is
now nothing but the uniform plain of the desert, broken
here and there by mounds of *débris* covered with sand ;
here it may be said with truth that the very ruins have
perished. Only in thought can the archæologist reconstruct vast buildings in accordance with the vast
material buried in disorder in the mud. The use of
bricks in building has been, to a greater extent than
political events, the auxiliary of Jehovah's wrath against
Nineveh and Babylon.

If the nature of the soil forced the Mesopotamian
architect to build with bricks, the neighbourhood of
rivers and canals for irrigation and the want of outlet
for the water obliged him at the same time to have
recourse to an expedient peculiar to Chaldæo-Assyrian
architecture. He had to raise the actual dwelling on

an artificial terrace removed from the level of a soil impregnated with unwholesome damp. This platform or basement of unbaked brick on which the building was placed is met with everywhere, not only at Nineveh and Babylon, but from the beginning in the sub-structures of Mugheir, Tello, Warka, and Abu Shahrein. In the palace of the *patesi* Gudea, the mass forms a sort of immense pedestal 39 ft. high, and nearly 655 ft. at the base ; at the present day the sides form in relation to the plain a slope of 164 ft. Formerly the platform was mounted by a gentle slope intended for horses and chariots, and by one or more flights of steps which broke the outline of the terrace. The stone staircases by which the terrace of the palaces of Persepolis is ascended, are still in place ; in Chaldæa and Assyria, where they were built of brick, they have almost everywhere disappeared. However, Taylor discovered two on the side of the platform of the palace of Abu Shahrein ; one has only twelve steps 2 ft. broad ; but the other was a monumental staircase of stone, 16 ft. broad, with a slope of more than 65 ft.

The edifice which surmounts the platform at Tello is of bricks cemented together with bitumen ; its exterior walls are 5 ft. 10 in. thick, and form a parallelogram 173 ft. long and 101 ft. broad. Like the palaces of Warka and Mugheir, its orientation is according to the Assyrian custom—that is to say, the angles are turned towards the cardinal points, not the sides as in the Egyptian monuments. The two longer sides bulge slightly towards the middle, thus describing two opposite elliptical curves—a peculiarity which gives to the plan of the edifice something of the appearance of a barrel, or of two trapeziums joined at the base. The outer surface of the walls is not everywhere uniform and flat ; the adjacent sides of the northern angle are ornamented by projections alternately curved and rectilineal—a system of decoration which has also been observed at Warka, among the ruins of the temple called Wuswas, and is found later in the Assyrian monuments. The great north-eastern façade exhibits

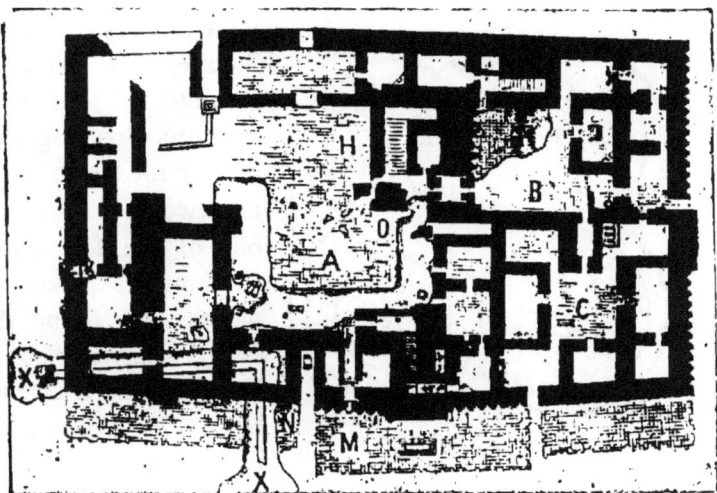

Fig. 2.—Plan of the palace at Tello (after Heuzey).

in the middle, besides the outward swell of which we have spoken, a projection 3 ft. 3 in. thick and 18 ft. long. The wings of this projection are formed of square pilasters and half-columns 1 ft. 7 in. diameter, which recall the clustered pillars of our cathedrals, and form one of the most interesting peculiarities of the primitive architecture of Chaldæa. Taylor * and

* *Journal of the Royal Asiatic Society*, vol. xv., p. 406.

Loftus * had already remarked, at Abu Shahrein and Warka respectively, pillars and half-columns of brickwork; M. de Sarzec has found the same architectural features in one of the secondary mounds of Tello, which he calls the *tell of pillars*,† and which seems to represent the ruins of the temple of the god Nin Girsu. Two of these pillars, which measured 6 ft. in thickness, and were separated by a space of 6½ ft., still consisted of twenty-four courses of bricks. " Each

Fig. 3.—Section of pillar (after Heuzey).

pillar," says M. de Sarzec, " is formed of a cluster of four round columns close together, and built entirely of brickwork. . . . If one of the four round columns is taken to pieces it is found that every alternate course is formed of a circular brick in the centre, round which radiate eight triangular bricks grooved at their interior angle, and rounded on the outer surface, so that they describe by their union a complete circle. In the next course the circle is composed, on the contrary, of eight triangular bricks ending in a point, which are united at the centre of the column, and of six other curved bricks which enclose the first eight. The space between the four circles thus formed is

* *Travels and Researches in Chaldæa and Susiana*, p. 175.
† *Decouvertes en Chaldée*, p. 62.

filled up with two large bricks hollowed out in the form of an arc of a circle, which fit exactly into it. These curious pillars, thus ingeniously constructed, recall the Egyptian order, modelled upon vegetable forms, which imitates four lotus-stalks in a bouquet; they show how skilfully the Chaldæans could dispense with the stone column. The base consisted of a square mass of bricks forming a pedestal projecting on all sides 2 ft. 11 in. beyond the shaft. The whole group was covered with a thick bed of plaster.*

Yet, whatever skill was displayed in the manufacture of these specially moulded bricks, round, triangular, or forming a section of a circle, pillars of this construction could not, like the Egyptian column, show sufficient solidity to support a heavy mass; they would soon have bent under the burden. Accordingly they could only be employed exceptionally and almost entirely for decoration, whether to support the roof of a grand staircase or to shelter the *cella* in which a deity delivered his oracles.

The defective side of Chaldæan architecture, therefore, consists in the lack of stone supports rising proudly into space like the Egyptian column, and upholding on their bold heads, quite as well as the thickest walls, the foot of the arch, the architraves, the roof, the upper terraces or the upper stories of the building. But the proof that the architects would have hewn columns of stone, if nature had furnished them with the necessary material, is just this ingenious artifice by which they succeeded in replacing them; and moreover they did not hesitate to employ small columns of wood or metal in the con-

* See Heuzey, *Un palais chaldéen*, pp. 37-58.

struction of small buildings, such as the shrines of their gods. A stela of King Nabu-ablu-iddin (about B.C. 900), found at Abu Habbah, represents the shrine of the god Samas, supported by small wooden pillars, covered with plates of bronze overlapping each other so as to resemble the trunk of a palm tree (see fig. 29). The base and the capital are alike; they are composed of a double volute shaped like a lotus-flower, approaching somewhat the Ionic capital; in short, the Chaldæans knew how to make use of the column in minor architecture.

One doorway at least was opened in each façade of the palace of Tello, but these openings were not on the axis of the structure, nor even symmetrical. The principal side (the north-east) had two entrances; the largest, nearly in the middle of the swell, had an opening 3 ft. 11 in. broad. It was constructed at a later period—that is to say, at the time near the Christian era when the Græco-Parthian kings of Characene conceived the idea of restoring Tello and installing themselves there. Like the Arab houses of our day, the outer walls of the palace of Gudea show no other openings; there are neither windows nor lights of any sort, admitting the air and the day, and looking out over the country or the town.

Let us now penetrate into the interior of the Chaldæan edifice, of which the blind and dumb walls leave in our imagination an impression of gloom and cold uniformity. The walls seem never to have exhibited the smallest architectural decoration; they are entirely bare, and only characterised from time to time by depressions and projections; no traces of mouldings, of

plinths, of cornices, and of those devices to which the
architects of all countries have recourse in order to
break the lines of the walls, and to call forth effects of
light and shade. It must be supposed that the interior
decoration of the palace consisted entirely of colouring
and hanging draperies. The thickness of the wall
varies from 8 ft. 6 in. to 2 ft. 7 in. All the partitions cut
one another at right angles, forming thirty-six square
or rectangular chambers; the largest measures 39 ft. 4 in.
by 12 ft. 2 in., and the smallest 10 ft. 11 in. by 9 ft. 9 in.
The disproportion which exists, especially in the state
saloon, between the length and breadth, the extreme
thickness of the walls, even of those which are the least
important in the structure, form essential peculiarities
to which we shall draw attention later in the Assyrian
edifices. At Nineveh it has been proved that it is the
thrust of the semicircular vaulting, which roofs the
chambers, that has forced the architect to bring the
parallel walls near to one another and to give them an
enormous thickness. Are we, in the absence of palp-
able proof, to draw the same conclusion with regard to
the palaces of old Chaldæa? Are we authorised to
assert that the vault was known three thousand years
before our era? In a word, how were the halls of
Gudea's building covered? Was it everywhere by
means of transverse rafters supporting a floor and a
terrace? or was it oftener by a bricked vault? As
far as we have read M. de Sarzec's narrative, or M.
Heuzey's studies on the excavations of Tello, we have
found no direct answer to this question. Perhaps the
present state of the ruins or the successive alterations
to which the primitive structure has been subjected do

not allow a categorical solution of the problem to be given. However, important indications authorise us to believe ·that the Chaldæans of the time of Gudea already understood the vault and used it for roofing their houses. In several parts even of the palace of Tello, M. de Sarzec found small vaulted passages, 3 ft. 3 in. high and 1 ft. 11 in.* thick, in a perfect state of preservation ; in one of the secondary mounds he brought to light a small vaulted drain which carried the sewage of the town far away *of. p.* into the plain. Taylor found, in an underground chamber of the necropolis at Mugheir, the most primitive kind of vault that has ever been known—that called the corbelled vault. In this false vault the courses of bricks ascend in parallel rows on each side until they meet

Fig. 4.—Corbelled vaulting at Mugheir (after Taylor).

one another, every fresh course projecting perceptibly beyond that beneath it, until the opposite courses touch and form one.

It was, then, as it seems, the Chaldæans who invented the vault ;† the want of timber compelled them in early times to contrive to defend themselves at once against the heavy rains and the ardour of a torrid sun ; the creation of the vault was in their case instinctive and spontaneous. They raised, two or three thousand

---

* E. de Sarzec, *Découvertes en Chaldée*, pp. 34, 35.

† See Perrot and Chipiez, *Hist. of Art in Chaldæa and Assyria*, vol. i., p. 222 [Eng. ed.].

years before our era, vaults and domes like those which are built to this day by the rudest masons at Mosoul or Bagdad. No doubt the present state of the Chaldæan ruins and the insufficient explorations which have been undertaken among them do not enable us to say whether these Proto-Chaldæans knew every kind of vault, as the Assyrians did in the age of the Sargonids, or the Babylonians at the epoch of Nebuchadnezzar ; but the remarkable perfection observed in their monumental structures, and in the very manufacture of the bricks, are so many arguments in favour of the inference that the palaces and houses of the Chaldæans in the time of Gudea were surmounted, for the most part, by semi-circular vaults or by cupolas, as were later, according to Strabo,* the houses of the Babylonians. The vaults supported a terrace formed of clay ; this layer of earth would be less thick over rooms roofed only with a ceiling of palm-beams and reed-matting. The ascent was by staircases, an example of which seems to have been found in the palace at Tello.†

While clearing away the material accumulated between the courts A and B, the workmen employed by the French explorer came into contact (at the point H) with a structure of baked brickwork, which proves that the Chaldæans at the remotest epoch had already invented one of the most interesting and characteristic elements of their architecture—the *zikkurat* or staged tower. The lower layers in the palace of Gudea alone exist, and are composed of two solid masses in stages one above the other. In its present condition the upper terrace is a mass 26 ft. square, 13 ft. less on all

* Strabo xvi. 1, 5. † E. de Sarzec, *op. cit.*, p. 37.

sides than the lower stage ; perhaps there still exists a third and lower step, which has not been reached by the soundings, which are imperfect at this point. The *zikkurat* of Tello was not in any case so lofty or so important a structure as those of the Ninevite palaces or those represented by the ruins of Babil or Birs Nimroud at Babylon. It was even much less considerable than that which Taylor observed at Abu Shahrein, and which was equally old. These towers always had, from the first, seven stages, each painted of a different colour, and connected with the worship of the sun (Samas), the moon (Sin), and the five planets of the astronomical system of the Chaldæans.

The disposition of the royal apartments showed a striking analogy with that which we shall meet with again· later in the palaces of Nineveh ; there were the convenience and comfort which we find in the palaces of modern oriental sovereigns. To the Chaldæans again we must give the credit of having invented that architectural arrangement which springs from the necessities of oriental li'e, and is so well fitted to its needs that for four thousand years it has never varied. There were in the palace of Gudea three interior courts (A, B, C, fig. 2), round each of which the rooms radiated, and from which they received air and light. Each of these three groups had its own entrance, and communicated with the next group only by a single passage easy to guard or to close. The group of chambers situated in the northern angle (C) was especially isolated and removed from the others ; it was the hareem or women's apartments. At the eastern angle (B) were the rooms composing the seraglio or *selamlik*—that is to say, the part of the palace inhabited by the king and his officers ; there was the saloon for official receptions, of which we have given the dimensions. This part of the royal dwelling communicated on one side with a state courtyard, measuring 55 ft. 8 in. by 68 ft. 9 in., and on the other with the outside by means of a smaller room serving as an antechamber ; beside the door opening on the façade, boxes or recesses had been arranged in which the guards were posted. The third group of chambers, on the south-east (A), formed the *Khan*—that is to say, the dependencies of the palace, the kitchens, the slaves' lodgings, and the stables.

All the rooms were paved with bricks ; they very rarely led into one another, and had an opening looking on to the court. The largest of the doorways, that which opened into the state saloon, was of the unusual breadth of 6 ft. 6 in. ; it was probably a folding door. Under each of the principal doors there was a great threshold of marble or alabaster, sometimes covered with an inscription and placed on a bed of bitumen and crushed bricks ; under this concrete, finally, cylinders of precious stone and talismanic amulets were generally found.

The leaves of the door turned on pivots, the point of which rested in a cavity hollowed out for this purpose in a great block of diorite. M. de Sarzec brought to the Louvre a large number of these natural blocks, which were found buried in the pavement so as only to rise an inch or two above the surface. On the smooth surface of each of them it is seen that the socket, hollowed out in the form of a conical cup, has

2

undergone an incessant friction; round the hole an inscription, sometimes circular, was engraved (fig. 5). To prevent the wooden pivot of the doors from wearing out too rapidly, it was enveloped in a metal sheath, which took the form of a funnel, and which was fixed to the wood by means of nails. One of these bronze cups has been found at Tello, still in place on the socket.[*]

Fig. 5.—Socket for pivot of door, from Tello (Louvre).

The discoveries of Loftus and Taylor show us how the façades and the rooms of the Chaldæan palaces were decorated. The principal façade of the buildings at Abu Shahrein and Warka had a mural decoration of a kind as primitive as it was singular.[†] First it was plastered with a thick layer of clay stucco; then, before this plaster was completely dry, cones of baked clay were buried in it, like metal nails. Only the head of these cones is visible on the surface of the wall, while the stem is plunged into the thick clay and sticks there

Fig. 6.—Terra-cotta cone from Tello (Louvre).

unseen. To the heads of these cones, disposed at regular distances, and acting perhaps also as talismans,

---

[*] E. de Sarzec, *op. cit.*, p. 59.
[†] Loftus, *Travels and Researches*, pp. 187-189.

various colours are applied ; they are black, red, white, or yellow. Moreover, each head is separated from its neighbours by coloured geometrical lines, so that it became to the eye the centre of a lozenge or a square.

If the interior of the rooms was lined in monochrome with white stucco, or with fresco painting, nothing of this decoration is left. But we have in sufficiently large quantities, although always much mutilated, the remains of another more original system of wall decoration, of which the Chaldæans are the inventors—that is to say, enamelled bricks. By applying a coloured paste, which the fire would vitrify, to one of the surfaces of the bricks before baking, a glaze or enamel was produced, closely united to the clay and immovably solid. It was again necessity and their ungrateful climate which induced the Chaldæans to have recourse to this ingenious method. They were in great need of a remedy for the want of stone and a means of preventing the heavy rains from spoiling the colours applied to the walls. They succeeded so perfectly in this that even at the present day the brilliancy of these glazed tiles is not affected. The colours with which they are painted are of the simplest, and vary little ; they are blue, white, black, yellow and red. Unfortunately, those fine fragments which have been brought to our museums are only so far interesting that they teach us the technical methods of a manufacture which involves that of opaque glass ; even those which are least mutilated contain at the most a few floral designs or portions of the figures of animals, and moreover these last are not older than the epoch of Nebuchadnezzar.

The trenches dug among the massive terraces of
Chaldæa have revealed other curious details of construction. We know, for instance, what steps were
taken to prevent the sewage of the houses or the rain-
water which fell upon them from filtering through the
platforms of crude brick on which the buildings stood ;
a rapid disintegration would have followed. They,
therefore, planned a complete system of water-channels
and drainage. In one of the mounds at Tello, M. de
Sarzec found a series of cylindrical pipes or tubes of

baked clay, fitted into one another, and
forming together a conduit for the
water.*

But the place where this method
has been carried out with peculiarly
ingenious skill is the necropolis at
Mugheir. The top of the platform,
in the body of which the tombs are
sunk, is covered with a brick pavement laid with special care, in which

Fig.   7.—Drainage
pipe at Mugheir
(after Loftus).

every chink is filled up with bitumen. Under this upper
crust the coffins are ranged in order, one above the other,
each one being placed separately in a small chamber.
At intervals brick tubes are met with, fitted into one
another and forming a sort of immense flue hidden
in the structure. The lower extremity of the pipes
opened into a drain ; the upper end, on a level with the
surface of the pavement of the terrace, was furnished
with a cap pierced with an infinite number of small
holes like a skimmer. Through these the rainwater
was carried off, and this system of drainage was so

* E. de Sarzec, *op. cit.*, p. 60.

wonderfully well understood and carried out, that it has remained intact to our own day, and, according to Loftus, the tombs have been so well preserved that they are found perfectly dry, including the bodies and their furniture. We shall see the Assyrians take similar precautions to preserve the terraces of the Ninevite palaces from the percolation of water.

The construction of a temple or palace was the occasion of a religious ceremony analogous to that which we call the laying of the first stone. In a hollow formed in the foundation-wall a cylinder of baked clay was deposited (fig. 8), on which an inscription was written describing the erection of the building and setting forth the piety and great deeds of the prince ; this cylinder was accompanied by various talismanic objects : cones and statuettes of bronze and baked clay, cylindrical seals, votive tablets, sometimes of silver or gold. Among the foundations of the palace of Gudea, M. de Sarzec found four of these cavities in the wall measuring 1 ft. 1 in. by 10 in. by 4 in. ; they still contained the cylinders and amulets deposited there.

Hiding-places of the same kind have been observed at Senkereh, at Mugheir, and among the ruins of almost all the Chaldæan and Assyrian buildings. The Assyrians themselves, when they wished to restore an old ruined temple, took pains first to find out the hiding-place of the foundation-cylinder or *timmennu*.

The last king of Babylon, Nabonidus, relates in one of the official inscriptions of his reign how he happened to find the *timmennu* of the earliest builders of the temple of the Sun at Larsa. King Kurigalzu (about B.C. 1350), and later Esarhaddon (B.C. 680—667), and

Nebuchadnezzar himself, had repaired this venerated sanctuary, and sought vainly for the hiding-place of the talismans. "Then I, Nabonidus, inspired by my piety towards the goddess Istar of Agade, my sovereign, caused an excavation to be made. The gods Samas and Rammanu granted me their constant favour, and I found the foundation-cylinder of the temple of E-Ulbar." It bore the name of the king Sagasaltias (about B.C. 1500). After reading the inscription, Nabonidus restored it to its place and himself made another cylinder to record his researches and his own works; he deposited it in the foundation by the side of the ancient cylinder. Modern explorers, no doubt also favoured by Samas and Rammanu,

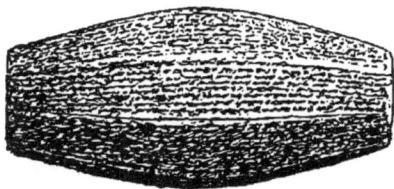

Fig. 8.—Foundation-cylinder from Khorsabad (Louvre).

found in a sufficiently good state of preservation the mysterious hiding-places and the precious objects which had been piously placed there 550 years before our era.*

II. STATUES AND BAS-RELIEFS.

The discoveries of M. de Sarzec at Tello, and those of other explorers in Chaldæa, allow us to go back almost to the origin of sculpture in Western Asia. Our museums possess, in fact, bas-reliefs and statues belonging to a rudimentary stage of art, the remote age of which is still attested by the archaic inscriptions which accompany them, and these most ancient monu-

* M. Babelon's statement that the cylinder of Sagasaltias was found by modern explorers with that of Nabonidus is unfortunately inaccurate. Only the records of Nabonidus were discovered. See Taylor, *Journal of the Royal Asiatic Society*, vol. xv.

ments are followed, as in the case of Egypt and Greece,
by other statues and bas-reliefs which, descending a
chronological scale across the ages, represent the
graduated phases of artistic progress in Chaldæa before
the Ninevite supremacy was imposed upon this country.
Among the fragments of sculpture at Tello, that which
M. Heuzey considers most primitive, and which should
be placed at the head of the productions of oriental
sculpture, is a bas-relief of greyish limestone, 10 in.
broad and 5 in. high. Four figures alone remain of
the complicated scene which decorated this stone panel.
One of them is seated, with
the profile turned to the
left ; it is a beardless man
rather than a woman, and
his face is half covered by
an exaggerated eye seen
from the front as in
children's drawings. His
hair consists of two long

Fig. 9.—Bas-relief from Tello
(Louvre).

tresses falling to his shoulders, and almost to be mistaken for the lappets of the high tiara with which he
is crowned. This tiara seems to be adorned with two
bulls' horns. The bust is draped with a large shawl
which leaves the right shoulder bare. The hand,
raised to a level with the face, looks like a simple fork ;
it holds a cup, as if the scene represented a libation, and
in fact we still see a part of the deity to whom the
offering is directed. On the right a bearded man with
square shoulders, crowned with a low cap, dressed in a
large robe without folds, holds in his right hand a sort
of club, with which he seems to deliver a blow upon the

head of his companion, whom he seizes by the hand.
It will be seen that the explanation of this picture is
exceedingly doubtful; but looking from the point of
view of the history of art, we must recognise in it
without hesitation a fragment which comes down from
remote antiquity. The relief is low, the outline of
the figures is timid and uncertain, the details are dis-
proportioned, as if the rude chisel which carved them
had been held in the unskilful hands of a child; the

design is full of elementary mis-
takes, though limestone is soft and
easily worked.

A more advanced art marks the
fragment of a bas-relief which M.
Heuzey called " the Eagle and Lion
Tablet," and which is dated by an
inscription mentioning the king Ur-
Nina (B.C. 2500). An eagle is seen
here with outspread wings standing

Fig. 10.—Bas-relief from upon a lion. The sculpture is
Tello (Louvre). equally flat and without modelling,
but the graceful outline of the figures is clearly chiselled,
and with a surer hand; the extremities of the wing
feathers of the eagle are indented, the body of the lion
is remarkably correct in outline, except the head, which
still remains barbarous.

A third stage of Chaldæan sculpture may be represented by the "Vulture Stela," on which the names of
two kings have been read, one of whom is the son of
Ur-Nina. The three fragments of this limestone stela
are carved on both sides. On one of them a flock of
vultures carry away human remains in their flight—

heads, hands, and arms. The human heads denote an
art which has left the gropings of childhood behind :
they are entirely shaved, the nose is always aquiline, the
eye of an exaggerated
size and triangular.
The vultures, more
rudely drawn, are
nevertheless well cha-
racterised by their long
curved beak and their
claws of exaggerated
length ; the markings

Fig. 11.—The Vulture Stela (Louvre).

of the feathers and wings are brought out. On another
fragment of the same stela it seems that we witness the
construction of a sepulchral tumulus. Fiq. 12

Men dressed in a short tunic, fringed, and tightened
at the waist, carry on their heads wicker baskets, pro-

Fig. 12.—The Vulture Stela
(Louvre).

bably containing earth to
cover the pile of corpses
heaped one upon the other
in symmetrical and alternate
rows. The third piece of
the same monument seems
to represent a scene of car-
nage. As for the back of
the stela, it is less ornamented ; however, on one
of the fragments (fig. 13),
a pole surmounted by an
eagle with outspread wings is seen, and then a large
human head, incomplete but highly interesting ; it exhibits, from an anatomical point of view, the same

character as the smaller heads which we have just
considered ; but its head-dress is a most curious
feature,—a sort of tiara decorated with bulls' horns.
"By an archaic conventionality," observes M. Heuzey,
"these two horns are seen in profile, curved forwards
and backwards ; but in reality they were attached to
the sides of the cap. ... The cap is also surmounted
by a crest of four large feathers, in the middle of which
rises a cone decorated with a quaint head also crowned
by a crescent ; this little decorative head, drawn in full

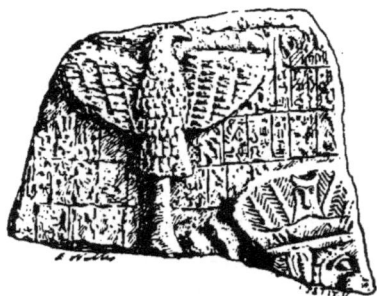

face, has an exceedingly
long and broad nose
without any sign of a
mouth, so that it may be
doubted whether it be
the head of a man or of
an animal."* The same
tiara is found with unim-
portant modifications on
Assyrian cylinders and

Fig. 13.—The Vulture Stela (Louvre).

bas-reliefs, in which it forms the head-dress of deities
or pontiffs.   The artistic superiority of the bas-reliefs
of the Vulture Stela over the monuments quoted previously is abundantly evident, and already allows us a
foretaste of the sober and vigorous art revealed to us
by the large statues found in the palace of Gudea.

It was in the most spacious court of the palace that
M. de Sarzec found assembled nearly all the Chaldæan
statues which he had transported to the museum of the
Louvre.   To the number of ten, they are of blackish
diorite with a bluish tinge ; all are headless and bear

* Heuzey, *Gazette Arch.*, 1884, p. 195.

inscriptions in the name of Gudea or of Ur-Bau. At
the moment of discovery they were lying on the slabs
of the court-yard,—on one side those which represent upright figures, on the other
the seated statues. A separate
head, appearing to belong to one
of the statues, was also found in
the same courtyard. The other
heads were unearthed elsewhere,
and it is impossible to say whether
they had been removed from the
headless statues that we know.
All these heads, though exhibiting
common characteristics, are distinguished from one another by

Fig. 14.– Chaldæan head
(Louvre).

peculiarities which disclose the surprising skill and the
fecundity of the Chaldæan genius at this remote epoch.
The man's head (fig. 14) found in the great courtyard is
of life-size, the hair and beard
completely shaven, as in certain
Egyptian statues. The eyebrows form an exaggerated projection above enormous eyes ;
the skull is remarkably elongated ; the mutilated nose alone
prevents us from having the
complete type of the Chaldæan
race, with its hard features and
thick, sensual lips.

Fig. 15.—Chaldæan head
(Louvre).

In a neighbouring tell M. de Sarzec found another
head of the same size and of an equally interesting
type. It is less severe in aspect than the preceding

one, but carved with equal skill. The face is round and almost smiling, the chin broad and powerful, the nose flat. The very original head-dress is composed of a woollen cap fitting closely to the head, and furnished with a thick border, which, turning up, forms a sort of crown ; the meshes of the woollen tissue are conventionally marked by a number of symmetrical rolls. Even at the present day in Lower Chaldæa the Christian priests of the Chaldæan rite envelop their heads in a turban of black stuff, which allows of a similar arrangement.[*]

Fig. 16.—Chaldæan statue (Louvre).

As for the headless statues whether seated or standing, they have all the same characteristics, exhibit an identical type, and are incontestably of the same school of sculpture. Here is a personage seated on a sort of stool not fully carved out ; he recalls involuntarily the Greek statues of the sacred way of the Branchidæ at Miletus, and is in the same religious attitude. A cloak without sleeves is crossed over his breast and thrown back over his shoulder ; a handsome fringe, delicately

[*] E. de Sarzec, Découvertes, p. 61.

carved, falls over the whole depth in front ; the hands
are clasped on the breast in the oriental posture of
meditation and devotion ; the bare feet are chiselled
with an attention to detail never to be surpassed in
later times, even by the Ninevite artists. On the
knees of the personage lies a tablet intended to receive
an inscription or a design. In fact, another statue
like this, though of smaller pro-
portions, holds on its knees a
similar tablet, on which the plan
of a fortress with its bastions and
posterns is engraved in outline,
just as an architect of the present
day would draw it. A graduated
rule, that is to say, one sub-
divided into fractions of unequal
but proportional length, $10\frac{3}{4}$ in.
long, is carved in relief beside the
plan, for which it serves as a scale ;
finally, at the side lies the style
with which the architect engraved
his design (see fig. 53). The
standing statues answer almost to
the same description ; they also

Fig. 17.—Chaldæan statue
(Louvre).

are bare-footed, with the hands crossed upon the breast
but the arrangement of the long shawl, which seems to
form the only garment of all these personages, becomes
more intelligible. The Arab still drapes himself in the
same fashion in his burnoos,—that garment, at once so
simple and so dignified, of the shepherd of the desert.
It is a piece of woollen stuff, the borders of which are
adorned with a fringe; it is folded in two, and wrapped

round the body obliquely, so that it covers one arm and
leaves the other bare ; the upper corner, held fast by
wrapping the garment once round, is enough to keep
the whole in place. We shall find this large shawl
again on the Ninevite bas-reliefs, just as we shall
observe the persistence and exaggeration of this sober
and nervous style, which, as early as the Proto-
Chaldæan epoch, lays too much stress on the muscles,
and lingers with an excessive fondness over anatomical
details.

The Chaldæan statues were intended to be seen all
round, and not laid flat against a wall ; they are completely finished behind as well as in front. Compared
with the statues found in the temples of Cyprus, for
instance, they show us that the artist has sought to
spare neither his time nor his trouble. Amid this
sobriety of treatment and this uniformity of attitudes
we feel that Chaldæan art is already far from the hesitation and incorrectness of the first age ; the chisel
attacks the hardest stone with vigour and success ; the
artist's hand is experienced and sure of itself. This
archaic art is above all realistic, and aims at a precise
and even affected following of nature. The bare
shoulder is modelled and copied with surprising truth,
the hands and feet are studied even to the knuckles,
the nails, the wrinkles of the skin. At the same time
the figures are thick-set and, it may be said, far too short
—a fact which contributes to increase the impression of
strength and muscular energy produced by an attentive
observation of them.

The suppleness of the Chaldæan genius at the time
of Gudea appears again in a singular monument of the

De Sarzec collection, which may be taken to be the foot of a vase rather than the base of a small column (fig. 18). Small figures in high relief, nude, and seated on the ground, lean against a cylindrical stem. The best preserved figure has an oval face of rare refinement, and of a type entirely foreign to that of the large statues; with his beard cut in a point, and his head covered with a woollen turban, he looks straight in front of him with a smiling aspect.; in all Assyrian sculpture no countenance of such originality could perhaps be found. We do not know what is the meaning of these little figures crouched round this sort of basin. They seem to hold the place of the winged bulls and lions or other fantastic genii, whom Assyrian art will soon

Fig. 18.—Foot of Chaldæan vase (Louvre).

multiply everywhere in the capacity of architectural supports or ornaments.

In front of the palace at Tello stood a large stone basin decorated with sculpture, some fragments of which have come down to us. This monolithic trough, 8 ft. 2 in. long by 1 ft. 7½ in. broad, served, perhaps, to water the camels and the flocks which halted at the gate of Gudea's dwelling; or rather, on account of its rich ornamentation, may we believe that it was a basin consecrated to the service of the temple, like the brazen sea in the Temple of Jerusalem, or the vase of Amathonte? However it may be, there were, on its two longer surfaces, in low relief, women with arms outstretched, holding magic vases, from which

Fig. 19.—Bas-relief from Tello (after Heuzey).

two jets of liquid gushed, on each side of an ear of corn, a graceful symbol of the proverbial fertility of Mesopotamia, enclosed by the sacred streams of the Tigris and Euphrates, which were adored under the name of Naharaim, the two rivers *par excellence.*

The fragment reproduced here (fig. 19) shows us that the Proto-Chaldæans already gave to flowing water the conventional form of undulating lines (see also fig. 34); the woman is drawn with surprising truth.* The same technical skill is remarked in a bas-relief from Tello, which represents a bearded personage, in full face, with a costume in which M. Heuzey has recognised

Fig. 20.—Bas-relief from Tello (*Rev. arch.*, t. i., 1887, p. 265).

the fleecy stuff called *kaunakes* by the Greeks.   Observe

* L. Heuzey, *Un palais chaldéen,* pp. 59-117.

the delicacy with which the Chaldæan artists treated
the costume and the beard. It may almost be said
that Mesopotamian art has no further progress to
make, and that it already shows its full proportions
at the fabulously remote epoch represented by the
antiquities of Tello.

There is less modelling in the figures which adorn
the upper part of the *Caillou Michaux* ; the relief upon
it is dry and flat, and the drawing affects a hieratic
stiffness which would suggest an epoch of decadence,
or at least a time when Chaldæan art was arrested in
its upward march. This monument, dated in the reign
of Marduk-nadin-akhi, King of Babylon about B.C.
1120, was perhaps a stone rolled down by the waters
of the river, which was made into a sacred object ;
the cuneiform inscription contains the donation of a
landed estate, settled as a dowry.* The curious figures,
under the protection of which this contract is placed,
show us, as they do in many cylinders, that at this
epoch Chaldæan mythology was turned to profit by the
artists, who knew how to unite human to animal forms
without falling into monstrosity or deformity, and to
give symbolical figures to the stars and to the invisible
genii conceived by their wild imagination. The drawing of these strange figures is not unskilful ; they
inspire terror without degenerating into the caricature
and grotesque forms which mark the images of the
gods among barbarous peoples. Chaldæan art is
as learned as the secrets of its mythology are complicated. Examine, for instance, this winged goat

* See the translation which I have given of it in Lenormant and
Babelon, *Histoire ancienne de l'Orient*, vol. v., p. 84.

lying before an altar ; the angular outlines of its horns

are rendered with truth, the
muscles of its legs, perhaps
badly placed anatomically,
are analysed in their smallest
details, and the movement of
this animal, which is making
an effort to rise, is very
natural, though lacking in
life and suppleness.   We
shall recognise the same
characters of dryness and
rudeness in the black basalt
stela of the
same king,
M a r d u k-
nadin-akhi.
Here, as in

Fig. 21.—The *Caillou Michaux*
(Cabinet des Médailles).

the *Caillou Michaux*, the relief is
flat,—nothing supple, graceful, or
amiable ; the Chaldæan genius cannot
smile.   Of those ample garments of
the Oriental, those draperies with
which the Greek artist will be able
to produce so powerful an effect, the
Chaldæan artist is satisfied with
scratching in outline, so to speak,
the folds and fringes ; he makes
heavy embroidered copes of them,
like those of Catholic priests.   But,

Fig. 22.—Stela of Ma-
duk-nadin-akhi
(British Museum).

in compensation, he looks at these embroideries
through a magnifying glass, and excels in analysing

and reproducing the richness of the tissue, the innumerable and complicated forms of the design. We can henceforth foresee that the sculptor, losing sight of synthesis so as to place his ideal exclusively in the infinitely little, will never rid himself of the narrow formula in which he so early imprisoned his talent. All his figures in statuary or in the bas-reliefs, so highly finished in detail, show as a whole a hieratic and conventional stiffness, which will unhappily descend as a heritage to the Assyrian artist.

III. Minor Sculpture and the Industrial Arts.

The Chaldæans could work in bronze as skilfully as in stone. M. de Sarzec has collected some bronze figures which, compared with other monuments already secured, allow us to fix some precise landmarks in the gradual development of the art of casting and chiselling metals in Chaldæa. A certain statuette of a man or woman (fig. 23) may be considered the most rudimentary attempt.*

Fig. 23.—Chaldæan statuette in bronze (Louvre).

It has simply the shape of a cylindrical stem, the upper part of which is furnished with two arms and a human head like the *xoana* of the Greeks. This head, surmounted by small horns, is strangely barbarous; it recalls the art of the men of the bronze age and the most rustic of the Cypriote terra-cottas. Progress is manifest in other bronzes—

* Perrot and Chipiez, *op. cit.*, vol. ii., p. 192 f. [Eng. ed.]

separated, perhaps, from the former by several hundred years. These are statuettes which, instead of being fixed on a base, end in a reversed and much elongated cone, which must have served to plunge them into a soft matter such as mortar. One represents a recumbent bull, the other (fig. 24) a kneeling man holding in his hands the base of the cone; he is

bearded and covered with the tiara with several pairs of horns, reserved for gods and genii. A third, lastly, is a woman carrying a basket on her head, whose body has remarkably the appearance of an elongated ingot. This canephoros, whose female form is only indicated by the breasts and the width of the hips, leads us naturally to speak of another cane-phoros (fig. 25), found at Afaj on the Euphrates, bearing the name of the king Kudurmapuk (B.C. 2000). It may be seen by this statuette that the art of working in bronze followed closely the progress of sculpture in stone. Though the

Fig. 24.—Chaldæan statuette (Louvre).

head and arms are still the work of half-trained artists, the head is very remarkable; the arch of the eyebrows and the eyes are treated as in the large diorite statues; the hair is completely shaved. The same characters are observed in a remarkable figure of a bearded priest, wearing a tiara of moderate height, dressed in a long tunic with flounced fringes.* Here

* Perrot and Chipiez, *op. cit.*, vol. ii., p. 195, fig. 106.

is a mutilated statuette from Tello (fig. 26) ; it is a god standing on a crouching lion ; the head of the roaring beast has a ferocious and natural expression, but the god's robe is cylindrical, without amplitude and and without modelling, and the artist has tried in vain to conceal this stiffness, which betrays his impotence, by engraving the fringes and rosettes of the drapery. Remark that the long hairs of the lion are treated like the woollen shag of the priest's cap which we examined just now (fig. 15). The animal has very small wings ; his forelegs are those of a bull, his hind-legs end in lion's claws ; the study of nature here is perfect, but in those conventional lines which are meant to express the swell of the muscles, we feel the tendency to exaggeration and trivial rudeness which we remarked in the statues.

In one of the smaller mounds at Tello, M. de Sarzec discovered a fragment of a large bronze statue. " It was," he says, " a life-sized bull's horn, of bronze plating mounted on a wooden frame, but the wood was carbonised by the action of fire."* He had also found a sword, which was stolen and destroyed by an Arab. But we can cite another weapon of the same kind in the possession of Colonel Hanbury ; the blade, curved

Fig. 25.--Canephoros of Kudurmapuk (Louvre).

* E. de Sarzec, *Découvertes*, p. 61.
† *Revue archéologique*, 1883 (3ᵉ série, t. ii.) pl. xx.

like a scythe, and triangular, bears a votive inscription in the name of the Assyrian king Ramman-
nirari, the son of Pudil (B.C. 1300). The curious
peculiarity of this weapon is that on one of its surfaces
a small recumbent deer is to be seen engraved, and this
is the maker's mark : from this time onward the jealousy
of craftsmen comes into play and declares itself by the
same measures as in our day.

Fig. 26.—Chaldæan statuette in
bronze (Louvre).

Surprising as the phe-
nomenon is at first sight,
Chaldæan pottery was far
from following the progress
of sculpture. The excava-
tions of Tello have enriched
the museum of the Louvre
with five hundred terra-
cotta cones, bearing the
name of Gudea and Ur-Bau,
but these are only industrial
products, without artistic
character, and belonging
to the brick manufacture. The necropoles of Warka
and Mugheir, where we might have expected to meet
with works of art, as in the tombs of Greece or
Etruria, have only furnished coarse vases which bear
witness to the complete inferiority of pottery among
the Chaldæo-Assyrians. They are all singularly barbarous and rustic, whether they come from the archaic
tombs of Warka and Mugheir, or issue from the
ruins of the palaces where, nevertheless, the art
of sculpture soars and displays itself in its perfect development. Assyrian pottery, even that of the

best epoch, resembles, sometimes so much as to be mistaken for it, the most archaic pottery of Greece proper and the Islands of the Ægean. But here it is only the beginning of art, the first effort of the potter who before long will fashion masterpieces ; there, on the contrary, these vulgar kitchen receptacles form the whole art, and represent at once the start and the finish.

This neglect of ceramics by the Chaldæo-Assyrian artists results from geological and climatic causes analogous to those which, as we shall see, developed sculpture in bas-relief to the detriment of sculpture in the round. It is especially owing to the bad quality of the clay in Mesopotamia, which, though quite fit to be turned into square bricks, has not a fine enough grain for the purpose of fashioning from it the fragile frame of a broad crater, or of a slim amphora, and still less for the purpose of lending itself to all the details of face and drapery in graceful and slender figurines like those of Tanagra, Cyme, or Myrina.

The cohesion of the Mesopotamian clay is so imperfect that the Babylonian terra-cottas which have come down to us crumble almost at the first touch, in spite of the process of baking to which they have been subjected. It is observed that, to give some consistency to the body of the vases and to prevent cracks, the potter has been obliged to mix the clayey paste with chopped straw. It was impossible then to make the sides thin, or to fashion them with art ; consequently it would not have been natural to decorate with rich and careful painting vases which could only be heavy and coarse. It was enough to trace out geometrical designs, bands of colour, ovals, symmetrical festoons round the neck of the amphoræ; nothing in this sort of decoration has been borrowed from the animal or vegetable world or from history, of which the artist could, however, make so wonderful a use in the decoration of metal vases, or of knicknacks in ivory, wood, or stone.

The Chaldæan terra-cotta figurines, however coarse they may be, are not entirely divested of interest for the

Fig. 27.—Chaldæan statuette in terra-cotta.

history of art and mythology, and M. Heuzey has been able to appreciate them with delicacy from this point of view.*

The statuettes collected in great quantities by Loftus, at Warka, are of solid clay, and were manufactured in a mould in one piece; the back is flat and modelled with the hand. The clay is of a greenish grey, or sometimes brown; it is well baked and very hard. The attitude of these grotesque little figures offers singularly striking analogies to the terra-cotta figurines of the first Egyptian dynasty; they are men in long robes, with their beards cut in the Assyrian fashion, women dressed in tight tunics and wearing falling head-dresses like the Egyptian figurines; their hands are clasped on their breast in the religious attitude which we know already from the Tello statues. It is, however, very difficult to give the precise date of these figurines, which, perhaps, for the most part, are not anterior to the time

* *Les figurines antiques du Musée du Louvre*, p. 1 ff.

of Nebuchadnezzar. Besides, we shall return to them later on. It is enough for the moment to observe how little varied and meagre was the theme worked out by the Chaldæan modellers in clay, at a time when sculpture and the other arts were nevertheless already most flourishing.

The monuments which we have just reviewed allow us to appreciate the degree of prosperity and perfection attained side by side with the higher branches of art by various industries in Chaldæa, such as tapestry, weaving, and the embroidery of stuffs. The stela of Marduk-nadin-akhi, for example (fig. 22), bears witness to the wonderful skill of the women of the royal hareem, or of the men employed in the workshop, whence issued that robe with golden fringe, covered with elegant designs and precious stones set in the web of the tissue, that tiara adorned with feathers and wide-open daisies, those sandals, the broad lozenge-shaped stitches of which can be counted.

M. Heuzey * has demonstrated that the stuff called *kaunakes* (καυνάκης) by the Greeks, who gave this name to a Babylonian garment, goes back at least as far as the epoch of Gudea. The representation of this woollen tissue shows several series of tufts arranged in rows one above the other; the principle of the manufacture of the *kaunakes* is the same as that of plush or velvet, only the woollen pile is longer and arranged less closely. This sort of material, invented by the Chaldæans, continued to be made by the Assyrians and Persians ; in this way the Greeks came to know it, and Aristophanes speaks of it in his comedy of the *Wasps*.

* *Revue archéol., mai-juin*, 1887.

Garments made of *kaunakes* are frequently met with on the Chaldæan monuments, especially on the cylinders, where they have been mistaken for robes of a gathered and gauffered material. They are worn both by women and by men, as is proved by the bearded personage whom we reproduced above (fig. 20), and a female statuette in alabaster which shows all the characteristics of Chaldæan art contemporary with the monuments of Tello (fig. 28).

Fig.28.—Chaldæan statuette in alabaster.

The tablet of the god Samas (fig. 29), found at Abu-Habbah (Sepharvaim), and dated in the reign of the Babylonian king Nabu-

Fig. 29.—Bas-relief of the tablet of the god Samas (British Museum).

pal-iddin (B.C. 850), shows together the two principal Chaldæan garments—that made of kaunakes, and that of a plain material, open in front, which we shall often meet with again in Assyria. Moreover, this bas-relief, if it is closely studied, throws a remarkable light on the different industries in wood, iron, stone and wearing material. The tabernacle in which the god Samas is seated on his throne seems to be an iron niche, the upper part being curved to imitate a shallow vault; in the front of the shrine there are small pillars of wood or iron; the stem is covered with scales in, imitation of the trunk of the palm-tree, and made, no doubt, of plates of metal laid over it; for base and capital there are volutes something like the Ionic capital. The solar disk, the symbol of the god, is supported by cords held in the hands of two genii, who seem to play a purely ornamental and decorative part. The throne of the god, and the table on which the radiated disk is placed, are elegantly

Fig. 30. Chaldæan head in steatite (Louvre).

sculptured pieces of furniture, and reveal a civilisation which strives after the highest refinement in its luxuries.

As for ornaments of precious metal, none have yet been found in Chaldæa, though we know that from the most distant ages gold and silver flowed into Babylon and the towns of Chaldæa as well as into Egypt. The goldsmith's art must have been on a par with that of the seal-engraver, the monuments of which are so numerous, as we shall now see. To these branches of art belongs a small head in steatite, carved in the round and forming the gem of the Tello collection; better than anything else, this head, treated in so

realistic and, at the same time, so highly finished a
manner, brings us into contact, so to speak, with the
brilliant superiority of the Chaldæan artist when he
devotes himself to these secondary forms of art, which
at the present day require the use of the magnifying-
glass, and in which we are at a loss whether to admire
most the patience of the artist, the steadiness of his
hand, or the delicacy of his talent.

IV. CHALDÆAN SEAL-ENGRAVING.[*]

Though we do not yet possess more than a limited
number of pieces of sculpture and statues, those
imposing witnesses of Chaldæan art in the time of
Gudea or Khammurabi, we can at least supply this want
by the numerous and varied productions of the seal-
engraver's art. The Chaldæans invented the carving
of precious stones, and no people ever made a more
constant use of those cylinders, cones and seals of
every form, on which are seen, engraved in lines fine
and deep, the same images which monumental sculpture
drew upon the walls of temples and palaces. These
stones carved in intaglio, whether hæmatite, porphyry,
chalcedony, marbles or onyx of every variety, were
worn round the neck, on the finger, on the wrist, or
fastened to the garment ; they were at the same time
prophylactic amulets against sickness or witchcraft, and
seals with which impressions were made at the end
of public or private documents.

The most ancient of the Chaldæan cylinders reveals
to our eyes the very origin of seal-engraving, the first

[*] See especially J. Menant, *La Glyptique orientale*, t. i., and L. de
Clercq, *Catalogue de sa collection*, fasc. 1-3.

attempts to carve the round, ovoid, or cylindrical gems of the necklaces of the stone age. The burin and the puncheon, handled for the first time, do not yet trace out more than zigzags, lozenges, straight and semi-circular lines crossing one another. Soon attempts are made to trace buildings, figures of animals, antelopes feeding (fig. 31), or fish. The joints and swells of the quadrupeds' bodies are represented by round holes, the limbs by simple strokes.

Soon, with greater mastery over his instruments, the artist—for we may now give him this name—will seek to reproduce on the cylinders the human figure, and then that of the divine beings or the heroes begotten of popular fancy, whose image is to increase the talismanic virtue of the

Fig 31.—Chaldæan cylinder (De Clercq collection).

stone. There are monsters standing on their hind-legs, struggling with one another, and giants killing lions or human-faced quadrupeds. M. Menant has remarked that the figures of animals are always represented in profile, while the human figures, with long beards, are in full face even when the body is in profile. There are double-faced genii, quadrupeds with a single head and two bodies. One of the most remarkable cylinders of this primitive epoch is, without contradiction, that of the rich De Clercq collection, the design of which we give here (fig. 32). Men and various animals are here seen : a goat with wavy horns browsing on the leaf of a tree ; a rhinoceros, antelopes, bulls, fish, an eagle, and some trees; two demons subduing fantastic animals, scorpions, and palm-trees. We think of the biblical scene of Adam and Eve in

Fig. 32.—Chaldæan cylinder (De Clercq).

the earthly paradise surrounded by all the living beings in creation.

Fresh progress is marked by the appearance of inscriptions at the sides of the figured scenes. Every possessor of a cylinder makes a point of having his name or that of a favourite deity engraved upon it. Accordingly the names of several *patesis*, who governed Chaldæan towns three or four thousand years before our era, have been found upon cylinders. The cylinder on which M. Oppert read the name of Asrinilu, *patesi* of Umalnaru (fig. 33), represents an episode in the Chaldæan epic. The hero Izdubar, with curly beard and hair, seizes with each hand by a hind-leg two lions hanging head downwards. The scene is completed by trees, an antelope, a small human figure, a lion-headed scorpion, a human-headed bull. What is here especially striking is the archaism of the cuneiform signs, formed of strokes,

Fig. 33.—Chaldæan cylinder (De Clercq).

which cross one another, but have not yet the form of wedges, which they are to assume later, and also the modelling and suppleness of most of the figures; the instrument is no longer felt through the work.

Chaldæan seal-engraving reaches its apogee with another cylinder of the De Clercq collection, which has the advantage of being dated, at least relatively: it bears the name of Sargani or Sargon the First, king of Agade, about 3800 years before our era. M. Menant mentions it as marking an important stage in the history of art. The picture, which is very simple, is composed of two symmetrical scenes: Izdubar, with one knee on the ground, on the bank of a river, holds with both hands the sacred ampulla, from which a

Fig. 34.—Cylinder of Sargani (De Clercq).

double jet of water escapes, and at which a bull with long striated horns comes to drink.[*] Here the artist possesses all the secrets of his art: never, at any epoch, will he be able to reproduce with greater delicacy and truth the powerful muscles of the bull and the giant. And as it must certainly be admitted that monumental sculpture advances as rapidly as seal-engraving, I do not know which should astonish us most—the degree of perfection to which the Chaldæans had carried the plastic arts, or the prodigiously distant epoch to which such monuments transport us.

[*] Heuzey, *Un palais chaldéen*, p. 91.

A cylinder in the museum at New York (fig. 35), which from the characters of the writing seems almost contemporary with that of Sargon the First, is executed with a still greater perfection. The play and graceful suppleness of the muscles of the bull and the lion are rendered with the precision which the direct study of nature brings, and with the ease which betrays an artist who can overcome technical difficulties.

If all Chaldæan cylinders could be classed chronologically and by schools, epochs of perfection or of decadence would no doubt be observed, and also greater activity in some artistic centres than in others, the choice of subjects being modified from town to town and from age to

Fig. 35.—Chaldæan cylinder (New York Museum, after Menant).

age. In the present state of our knowledge we can only hazard conjectures with regard to this. M. Menant looks upon the cylinders which represent the goddess Istar holding her child upon her knees and receiving the homage of the faithful, as issuing from the workshops of Uruk (Erech); it is the prototype of the divine mother whose worship is to spread even into Greece. At Ur cylinders of very different types, but of a dry execution, which is rather a mark of decadence than of archaism, were manufactured : there are scenes of worship or initiation into mysteries, and sacrifices, among which that of the kid

is the most frequent.   On certain monuments M. Menant
recognises a representation of human sacrifices : the
most marked scene of this kind shows us a sacrificer,
who, raising his right hand, brandishes a dagger over
a kneeling child, whom he seems to prepare to slay,
in the presence of a pontiff and of the statue of the
god.   One of the commonest figures on Chaldæan
cylinders is that of the goddess Istar, sometimes decked
with rich ornaments, sometimes entirely naked, in full
face, with her hands clasping her breasts : this last
type, profusely reproduced by the modellers in clay,
was perpetuated all over the East up to the time of the
Greek and Roman supremacies.

CHAPTER II

ASSYRIAN ARCHITECTURE.

ASSYRIA, because she lies nearer to the mountains than Chaldæa, and because the use of stone, without ever being exclusive, was more frequent in northern than in southern Mesopotamia, has left us important ruins which have already been partly explored, and which allow us to reconstruct the forms of her architecture, without material gaps, from the ninth to the seventh century before our era. In temples, palaces, staged towers, and fortresses, the art of building is revealed to our eyes by means of the excavations of which Nineveh and its environs have been the object. But nothing is left of private architecture, and the same must be said of sepulchral architecture, or rather this latter did not exist in Assyria, which has only yielded to our explorers a few jars filled with bones. The corpses were generally carried away into Lower Chaldæa, which continued to be for long ages a sort of *Campo Santo*, or vast cemetery at the service of the inhabitants of all Mesopotamia. Down to the present day, the Persians, even of the most distant provinces, make a point of having their dead buried at Nejef and Kerbela, near the mosque of Ali, the great saint of the Shiite Mussulmans. This traditional superstition is turned to profit by a company of carriers, who annually

transport more than ten thousand corpses. The necropolis of Mugheir and the surrounding tells belongs
therefore both to Chaldæa and to Assyria ; corpses are
piled up there by hundreds of thousands, but beyond
the system of drainage, organised in order to catch the
rain-water, it offers nothing of great interest. There
were no sepulchral monuments ; and as for the tombs
themselves, they are generally little brick structures
with nothing remarkable about them ; the furniture
consisting of terra-cotta vases and figurines, amulets
and cylinders, is of the
most wretched description.
   The principal buildings
of Assyria, which have been
methodically and almost
completely explored, are
those of Khorsabad, some
leagues to the north of
Nineveh, and those of
Kouyunjik and Nimroud.

Fig. 36.—Tomb at Warka (after
Taylor).

Several hillocks in which a collection of important structures would with equal certainty be found, such as the hill
of Nebi Yunus, where Arab tradition fixes the tomb of
the prophet Jonah, and Arvil on the site of Arbela, have
not yet been tested by the explorer's pick ; others, such
as the artificial mounds of Kalah Shergat, Balawat, and
Karamles, have only been incompletely explored, and
though epigraphic material, extremely valuable for
history, and bas-reliefs of the highest artistic interest,
have been extracted from them, from the architectural
point of view at least their imperfect excavation teaches
us nothing new.

The Babylonian buildings of the epoch of Nebuchadnezzar and Nabonidus must have resembled the Ninevite
palaces and temples in form and architectural arrangement ; but up to the present time we can only speak
of them by conjecture, or according to the inexact
descriptions of Greek travellers, and we cannot regret
too much that the enormous Babylonian tells, such
as those called the Kasr or Palace, Tell Amran,
Babil and Birs Nimroud have yielded hardly anything
yet of their archæological treasures. We must, then,
for the present, confine ourselves to the description
of the ruins of Khorsabad, Nimroud, and Kouyunjik,
in order to reconstruct the principal forms of Mesopotamian architecture at the most splendid period of the
Ninevite empire.

§ I.   PRINCIPLES OF CONSTRUCTION.

The limestone which is furnished in abundance by
the lowest spurs of the mountains of Kurdistan enabled
the architects of Nineveh not to employ brick exclusively, and sometimes to erect walls of trimmed ashlar.
They used limestone especially for the basements of
the buildings, which were more particularly exposed to
the action of damp, so fatal to crude brick ; they also
had recourse to it for the construction of the ramparts
of the royal palaces. But even here, on account of the
dearness of the materials, which it was necessary to
seek at a distance and to spend much time in hewing,
stone is only employed for the outer facing of the
wall ; the builders use it sparingly, and are as niggardly
of it as they are prodigal of brick. Accordingly, the

walls which enclose the terrace of Sargon's palace at Khorsabad are only of stone on the surface; the interior, or rather the nucleus of the structure, is of brick. The blocks on their external and visible surface are of variable length, but are placed upon one another in very regular courses of equal height and with crossed joints. Headers penetrate like wedges into the mass of the terrace to ease the layers of brick and bind them to the stone structure. In the lower courses of the rampart of the palace

Fig. 37.—Masonry at Khorsabad (after Place).

at Khorsabad there are regularly hewn blocks from 8 ft. 2 in. to 9 ft. 10 in. square; the blocks diminish in volume in proportion to the nearness of the layers to the summit of the rampart, which was 59 ft. high, including the battlements, which formed a parapet all round the terrace.

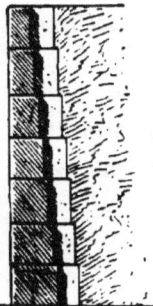

Fig. 38.—Section of wall at Khorsabad (after Place).

The interior or exterior walls of the building which stood upon this gigantic base had no need to fear the infiltration of water or the attacks of enemies: their solidity might be lessened without inconvenience, by economising the stone. As a matter of fact, they are of brick, baked or crude, and stone is scarcely employed in them except for the lining and paving of a few rooms. In that case great slabs of limestone or gypsum are set upright as a plinth against the lower part of the wall, to preserve it from corrosion; they are adjusted end

to end by the edge, and it was sufficient, in order to
fix them, to pour between their posterior surface and
the wall mortar which often only imperfectly adhered :
the outer and only visible surface of these slabs
was decorated with bas-reliefs which served for the
adornment of the halls. As for the walls themselves,
they were straight and perpendicular in contrast to
those of the Egyptian buildings, which, seen from
without, seem to lean inwards, and give to the whole
building the appearance of a truncated pyramid. The
Assyrian walls rise vertically, even when they enclose
vaulted chambers, or when they form part of staged
pyramids ; each stage forms a perpendicular terrace,
not a sloping one.

It has been observed that the partitions which separate
the halls sometimes look like one block set up on end ;
the joints and the courses of the brickwork cannot
be detected, to such an extent have the constructing
materials been soldered together in a perfect amalgam
of beaten clay. This peculiarity, noticed by Victor
Place at Khorsabad, can only be explained by admitting
that the bricks were employed in the building while
they were still saturated with water, and before the process of drying was finished. Their natural dampness,
added to that of the clayey mortar which bound them to
one another, has formed a sort of muddy paste which
must have taken years to harden, but which was particularly effective against the disintegration of the wall,
since it became in this way entirely homogeneous. It
was the extraordinary thickness of these walls which
prevented them from giving way under their own
weight, and even allowed them to uphold those heavy

beds of clay which form the vaults and terraces of the
houses. They thus protected the halls most effectively
from the ardent heat of the sun. At the present day
the inhabitants of Bagdad and Mosoul take refuge,
during summer, in their *sirdab*, a half-underground room
with extremely thick brick walls, the single opening of
which looks to the north. The people of Nineveh and
Babylon, subject to the same climatic conditions, certainly acted in the same manner. As for the princes,
they had, to defend them against the sun, walls from
13 ft. to 26 ft. thick, and vaultings as enormous as the
walls. Nevertheless, the mode of building with clay
which we have just noticed was very defective ; this is
the weak side of Ninevite and Babylonian buildings,
and we understand why the kings are unceasingly
obliged, as they relate in their inscriptions, to repair
or rebuild walls which crumble under the dissolving
action of water from the sky.

The unusual thickness of the walls, the long, narrow
form of all the chambers, are also justified by the employment of the vault as the essential element of the
Assyrian buildings. V. Place unearthed at Khorsabad a
great doorway surmounted by a semicircular arch. The
sides of the doorway, as well as the arch itself, are of
brick ; there are three rows of voussoirs one above the
other, forming as it were three concentric door-frames
half-fitting into one another. All the voussoirs, which
have issued from a single mould, have a slightly
trapezoidal shape, like the stone voussoirs of our most
carefully built edifices. The height of the doorway,
under the keystone, is 19 ft. 8 in., and the breadth 11 ft.
At other points, Place recognised that the enormous

accumulation of materials which filled up the halls could only come from the falling in of the clay vaults. Some blocks still, at the time of the excavations, formed an arch, sometimes several yards in diameter, solid enough to serve as shelter for the shepherds of the neighbourhood; they were, on the concave side, covered with carefully laid stucco, or with paintings in fresco —a circumstance which proves positively that these blocks are sections of crumbled vaults.

Fig. 39.—Vaulted and domed houses (after Layard).

The square chambers were surmounted by a dome; there are in the palace of Sargon two of these rooms as much as $44\frac{1}{2}$ ft. square. In a bas-relief discovered at Kouyunjik (fig. 39) a group of houses figures, among which some are surmounted by hemispherical cupolas, others by elongated domes in the form of sugar-loaves. The houses of Babylon were vaulted, as Strabo tells us. The Mesopotamian palaces of the Achæmenid, Parthian, or Sassanian epoch, the halls of which are surmounted by domes which scarcely yield in boldness to those of St. Sophia, evidently only handed on the Assyro-Chaldæan tradition which is also represented before our eyes by the modern houses of Mosoul, Bagdad and southern Persia. The technical methods of contemporary masons also do not fail to make known to us what steps their ancestors of the time

of Sargon or Nebuchadnezzar took to supply the want of
wood, and in consequence to do without a previous arched
framework : travellers tell us that they have observed
the commonest workmen of the country erecting their
hemispherical or elliptical cupolas by layers in rings,
laid one above the other, and narrowing in proportion
to their nearness to
the keystone; it is
the same principle as
that of the corbelled
vaulting.

The place where it
has been possible to
observe the employ-
ment of the vault in
the architecture of the
Assyrian palaces, is
in the very bowels
of the basements of
these edifices. A vast
corridor, surmounted
by a semicircular
vaulting, was disco-
vered by the English

Fig. 40.—Vaulted drain (after Layard).

explorers, in the flanks of the mound of Nimroud ;
the lower courses are of enormous slabs of stone, all
the rest is brick.   In the scientific system of drains
which carried off the sewage of the palace of Sargon,
Place distinguished every kind of vaulting : the
pointed or ogival vault, the semicircular vault, the flat-
arched vault, the shallow vault, the elliptical vault.
Never, at any point in their history, did the Egyptians

or the Romans push the application of the vault to an
equal degree of perfection. In most of the halls of
Sargon's palace a slab pierced with a hole was remarked
in the middle of the bricks which form the pavement:
this was the orifice of a vertical conduit opening into a
vaulted drain concealed in the terrace. One of these
drains had an ogival vaulting, the description of which
we will borrow from MM. Perrot and Chipiez.* "The
bricks composing it are trapezoidal in shape, two of
their sides being slightly rounded—the one concave, the
other convex. The radius of this curve varies with each

Fig. 41.—Vaulted drain at Khorsabad (after Place).

brick, being governed by its destined place in the vault.
These bricks go therefore in pairs, and as there are four
courses of bricks on each side of the vault, four separate
and different moulds would be required, besides a fifth,
of which we shall presently have to speak. The four
narrow sides of these bricks differ sensibly from one
another. The two curved faces, being at different
distances from the centre, are of unequal lengths; while,
as the lower oblique edge is some inches below the upper
in the curve, these two edges have different directions.
In their disinclination to use stone voussoirs the Assyrian

* *History of Art in Assyria and Chaldæa*, vol. i., p. 228 f. [Eng Ed.]

builders here found themselves compelled to mould bricks
of very complicated form, and the way in which they
accomplished their task speaks volumes for their skill."
The two upper voussoirs meeting and touching one
another by one of their corners, the triangular space
left empty between their edges was filled up either by
wedge-shaped bricks or by mortar. The drain which
we have just given as an example is 4 ft. 7 in. high
under the keystone
and 3 ft. 8 in. broad ;
the explorers were
able to follow it to
a length of 216 feet.
To facilitate its con-
struction the archi-
tect conceived the
ingenious idea of
building it upon an
inclined plane—that
is to say, that all the
rows of voussoirs,
instead of being

Fig. 42.—Vaulted drain at Khorsabad.
Slope of the bricks (after Place).

perpendicular, lean considerably backwards, and are
supported one upon the other ; this system, which did
not at all affect the solidity of the vaulting, allowed the
builders to do without circular wooden frames.

So much technical skill devoted to the construction
of simple subterranean conduits makes us particularly
regret that the deplorable quality of the material did
not allow the vaults and domes of the palaces to exist
till our day. However, there were not only vaulted halls
in the Ninevite buildings ; a certain number of them were

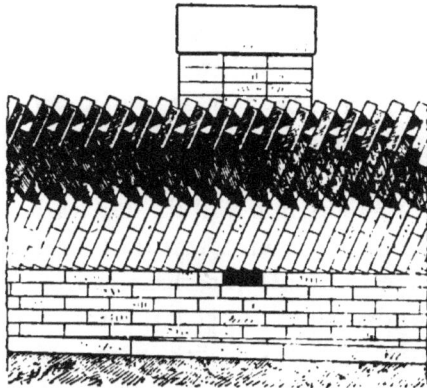

covered by flat roofs formed of beams of palm-wood, poplar-wood or cedar-wood, which supported light terraces. The bas-relief at Kouyunjik which we cited above shows us flat roofs side by side with parabolic and spheroidal cupolas. Nevertheless, what we said about the use of stone in the Ninevite structures we can repeat here on the subject of timber. Nineveh, not being too remote from the wooded mountains of Armenia, Kurdistan and Masius, where forests of pines, beeches, and oaks grow, did not deprive herself of the use of these woods in her structures ; she had panelled halls in her palaces, and, at the apogee of her power, when thousands and thousands of slaves placed their strength at the service of her monarchs, she had the timber of the Amanus and the Lebanon transported into her buildings. The king Assur-nasir-pal (B.C. 882-857) relates in one of his inscriptions that he had an enormous quantity of pines, cedars, and oaks cut down in the Amanus and the Lebanon in order to have them carried to Nineveh, and to employ them in the construction of his palace and the temples of his favourite gods. Other princes, such as Sargon, Sennacherib, Assurbanipal and Nebuchadnezzar, make the same boast of having utilised, in the buildings which they erected or repaired, beams brought from the Amanus and the Lebanon. " I caused the tallest cedars of Lebanon," says Nebuchadnezzar, "to be brought to Babylon ; the sanctuary of E-Kua, in which the god Marduk dwells, was freshly covered with beams of cedar-wood." * This is the wood of resinous nature, " the odour of which is good," add the inscriptions.

* Lenormant and Babelon, *Hist. Anc. de l'Orient*, vol. iv., p. 411.

At the British Museum fragments of a cedar beam, collected among the ruins of Assur-nasir-pal's palace at Nimroud, are preserved. Who will ever be able to say what efforts and how many human lives were required to transport these gigantic rafters across a rough country without any roads for traffic, from the Lebanon as far as the banks of the Tigris and Euphrates? Accordingly it may be affirmed that the use of wood was always exceptional in the Chaldæo-Assyrian structures; it was never introduced except as an exotic element, of which the monarchs boast on account of its rarity. The climate and the nature of the Mesopotamian soil were better suited by thick vaultings, which, then as at the present day, never ceased to be the rule there.

Quite as little as the Chaldæans, and for the same motives, did the Assyrians make a frequent and regular use of the column as an element of their architecture. Victor Place notices, like the explorers of Lower Chaldæa, several façades in the palace of Sargon adorned with pilasters and half-columns of brick, projecting beyond the plane of the walls, and having no object except to relieve the monotony of the structure. Perhaps, too, these half-columns, which are found in groups of seven, had, like the two famous pillars in the Temple of Solomon, a mystical and symbolical meaning, the number seven playing an essential part among the mythological conceptions of the Chaldæo-Assyrians. Elsewhere a few bases of columns and a few monolithic capitals have been found, which prove that the Assyrians used stone supports for monumental porches, as we ascertained in the palace of Tello. A fragment of a bas-relief preserved at the British Museum, and coming from the palace of Assurbanipal, shows us (fig. 43) the façade of a great building adorned with a projecting roof, supported by four pilasters and four columns.

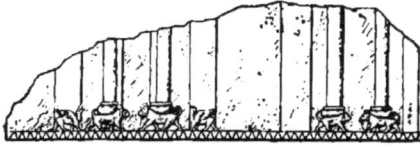

Fig. 43.— Façade with pilasters (from bas-relief in British Museum representing Babylon).

The base of these columns rests on the back of gigantic lions, which seem to advance to meet one another, two and two. On the back of the lion the architect has placed a coussinet, surmounted by a torus and by the stem of the column. In the ruins of the palace of Kouyunjik, four bases of columns were found still in place, and seeming to belong to a covered gallery; there were also two small winged bulls with human heads, crowned with the tiara, and supporting on their back a spheroidal base decorated with geometrical designs in relief. At Nimroud Sir A. H. Layard noticed also two crouching sphinxes bearing bases of columns (fig. 44); according to the same architectural principle the foot of the arches rested upon the gigantic bulls which flanked the chief entrances of the palaces.

Fig. 44.—Base of column (after Layard).

The stem of the columns was probably of wood, painted or covered with a metallic envelope. Round the inner courtyards there were, as in the courts of oriental palaces in our own day, porticoes formed of cedar beams resting on bases analogous to those which we have just noticed. Strabo * reminds us that in Babylon beams of palm-wood were used in the construction of houses: "They are careful," he says, "to wrap round each palm-wood pillar with rush-cords, which are then covered with several coats of paint." Things were not done quite in this way in the houses of the rich and in princely residences. A fragment of a cedar beam of the size of a man was discovered at Khorsabad.

Fig. 45.—Assyrian capital (after Place, *Ninive et l'Assyrie*, pl. 35).

It was still overlaid with a plating of bronze decorated with designs in *repoussé*, which imitate the bark of a palm-trunk.

An enormous block of limestone, 39 ft. 3 in. high brought to light at Khorsabad, comprises an entire capital and a part of the stem at the same time (fig. 45): it is almost the only Assyrian capital known. It affects the spheroidal form, and its convex part is decorated with a double line of curved festoons in relief; there was a similar ornament, no doubt, at the base. Several capitals from Warka are also preserved at the British Museum, but they were found among ruins of the Sassanian epoch. Nevertheless the resemblance which some of

Fig. 46.—Capital of Sassanian period from Warka (British Museum).

* xvi., 1, 5.

them bear to the architectural features of the bas-reliefs is so close that they are probably representatives of a style inherited from a former period. They are of that form, so well known in the sculptures, which has the character of the Ionic order, and was probably its original.

In imitation of their southern neighbours the Assyrians used the column especially in chapels of little importance, in which the supports had no vault or terrace to uphold. Bas-reliefs from Khorsabad and Kouyunjik represent sanctuaries the roof of which is supported by small columns with a base and a capital, which partake at

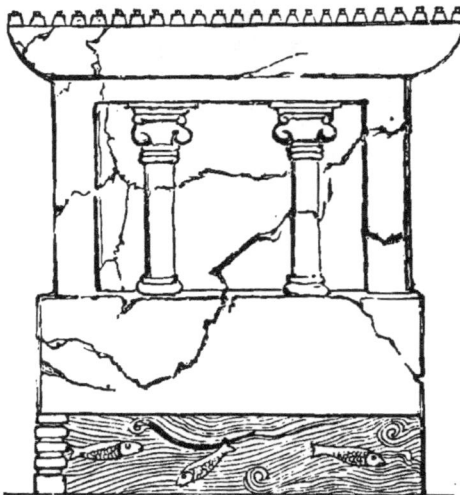

Fig. 47.—Shrine with columns (Botta, *Les Monuments de Ninive*, pl. 114).

once of the Ionic and of the Doric order of the Greeks (fig. 47). These little structures recall the Chaldæan shrine of the god Samas (fig. 29). An object which appears to be the base of a small column exists in the Nimroud Gallery of the British Museum. It is of sandstone, and, to judge from its size, it must have formed part of a small chapel or shrine, such as we see in the sculptures. The ornamental design upon

it is partly similar to that of the large capital figured
above, but presents some variations from it.   There is
a small hole into which the pillar was doubtless fastened
by a peg or metal dowel.

   The Assyrian palace, like Arab houses, developed
itself entirely in area, and not in height ; there was
rarely a second story on the platform.   Nevertheless
such a second story exists sometimes ; it is then open
at the sides, and the roof is supported by small columns.
These columns, of wood rather than of stone or brick,
form a gallery over
the   façade,   and
they are adorned
at   their   upper
extremity with a
double volute as
a   capital.   Bas-
reliefs   show   us
houses thus sur-
mounted   by   a
colonnade,   which

Fig. 48.—Base of small column
(British Museum).

supports a light, flat roof of wooden beams.   At the
present day, houses in Kurdistan are still built on the
same lines, and show an identical arrangement in two
stories; the lower without windows, the upper open at
the sides.

   In a word, the Assyrians, like the Chaldæans, not
having at their disposal building-stone in great abundance, were obliged to construct their edifices almost
exclusively of brick, the capabilities of which they tried
to the utmost.   The result of this was that they never
had those halls of columns which are the triumph of

columns

Egyptian architecture. However thick one may suppose pillars of brick, or columns formed of bricks moulded in the shape of segments of a circle, to be, these supports will never offer the same guarantee of solidity as the stone column. Wherever a heavy burden, such as a vault or a terrace, had to be supported, great walls were raised of an extraordinary thickness, which it would have been imprudent to pierce with windows capable of diminishing its resistance. Air and light only penetrated into the apartments by the doors ; often, too, an opening was contrived at the summit of the vault or dome, formed of a cylindrical pipe of burnt clay carried through the entire thickness of the structure.

§ II. PALACES.

The town of Dur-Sarrukin (the Fortress of Sargon) stood three leagues north of Nineveh, on the Khaswer, one of the branches of the Tigris, where the Kurdish village of Khorsabad has been built. Discovered in 1843 by E. Botta, French Consul at Mosoul, it was almost completely excavated by this illustrious explorer and his successor, Victor Place, and it is from Khorsabad that most of the Assyrian monuments in the Louvre come. It was the custom that each of the Ninevite monarchs should have a special palace built at some distance from the great Assyrian capital, and this became the royal residence round which stood the dwellings of the court-officers, the guards, the servants, and all persons who depended upon the prince or lived at his expense. Dur-Sarrukin was built by Sargon, the father of Sennacherib, about the year 710 before

our era. The palace and the town which was annexed
to it formed a group of structures contained within a
fortified enclosure (fig. 49) the plan of which was a
square of 5905 feet.

The wall of circumvallation, the angles of which
pointed to the four quarters of the heavens, as in the
Chaldæan buildings,
was crowned with bat-
tlements and pierced
by eight gates pro-
tected by towers.

The king's palace
(fig. 50) stood almost
in the middle of the
north-eastern façade,
and a part of its struc-
ture which projected
beyond the ramparts
had the appearance
of an enormous bas-
tion. The structure
of this palace was
supported by a plat-
form which formed

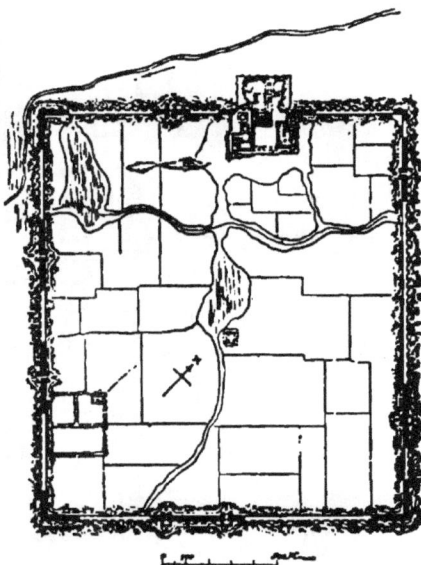

Fig. 49.—Plan of Dur-Sarrukin
(after Place, pl. 2).

an acropolis nearly twenty-five acres in area. The
mass of clay which had to be brought to raise the
terrace and the walls of the palace has been esti-
mated at 48,233,000 cubic feet. The platform over-
looked the town, and was reached by staircases,
destroyed at the present day, but which must have
been analogous to the monumental staircase which
formed the ascent to the palace of Sennacherib, and

the traces of which Sir A. H. Layard recognised.
As at Tello, a gentle ascent on an inclined plane was
formed for the passage of vehicles. The royal apartments built upon the terrace comprised no less than

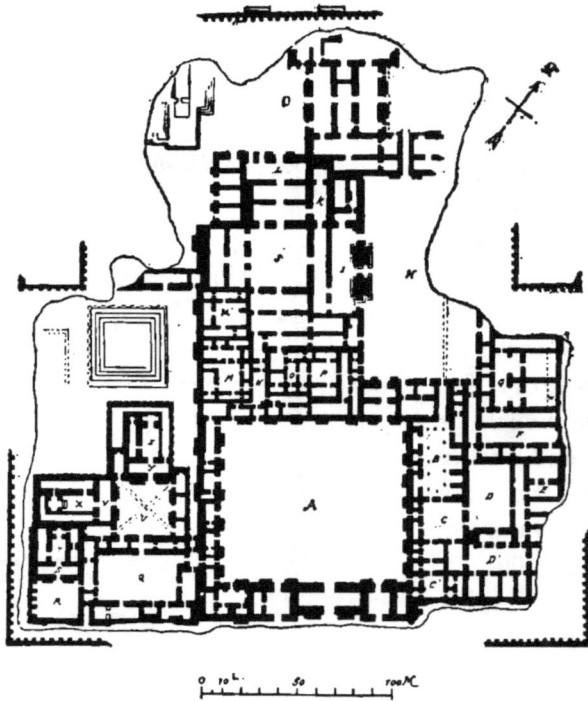

Fig. 50.—Plan of the palace of Sargon (after Place, pl. 7).

two hundred and nine more or less spacious rooms,
the walls of which, laid bare by Botta and Place,
are still sometimes twenty-six feet high and always
reach at least ten feet in the parts most demolished. It
was not easy to determine the destination of these
different halls. However, by comparison with the

present Turkish and Persian palaces, in which an
analogous arrangement has been perpetuated, with the
same usages, the following parts have been distinguished at Dur-Sarrukin as in the palace of Tello : the
seraglio, that is to say, the reception-rooms and the
dwelling-rooms of the prince and the men attached to
his person ; the *hareem*, or apartments of the women and
their children ; the *khan*, or the residence of the slaves,
the kitchens, the stables, and the offices.   The *seraglio*,

Fig. 51.—South-eastern façade of the palace of Sargon
(restoration by Place, pl. 20).

the most luxurious and most highly decorated part,
included ten courts and more than sixty rooms, adorned
with those bas-reliefs in stone which are now the glory
of the Louvre.   They were paved with square bricks
fixed in bitumen.   Where the ground was not to be
covered with carpet, as before the door, there was a
stone pavement in which the designs, skilfully carved
in relief, imitated those of the carpets themselves.   To
the buildings of the seraglio, situated on the north-east,
is attached the staged tower of which we shall speak
farther on.   The principal court of the seraglio had an

area of 3,202 square feet, and eight doors formed a means
of communication between it and the rooms of this part
of the palace; most of these openings are flanked with
colossal lions or bulls supporting the feet of semicircular
arches. The *hareem*, which occupied, on the south, a
surface of more than 94,726 square feet, formed a group
of structures communicating with the rest of the palace
by two doors only. It was, with its lofty blind walls, a
sort of prison in the very bosom of the fortress. Within,
there were several courts and isolated suites of rooms,
in which the apartments of the women were separately
arranged. The walls of the principal court must have
been decorated with true Asiatic luxury, for the foot of
these walls, when they were laid bare about fifty years
ago, was still covered with a lining of enamelled bricks
representing animals and mythological scenes. It was
here that the shaft of a column was found, of wood
covered with a bronze sheath, so that it is not rash to
affirm that this court was furnished with a portico all
round, and perhaps even with an upper story with open
sides. The *khan*, situated towards the eastern angle of
the structure, occupied an even larger space than the
hareem; the treasury or *bit kutalli*, the cellars, granaries,
and storehouse of domestic utensils, have been distinctly
recognized, as well as magazines of objects of all sorts,
carried off as plunder by Sargon in his expeditions, and
weapons of the chase and of war: in the very stables,
the presence of iron rings fixed in the wall has been
ascertained, to which horses and camels were attached:
lastly, the small but numerous rooms of the servants and
slaves have been excavated. Ctesias brings the number
of persons attached to the service of the palace of the

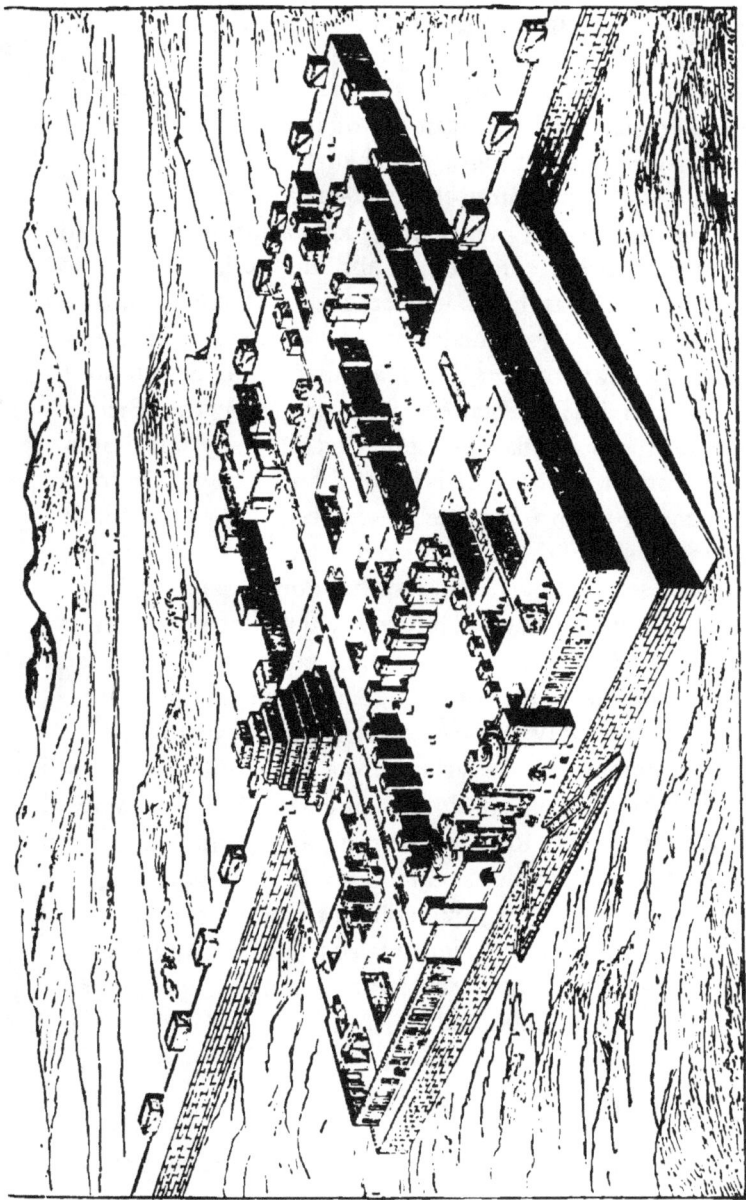

Fig. 52.—Bird's-eye view of the palace of Sargon at Khorsabad (restoration by Place, pl. 18 *bis*).

kings of Persia up to fifteen thousand : it may easily be
supposed that an equal number of hands was employed
at the court of the haughty king of Nineveh.

The palace of Sargon, the best-preserved of Assyrian
edifices, and that of which the excavation was directed
with the greatest consistency and method, deserved to
be taken as the most perfect type of the Ninevite
palaces.   The researches of the English explorers,
Sir A. H. Layard, Sir H. Rawlinson, G. Smith, and
H. Rassam, have procured, it is true, for the British
Museum the incomparable galleries of Assyrian monuments known as those of Nimroud and Kouyunjik from
the name of the principal tells explored ; they have made
known the site of the royal residences of Assur-nasir-pal,
Shalmaneser, Sennacherib, Esarhaddon, Assur-bani-pal,
and exhumed the fine sculptures which decorated their
halls ; but from the architectural point of view these
excavations teach us nothing remarkable and original,
or rather they only confirm what we know of the art of
building among the Assyrians from the study of Khorsabad ; the elements and principles of building show
themselves to be identical throughout, and, save for
secondary modifications and variable proportions, it
may be said that the arrangement and adornment of
Assyrian palaces were everywhere the same, and issued
from an uniform type created in Chaldæa, which was
never remarkably modified.

§ III. Temples and Staged Towers.

It was also in Chaldæa, as we have seen, that those
towers in stages (*zikkurat*) were invented, painted in

bright and varied colours, which constitute one of the original features of Mesopotamian architecture. If the staged towers of Mugheir, Tello and Abu Shahrein, are too much destroyed for us to be able to restore their different steps except in thought, we are sure, nevertheless, that these old Chaldæan edifices were similar to the towers the lower stories of which were excavated at Kouyunjik, Nimroud, Khorsabad, and finally at Babylon, where stood, from the remotest antiquity, the two famous temples called E-saggil and E-zida, and where Nebuchadnezzar built, according to the testimony of his inscriptions, the famous Tower of the Seven Lights. Who can say whether this architectural form was not inspired by the sight of the pyramids in steps of the Nile valley ? In any case the Greek historians agree in affirming that the staged towers were of a height comparable to that of the loftiest Egyptian pyramids, and the mass of the mounds of débris which represent the ruins of these towers is a sure warrant of this assertion. Birs-Nimroud at Babylon is still, at the present day, 235 feet high, and it has certainly lost at least half of its primitive height. The ruin of Babil is still 130 feet high. What European monument is there, even if built of hewn stone, which, after crumbling in upon itself, would reach 130 feet after thirty centuries of ruin and decay ? It is improbable, then, that Strabo deserves to be taxed with exaggeration when he assigns the height of a stadium or 591 ft. 9 in., to the temple of Bel at Babylon. Herodotus describes the same building in the following manner : " This temple is square, and each side is two stadia in length (1,183 ft. 6 in.). In the centre is a massive tower, of one stadium in

length and breadth; on this tower stands another
tower, and another again upon this, and so on up to
eight. A spiral staircase has been built outside leading
round all the towers. Towards the middle of the
ascent there is a room, and there are seats upon which
visitors rest; upon the last tower stands a large shrine,
in which is a large bed with rich coverings, and near it
a golden table." Modern excavations enable us to
affirm that this description is exact in all points, and
that all the staged towers of Assyria and Chaldæa were
constructed upon the same principle.

The *zikkurat* of the palace at Khorsabad, placed to
the east of the seraglio buildings, has still at the present
day three complete steps and the beginning of a fourth;
the first describes on the ground a square of 141 ft.
each way; each stage is 20 feet high, which gives us
reason to believe that the structure was as high as it
was broad at the base—a peculiarity already noted by
Herodotus and Strabo in the temple of Bel. The
stages laid bare by the French excavations were still
partly coloured by means of enamelled stucco, the
lowest stage white, the second black, the third reddish
purple, the fourth blue. Among the ruins of the tower
were found numerous fragments of enamelled bricks,
coloured vermilion, silver grey and gold, which proves
that the tower had seven stages of different colours. It
has been remarked that Herodotus (i. 98), gives to the
fortress of Ecbatana, in Media, the arrangement of a
gigantic tower in stages, the colours of which are similar
to those of the *zikkurat* of Khorsabad. There were,
according to him, seven concentric enclosures, the
most spacious being as large as Athens, while the

battlements of each enclosure rose higher than those
outside them. " The battlements of the first wall are
of white stone ; those of the second of black stone ;
those of the fourth blue ; those of the fifth vermilion.
. . . The two last walls are plated, the one with silver,
the other with gold."

The explorers of Mugheir thought that they recognised, in spite of the bad state of the ruins, that the
sikkurat of Ur was constructed in such a way that the
stages did not rise exactly in the middle of the square
platform of the lower
stage which served
as their base ; they
were nearer to one
of the sides, so that
they present on one
side much narrower
terraces than on the
other three. This
observation is con-
firmed by a bas-relief

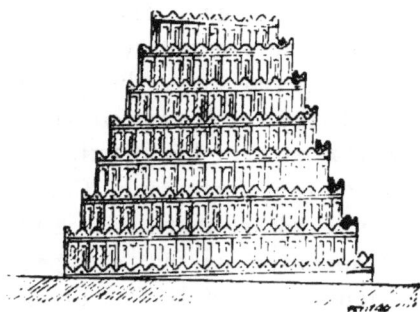

Fig. 53.—The staged tower of Khorsabad
(restoration by V. Place).

in the British Museum, unfortunately very rough, in
which, however, we distinguish clearly the greater width
of the terraces on one side and their corresponding
narrowness on the other. On the other hand the slope
of each terrace proves that it ascended like a screw, and
that there was no staircase cut in each of the stages to
put them in communication with each other. This is,
moreover, what is observed at Khorsabad : the ascent
to the summit of the ruins of the fourth stage is by a
quadrangular sloping path which mounts gently as it
winds round in a spiral form.

Diodorus Siculus informs us that the top of the staged towers was occupied by statues, for which the zikkurat would only form a sort of pedestal : " At the summit of the ascent," he says, " Semiramis placed three golden statues wrought with the hammer." These statues were perhaps in the interior of the sanctuary which generally crowned the building; everything makes it probable also that little chapels were constructed at each stage in the thickness of the structure, and that each of them was consecrated to the stellar deity of whom the colour of the stage was emblematic. The chapel on the summit was covered by a gilded cupola, which glittered under the glorious sunlight of the pure eastern sky, and dazzled all beholders. Nebuchadnezzar relates in his inscriptions that he overlaid the dome of the sanctuary of Bel Marduk " with plates of wrought gold so that it shone like the day." Does not Herodotus tell us that the last stage of the citadel of Ecbatana was gilded ? Finally, Taylor picked up among the ruins on the summit of the *zikkurat* at Abu Shahrein, a large quantity of thin plates of gold, still furnished with the gilded nails, which had served to fix them to the walls.

Besides these sanctuaries erected on the top of staged towers, in which the priests passed the night in watching the courses of the stars, there were other temples not provided with similar basements. Thus, on a bas-relief from the palace of Sargon, we see a representation of the pillage of the temple of the god Haldia at Musasir, in Armenia (fig. 54). This sanctuary, built upon a terrace like that of a palace, has a façade decorated with a triangular pediment, like a Greek

temple. Instead of a portico with columns to support
the pediment, there are thick pilasters to the number of
six, adorned at intervals with projecting horizontal lines,
and with disks, which are seen upon the façade also, and
may be taken for votive bucklers. Between the two
middle pilasters is the door of the temple, the opening
of which is enclosed by an architrave in stone ; on each
side of the door and of the same height as it, are two
colossal genii in human form, carved in stone and hold-

Fig. 54.—Temple of the god Haldia
(after a bas-relief at Khorsabad, Botta, pl. 141).

ing lances, the points of which rise even higher than
the pillars; behind them are lions ; lastly, some distance in front of the door, two gigantic basins,
probably of bronze, resting on tripods, recall the great
vessel found before the façade of the palace of Tello,
the brazen sea in the temple of Solomon, the vase from
the temple of Amathus : they were basins for lustral
water.

The description given by Herodotus and the author of
Bel and the Dragon of the famous temple of Bel-Marduk,

in Babylon, acquaints us somewhat closely with the
interior arrangement of the chapel which crowned the
zikkurat.   There was nothing, Herodotus relates, in the
way of furniture but a bed and a golden-table ; the walls
were panelled with plates of gold, silver, and ivory.   The
evidence of the Greek historian is confirmed by the text
of the cuneiform inscriptions : " I conceived the idea,"
says Nebuchadnezzar, " of restoring E-saggil, the temple
of Marduk.   I had the tallest cedars brought from
Lebanon ; the sanctuary of E-kua, in which the god
dwells, was covered with cedar beams and overlaid with
gold and silver."   Elsewhere relating the construction
of the tower of Borsippa, where stood the temple of
E-zida consecrated to the god Nebo, the same prince
expresses himself as follows : " In the middle of Borsippa I rebuilt E-zida, the eternal house.   I raised it to
the highest degree of magnificence with gold, silver,
other metals, stone, enamelled bricks, beams of pine
and cedar wood.   I covered with gold the wood of
Nebo's resting-place.   The posts of the door of oracles
were plated with silver.   I encrusted with ivory the
posts, the threshold and the lintel of the door of the
resting-place.   I covered with silver the cedar posts of
the door of the women's chamber."   On the golden
table in the temple of Marduk, Nebuchadnezzar lays, as
he recounts himself, offerings of every kind : honey,
cream, milk, refined oil ; to draw upon himself heavenly
blessings he pours out great draughts of the wine of
different countries into the goblet of Marduk, and
Zarpanit the Babylonian Astarte.*

* Lenormant and Babelon, *Hist. anc. de l'Orient,* v. iv., p. 412.

§ IV. Towns and their Fortifications.

In his description of Babylon, as Nebuchadnezzar and the kings of his dynasty made it, Herodotus expresses himself as follows : " This city, situated in a vast plain, forms a perfect square of which each side is 120 stadia long, so that the circumference is 480 stadia." Pausanias says that Babylon was the greatest city that the sun had ever seen in his course ; Aristotle seems to compare it to the Peloponnese in size.* Classical authors also assign to the walls of the Chaldæan capital a height of 200 royal cubits (342 ft.) and a thickness of 85 ft. They are said to be pierced by a hundred gates, flanked by two hundred and fifty towers and protected by a large moat, into which the waters of the Euphrates were turned. The exactness of these descriptions, which at first might seem hyperbolical, has been confirmed, as far as the thickness of the walls is concerned, by the excavations at Khorsabad, the ramparts of which are 78 ft. and even 90 ft. thick where they are furnished with bastions. The extent of the city itself was verified on the spot between 1852 and 1854 by the French expedition to Mesopotamia. The great enclosure of Babylon, that is to say, the enlarged Babylon of Nebuchadnezzar, according to M. Oppert, is 199 square miles in area—that is to say, seven times the extent of the fortified enclosure of

---

* What Aristotle really says is: " It is not a wall that makes a city, for the Peloponnese might be enclosed within a wall. Babylon, perhaps, is a city of such sort, and so is any other, the walls of which enclose a nation rather than a city. They say that when Babylon had been taken for three days part of the inhabitants were unaware of the fact."—Pol. i. 3.

Paris. A raised road, 196 ft. broad, ran along the interior of this rampart, and separated it from the interior wall, itself four times as long as the circumference of Paris; the two concentric walls bear in the cuneiform texts the names of Imgur Bel and Nimitti Bel. A view of the walls of Babylon seems to be given in one of the bas-reliefs from Kouyunjik, which represent

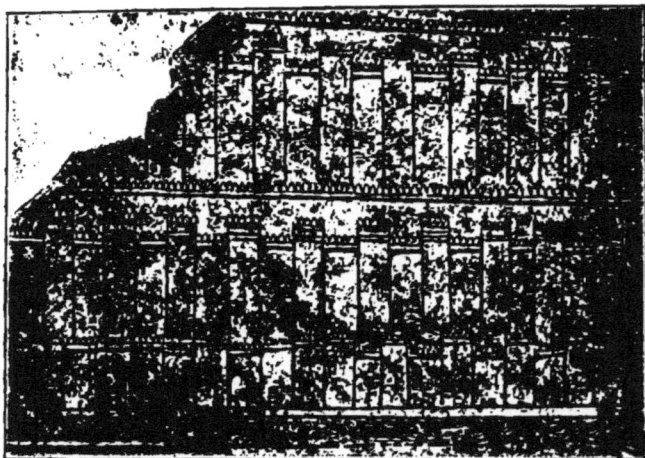

Fig. 55.—Walls of Babylon (British Museum).

the campaign of Assurbanipal against his brother Samas-sum-ukin, king of Babylon (B.C. 651-648). Nebuchadnezzar says that his own father Nabopolassar began to build the walls, and that he himself finished them; but this does not mean that the earlier city, called by Herodotus the Royal City, was not surrounded, as in the bas-relief, by a double wall like the later. Diodorus says that Semiramis surrounded the western part of the city with three walls, and two of these are identified by M. Oppert.* Fifty principal streets, twenty-five of which were parallel to the Euphrates, and twenty-five at right angles to it, leading to the hundred gates, divided the city into regular squares; a single bridge, formed of wooden planks resting on stone piles, was thrown across the Euphrates, which cut the city in two diagonally. The limits of the wall of Nineveh are not yet exactly known; but the testimony of the Bible gives us reason to believe that this city scarcely yielded in point of size to Babylon. The best mode of reconciling the statements of modern explorers with those of the Book of Jonah and the historian Ctesias, is, perhaps, to adopt the suggestion of Schrader,† and to suppose that "the Great City" of Genesis x. 12 was a group com-posed of the four towns

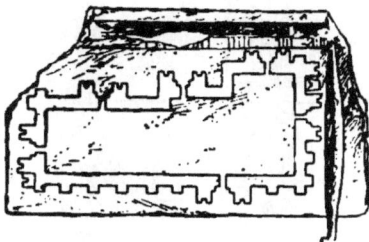

Fig. 56.—Chaldæan plan of a fortress.

there enumerated, of which Nineveh proper was the chief, and gave its name to the whole group.

In the absence of textual evidence, the very sculp-tures of the Assyrians place before our eyes numerous fortresses in plan or in a bird's-eye view. One of the statues from Tello represents the patesi Gudea as an architect, holding on his knees a tablet on which is carved in outline the plan of a stronghold (fig. 56). There are six gates flanked by towers, and the walls are surmounted by battlements. In all the bas-reliefs

* *Exp. en Mésopotamie*, t. i., p. 194 ff.
† *Cun. Inscr. and the O. T.*, vol. i., p. 79.

in which sieges are represented, the fortress is seen to
be composed of several concentric walls supported by
towers of greater elevation than the rampart from
which they [project, and surmounted by denticulated
battlements (figs. 58 and 74), which stand out on
corbels beyond the perpendicular surface of the wall.

Might we not imagine ourselves in presence of a
naïve miniature of the middle ages, representing the
siege of a feudal castle, when we examine in the
galleries of our museums
these Assyrian bas-reliefs,
on which are carved the
sieges of fortresses, which to
defend themselves against
battering-rams, arrows, and
projectiles of all sorts, are
provided with redans and
round towers, battlemented,
pierced with loopholes, and
furnished with a system of
defence which looks like
ourdeys and machicolations?

Fig. 57.—Assyrian plan of a fortress (from a bas-relief in the
British Museum).

As in the middle ages, a gate is never opened in
the wall of a fortified enclosure without being provided with a drawbridge, sheltered by two strong
towers, and defended by a projecting structure composed
of another rampart and two new bastions. The gate
is the weak point; it is the flaw in the cuirass,
the natural breach by which the enemy might enter:
every system of defence is there ingeniously accumulated, and the walls are thicker at that point. These
tall towers, these thick walls were guarded by bodies

of soldiers always on the look-out, who found here a pleasant shade to protect them from a scorching sun, to which even the inhabitants of the city found their way when they met to dis-cuss their affairs or to converse upon the news of the day. On each side of these long pas-sages recesses were made, and even actual halls for the guards. Several of the dramas related in the Biblical books are developed in such places, under such vaults. The present state of one of the en-trances of Khorsabad enables us to ascertain that the custom of as-sembling at the city gate goes back to the time of the Chaldæo-Assyrians. This gate was still sur-mounted by its semi-circular arch decorated with an archivolt in

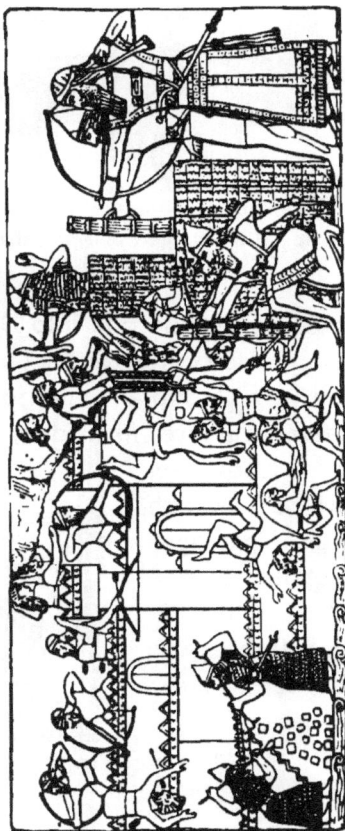

Fig. 58.—Siege of a fortress (from a bas-relief in the British Museum).

enamelled bricks. The structure formed a projection of 82 feet from the wall; built on a rectangular plan, it was itself pierced by an opening defended by two projecting bastions. After passing through this first structure, a court was reached which gave access to the opening

in the rampart proper flanked by two square towers
Through this gate a second court was reached, separated

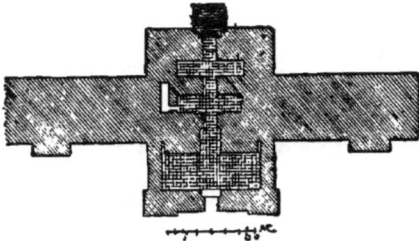

Fig. 59.—Plan of a gate at Khorsabad
(after Place. pl. 18).

again from a third
court by a new open-
ing; lastly, the wall
at the bottom of this
third court had again
an aperture which
gave access to the
town. Thus it was
necessary to pass
successively through
four doors to penetrate into Dur-Sarrukin, and a structure, symmetrical with that on the outside, projected
from the wall into the interior of the fortress. These
massive structures formed by themselves a real stronghold, 22,965 feet
square, with
vaulted passages
and galleries, the
chief of which is
not less than 278 ft.
long. It is clear
that such buildings,
which would in-
variably serve as

Fig. 60.—Gate of Khorsabad (restoration
by Place, pl. 8).

meeting-places, form fresh and cool retreats in countries
where the heat is such that it was impossible to gather
in the Forum or in the Agora, as at Rome or Athens.

CHAPTER III.

ASSYRIAN SCULPTURE AND PAINTING.

§ I. Statues, Stelæ, and Obelisks.

The brilliant period of Chaldæan statuary, which reached the apogee of its development in the monuments of Tello, came to an end with the fall of the petty principalities which flourished in Lower Mesopotamia before the Ninevite supremacy. Chaldæan statuary did not emigrate to Assyria with the other arts, or rather the Assyrians disdained to receive it. The principal cause which prevented this art from developing among the Ninevites was the nearness of the alabaster quarries, and the absence of marble, diorite, porphyry and other kinds of stone which allow of being carved in the round. Alabaster can only be hewn in thin, flat pieces, which, for this reason, lend themselves admirably to be carved in bas-relief, but are unsuitable for statuary. An alabaster statue of ordinary human proportions would be extremely fragile, and would run the risk of crumbling away in flakes, at any rate in the thinnest parts, such as the feet and hands. On the other hand, the abundance of alabaster in the neighbourhood of Nineveh caused the Assyrians to dispense with the importation from distant countries, at great cost, of blocks of diorite and porphyry like those which the Chaldæans, who

possessed neither alabaster nor any other stone, were
obliged to procure at any price. At least we must
admit that up to the present time the excavations in
Assyria have scarcely yielded to our curiosity anything
that can enable us to assert that statuary flourished in

Fig. 61.—Statue of Assur-
nasir-pal (British Museum).

Northern Mesopotamia. On
the contrary, the few Assyrian
statues that have come down
to us prove the poverty and
neglected condition of this
branch of sculpture. The
principal objects that can be
cited are two statues of the god
Nebo at the British Museum,
a statue of the King Assur-
nasir-pal (B.C. 882—857), and
two other figures of priests
which took the place of
Caryatids at Khorsabad.

The statue of Assur-nasir-
pal represents this king dresse
in a long robe without folds
and devoid of ornament, which
almost gives him the appearance of a cylindrical Terminus.
His beard and hair lie close to
his head and neck, and in each part it is evident that
the artist, through want of skill or on account of the
difficulties he felt in dealing with the block which he
had to fashion, did not dare to attribute to the limbs
a suppleness and ease that would have damaged their
solidity, nor to give to the beard and the delicate parts

of his work a finish which would have run the risk of splitting the stone.

The fringes of the robe are only indicated by slight strokes of the burin ; the arms are united to the bust, and so are the scep- tre and the crook which the monarch holds in his hands.

The Atlantes found in front of the enamelled walls of the hareem at Khor- sabad seem to have been employed in the structure as true columns ; on their head-dress they sup- port a square plinth which bears witness to their architectu- ral function ; their figures are of more than human stature. From the sacred vase which they press reverently to their

Fig. 62.—Statue in the hareem at Khorsa- bad (after Place).

breast, and which we have already seen in Chald æa, flow four streams, which recall the four rivers of Paradise in Genesis ; two of these liquid jets fall directly upon their feet, while the two others, rising over their shoulders, fall down their back to their feet in slightly undulating bands.*

* Heuzey, *Un Palais Chaldéen*, p. 81.

The scenes upon the bas-reliefs in the interior of the
palace chambers sometimes represent processions in
which deities, standing or seated, are carried upon
litters by priests or slaves (fig. 114): so there were

Fig. 63.—Stela of Samsi-Rammanu
(British Museum).

statues at Nineveh. It is
doubtful, however, whether
these discoveries give any
other impression of Assy-
rian statuary than that
which we have described.

Instead of statues, the
Assyrians often erected
stelæ and obelisks—a kind
of monument which holds,
so to speak, the middle
place between statues and
bas-reliefs. Among the
stelæ the most finished type
is that of King Samsi-Rammanu ,III. (B.C. 822—809).
It is a monolith of slightly
trapezoidal form, rounded
in the upper part. The
sides are covered with a
cuneiform inscription which
relates year by year the

military exploits of the prince. On the anterior surface,
surrounded by a border which forms a frame, the king,
in high relief and seen in profile, stands in adoration
before the planetary symbols. It is clear at the first
glance that the artist has been bolder than he would
have been in dealing with a statue in the round. The

feet and arms are freer and not held so closely to
the figure ; far from treating the details of the costume
roughly, he takes pleasure, on the contrary, in laying
exaggerated stress upon them.

In the British Museum are small stelæ of a later
date, bearing figures of Assur-bani-pal (B.C. 668—666).
They show the king holding a basket upon his head, in

Fig. 64.- Stela of Assur-
banipal (British Museum).

Fig. 65.—Obelisk
of Shalmaneser
(British Museum).

the same attitude as the early Canephoræ of Chaldæa
(see above, p. 37, fig. 25).

Assyrian obelisks, which have nothing in common
with the gigantic Egyptian monoliths to which this
name is given, are, like the stelæ, large boundary
stones set up in honour of the exploits of some prince,
sometimes on the very field of battle, or on the ruins
of a conquered town. The most complete and best
preserved of these monuments is the obelisk of

Shalmaneser III. (B.C. 857—822) found at Nimroud. This is a monolith scarcely more than 6½ feet high ; it is a square pillar, slightly pyramidal in form. The upper part is arranged in steps which recede from one another on all sides; the summit forms a platform, and has nothing to surmount it : perhaps a statuette of the king or his favourite deity formerly stood there. The four faces of the obelisk are covered with inscriptions and bas-reliefs arranged in rows one above the other. The lower part, which is entirely bare, must have been buried up to a certain point in the ground.

As we see, the stelæ and obelisks, which take the place of statues, are in a technical point of view derived from the bas-reliefs. If any Assyrian statues are brought us by future discoveries, they will always be few in number, and poor and timid in style; there is nothing among them to be compared to the Chaldæan statues, and above all nothing to be placed side by side with the innumerable Egyptian statues, the style of which sometimes almost attains to the perfection of Greek art ; Assyria also was destined to approach this ideal, but only in bas-relief.

Such was the logical consequence of the natural difference of the environments in which the empires of Egypt and Assyria, those two poles around which the whole of the ancient East gravitates, were evolved. On the banks of the Nile, stone suited for sculpture exists in profusion, and as there was abundant material in the hands of the artist, he was able to devote himself to incessant experiments, essays and trials, which, pro- gressively repeated from generation to generation, only stopped at the threshold of Greek art. In Mesopotamia there was little or no stone to carve; it was only rarely and at great expense that precious blocks were brought with much trouble from a long distance, and these were too dear and too scarce to allow of numerous experiments.

§ II. Bas-Reliefs.

To conceal the poverty of the material of their brick or clay structures, the Assyrians, as we have said, conceived the idea of lining the walls with thin slabs of limestone or gypseous alabaster of a yellowish shade,

Fig. 66.   Assur-nasir-pal sacrificing a bull (Bas-relief in the British Museum).

which they extracted at small expense from the neighbouring mountains of Nineveh. These slabs could be sculptured and polished with marvellous ease.

The most ancient bas-reliefs that the excavations in Assyria have brought to light come from the palace of Assur-nasir-pal (B.C. 882—857) at Calah (Nimroud). What a distance there is between this epoch and that of the ruins of Tello! But from the reign of this prince to the fall of Nineveh, towards the end of the seventh century—that is to say, during three centuries —there is an abundance of documents for the history of

sculpture; they have been disinterred principally from
the palaces of Assur-nasir-pal, Shalmaneser, Samsi-
Rammanu, Rammanu-nirari, Tiglath-Pileser, Sargon,
Sennacherib, Esarhaddon and Assurbanipal,—palaces
which these princes had built in order to immortalise
their fame, and the walls of which they covered with
the scenes of their valour and the narrative of their
exploits.

Besides the interior walls of the chambers, no bas-

Fig. 67.—Genius with the beak
of an eagle (Bas-relief at the
Louvre).

Fig. 68.—Two-winged genius
(Bas-relief at the British
Museum).

reliefs were found in the palaces except on the principal
façade. These sculptures on the façade have peculiar
characteristics upon which we must lay stress. In
the first place, they are exclusively devoted to religious
and mythological subjects : not the smallest allusion is
found to the exploits of the prince. They represent
especially divine heroes, winged genii with human
bodies and eagles' claws and beaks, winged lions and
bulls which guard the royal residence and defend the
approaches to it, whether against evil spirits or against

foreign invasion. Accordingly the figures in these exterior sculptures are of colossal proportions, as it is fitting for gods and heroes. There was also a reason drawn from the laws of perspective in this enlargement of the figures, since the façade of the palace was intended to be seen at a greater distance. The winged bulls at the Louvre, which come from Khorsabad, are from 13 ft. to 16 ft. high. The groups which represent Izdubar, the Assyrian Hercules, strangling a lion under his arm, are as much as $19\frac{1}{2}$ ft. The Assyrians multiplied their winged bulls at the entrance of the doors. Twenty-six pairs of them were found in the palace of Sargon, and as many as ten in a single façade of the palace

Fig. 69.—Four-winged genius, Khorsabad (Louvre, 9 ft. 10 in. high).

of Sennacherib. Assyrian texts speak of them as *kirubi* (cherubim?) or *sedi* (genii). The considerable projection of their figures from the walls makes them partake of the bas-relief and of the statue in the round at the same time. Some of these bulls have a relief of about 8 in.; placed at the corner of the doors to support the archivolt, they seemed, like Atlas upholding

the world, to bear upon their heads the whole mass
of the building. Carved on two sides, they are like
statues half-buried in the thickness of the wall. They
were generally arranged in fours, two being on the
plane of the wall, facing one another on each side of
the door, and the other two facing the visitor as he
entered, while their heads stood out from the façade
and their hinder parts remained inside the passage.
The visitor arriving from without saw before him at

once the bodies of
the first two in profile
and the full face of the
two others.   Before
the building or within
the doorway he still
saw at the same time
full faces and bodies
in profile.   By an
illusion, he seemed
to behold continually,

Fig. 70. Winged and human-headed lion and in every posi-
(British Museum).
tion, the whole of a

bearded monster, with his thick mane on his chest, his
neck furnished with tufts of hair, his legs, in which
the muscles, speaking emblems of material strength,
are powerfully marked, his wings formed of rows of
plumes, and reaching, like gigantic fans, as high as the
archivolt.

Except in the palace of Sennacherib, these winged
bulls, in order that the illusion may be more complete,
are represented with five legs ; two hind legs and three
fore legs, of which two are straight and one is bent.

The object of this trick was always to show four legs, whatever might be the position of the spectator. In fact, standing before the beast, the spectator sees his two fore legs ; on the side, one of these two being no longer visible, the artist has replaced it by a third which is seen in profile in the background. This quaint device of the Assyrian sculptor is never met with in Egypt.

The philosophical idea expressed in these bulls and lions, these impassible and majestic sentinels, is that of physical strength, calm and sure of itself; it is the conception of the Egyptian sphinxes and of the Græco-Roman Hercules in repose, with a half-smile upon his face. Only, while in the Greek Hercules the human element alone comes in, and in the Egyptian Sphinx there are only two elements, the man and the lion, four, and even more, are found in the Assyrian *Kirubu* : the man, the bull, the lion, and the eagle. The artist's chief merit is that he was able to give fair proportions to this fantastic beast, and to combine these various elements

Fig. 71.—Front face of a winged bull from Khorsabad (Louvre).

which he borrowed from nature, so as to create a figure of harmonious forms, in which nothing shocks the taste, and the expression of which is noble, majestic, and natural. To us, though we are the children

of another civilisation, nothing seems grotesque or
deformed in these fine and vigorous creations of the
Assyrian genius, which could, as skilfully as the
Egyptian genius, associate the human form with the
animal form in the symbolic representation of deity
and of supernatural beings.   It is on the banks of the
Tigris that we find the prototypes of the Loves, the
Centaurs, the Chimæras, the Sphinxes, the Gryphons,
the Pegasi, the Hippocampi of Greek art.

It has been calculated that the series of bas-reliefs

Fig. 72.   Battle scene (Bas-relief from Nimroud, British Museum).

from the halls of Sargon's palace at Khorsabad, placed
end to end, would form a line a mile and a half
long.   Those who have visited the British Museum
will remember the Nimroud and Kouyunjik galleries,
and the Assyrian Basement, each one of which is larger
than the Assyrian gallery at the Louvre.   What a
quantity of material for writing the history of Assyrian
sculpture during three centuries is here in our hands!
In the interval between every campaign, that is to say,
between two springtides, the king had bas-reliefs sculptured to exhibit before men's eyes his prowess in the

chase or in war, and the manifold episodes of official
life.   Taken as a whole, the sculptures in the interior
of the palaces are always in honour of the prince.
Everything is for the king, who symbolizes the life of
his whole people ; he does everything, and nothing is
accomplished except by his hands or by his orders ;
nowhere is the ferocious egotism of Eastern monarchs
more conspicuous than in these bas-reliefs.   Egyptian
sculptures often contain scenes of civil life from which

Fig. 73.—The Assyrian army in a mountainous country (Bas-relief
from Nimroud, British Museum).

the Pharaoh is excluded : agricultural labour, games,
festivals, public markets, and many other episodes in
the existence of the ancient Egyptian Fellaheen.   In
Assyria we find nothing of this sort ; the speaking
walls repeat, without a moment's pause, the warlike
chronicle of the kings.

   This exclusively official side of the Ninevite sculptures
compelled art to confine itself to abstract types, created
once for all, which, multiplied to satiety, produce a
certain fatigue in our minds.   There is no more pro-

7

portion or scale in the Assyrian bas-reliefs than among
the Egyptians or the Chinese ; perspective is absent,
or rather the artists made vain efforts to calculate and
reproduce its effects.   Men are taller than the chariots
that they mount and the horses which draw them ; they
even overtop the fortresses that they besiege.   As in
Egypt, the king is always represented as taller than his
ministers, and in general the Assyrians are taller than

Fig. 74.—Siege of a fortress (Bas-relief from Khorsabad, Louvre).

their enemies.   Greek heroes, in classical art, are also
often taller than the warriors who surround them ; the
same facts have been remarked in Chinese art.   The
practice is naïve, but it is common to all arts and easily
explained by the absence of perspective.   At the present
day, when our artists can at their pleasure arrange
several planes in their pictures, and produce distances
and backgrounds in the scenes which they wish to
render, they are satisfied to make the important scene
stand out and place the principal actors in the fore-

ground.   Before perspective was understood and many planes could thus be created, there was no means of bringing out the principal actors except the device of a disproportionate enlargement.

Generally speaking, the Assyrian artist shows a fondness for picturesque spots, mountains, and rivers. But he renders them with the strangest errors in the relative proportions of the objects: for instance, the

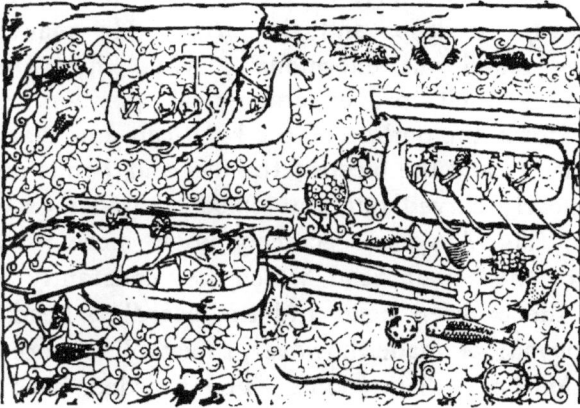

Fig. 75.—Navigation scene (Bas-relief from Khorsabad, Louvre).

fish among the waves are as large as the boats; the birds in the forests are as large as the trees or the hunters; the vultures on the field of battle are as big as the horses.

When the artist wishes to reproduce the human countenance, he always places the eye in full, even when the face is in profile.   When the sculptor is obliged to represent his figures in full face, or in any other attitude than the simple profile, he is much embarrassed, and shows his hesitation and his incapacity ; unable to foreshorten the feet, he draws them entirely in profile, while the whole of the upper portion of the body is in full face—an error which gives an appearance of dislocation to the figure. He turns the heads round as if they were put on the wrong way ; the hands present the same deformity : it might sometimes be supposed that the artist has put them on backwards.

The principal efforts of the sculptor were aimed at the head, the legs, and the arms. He makes the muscles stand out enormously, while they are not always in their proper anatomical position. Bold curves form the outline of the knee-cap and mark the leg-muscles and the biceps ; the feet and hands are not only clearly carved out, but chiselled to an excessive depth. The Assyrians scarcely knew more than two types of the human head, which they constantly reproduce : the bearded head and the beardless head. An attempt may be made, however, to establish more exact definitions and distinctions. The bearded head may wear its hair curled in very short ringlets, or else the beard and the hair may be twisted in parallel and symmetrical tresses : this last form is reserved for figures of gods, heroes, kings, the chief functionaries of the court, and soldiers. The beardless heads must be recognised as the type set apart to represent eunuchs. These personages, some of whom played an important part at court, like the Kislar-Agha, or chief of the black eunuchs at Constantinople, are characterised by their fleshy and sensual countenances.

Among the works of Chaldæan and Egyptian art there are faces which belong to old men, to young men, and to children. In Assyria it may be said that the faces never change, or rather three or four fixed types are exclusively met with : kings, officers, slaves, and even gods, have all the same physiognomy, which belongs to the age between youth and maturity. When children are met with, they have a prematurely old appearance, and their stature alone distinguishes them. The Ninevite artists rarely repre- sented women, and when they did so proved their abso- lute inexperience. Their veiled women have vulgar fea- tures, from which all ideas of physical beauty are banished. Examine the scene in which King Assurbanipal and one of his wives are drinking from goblets (fig. 77).

Fig. 76.—Eunuchs (Bas-relief from Khorsa- bad, Louvre).

The face of the queen is almost masculine in appear- ance ; even her hair is dressed like that of men ; she wears a peculiar diadem, and is draped in sumptuous robes, embroidered and enriched with jewels.

The Assyrian sculptor had not the skill to draw a true portrait and to study individual likeness, except perhaps in certain royal heads.* Nor had he the skill

* Menant, *Remarques sur les portraits des rois assyro-chaldéens*, 1882.

to give to the types which he created the least expression, betraying any motion whatever of joy or sadness :
his figures remain impassive, whether taking part in
joyous banquets, in the excitement of hunting, in
battle, or even amidst the most atrocious tortures.

Fig. 77.—Assurbanipal and his queen (Bas-relief from Kouyunjik,
British Museum).

The countenance of the Assyrian is always imper-
turbable, never laughs and never weeps ; the gestures of
his arms alone are designed to express and interpret his
impressions.   The hand raised and drawn back to the
height of the nape of the neck is a sign of introduction or of an appeal; the hand raised in front of the
mouth is a sign of mourning and of violent grief; the

hands held in such a way that one grasps the wrist of
the other, make a gesture which implies an acknow-
ledgment of servitude and absolute submission, due
only to the sovereign or to the gods. Assyrians are
sometimes seen in the act of prayer, raising one hand
as high as the face, while the
other hangs loosely by the side ;
but some adopt the Christian
posture in prayer, raising their
two hands and pressing the
palms against one another.

As the bas-reliefs of the
Ninevite palaces are specially
devoted to the representation of
the military campaigns of the
kings against foreign nations,
the artist has often been led
to draw men or women of
distant countries, distinguished
from the Assyrians by their
national costume or by certain
ethnographical characteristics.
It is sometimes possible to
understand these distinctions between Assyrians and foreigners
in the sculptures : for instance, the Jewish type could
scarcely be better expressed at the present day than it
is in the figure of one of the captives coming to make
their submission to King Sennacherib in his camp
before the walls of Lachish (fig. 78).

Fig. 78.—Jewish type, from
a bas-relief from the palace
of Sennacherib (British
Museum).

Moreover, with regard to the human form, the scope
of Assyrian sculpture was greatly limited in conse-

quence of the false modesty of the East, which was in

Fig. 79.—Assurbanipal in his chariot (Bas-relief from Kouyunjik, Louvre).

existence in ancient times as it is in our own day among

the Arabs, and prevented the artist from studying the human frame in the nude and in the living model. The Assyrian, like the Arab, is always draped in his thick burnoos, and this fashion, observed with religious strictness, contributed to no small extent to the sudden arrest of the progress of art.   The long linen tunic, garnished with embroideries, only allows the head, feet and fore-arm to be seen ; the working dress of the slaves, or sometimes the tunic of the soldiers, descends no further than the knee; the large fringed shawl, when it is worn, envelops the body like the Arab burnoos and the Roman toga.

The Assyrian, therefore, in consequence of a Semitic prejudice, could never

Fig. 80.—Sargon (Bas-relief from Khorsabad, Louvre).

express natural and ideal beauty : herein lies his inferiority in comparison with the Egyptian sculptor ; we know from thousands of examples how the artists of Thebes or Memphis treated the human torso, and several of their statues and even of their bas-reliefs are masterpieces.   Rarely has the Ninevite sculptor ventured to represent the human form in the state of

nudity, except in the case of the goddess Istar, and in
that of a few figures of slaves or of corpses lying on
the battle-field; and these exceptional cases betray
his complete want of experience.

He tried to remedy the defect which we have just
indicated by striving after perfection in details. No
art has treated with greater complaisance and refinement
all the features of the costume, not forgetting a single
tress of the hair or a single fringe in the drapery. Here
is, for instance, a bas-relief from Khorsabad (fig. 80),
which represents Sargon attended by an eunuch. Observe with what inimitable perfection the embroidery of
the tiara, of the mantle decorated with rosettes, and of
the robe with its elegant diaper pattern is rendered;
the silky softness of the fringes in the eunuch's dress is
almost to be felt. The hands and feet, beard and hair,
of the two figures, are treated with the delicacy of a
cameo. Secondary matters thus assume an exaggerated
importance detrimental to the effect of the whole; the
muscles are so strongly marked that they become monstrous; the relative proportions of the different parts
of the body are no longer conformed to nature. In this
respect again Assyrian sculpture remains greatly inferior
to its rival on the banks of the Nile. It cannot be too
often repeated that the minute study of detail and devotion to the infinitely little ruined Assyrian art by helping
to make it forget the general features of the work; the
sculptor, led astray by this false object, looked at his
figures too closely, omitting to improve their proportions and to give them more suppleness, life, and
movement; even when most finished, they always give
us an impression of geometrical stiffness.

If the direct study of bodily forms was neglected by the Assyrian artist in the case of human beings, it was not so in the case of animals. Accordingly Ninevite sculpture shows itself to far greater advantage in the representation of the animals of different kinds found in Mesopotamia. In this province it may claim a considerable superiority over Egyptian art, and reaches, in the time of Assurbanipal, that is to say, at the moment before the fall of Nineveh, a degree of perfection which

Fig. 81.—Wounded lioness (Bas-relief from Kouyunjik, British Museum).

may sustain comparison with the finest creations of Hellenic art. Its masterpiece is the figure of a lioness succumbing to the shafts of the hunters, from the palace of Assurbanipal at Kouyunjik. Her spinal column is broken by an arrow which pierces it through ; the blood gushes in streams from the wound, but though on the point of expiring, the savage beast makes a heroic effort to raise herself upon her forelegs and to utter a last roar. In order to render this dramatic attitude with so much truth, the artists must often have followed the royal hunting expeditions and witnessed terrible scenes in the deserts where the wild beasts had their haunts. Other bas-reliefs show us, with an almost equally successful execution, lions springing on to the royal chariot, dashing boldly towards the boats which plough the waters of the river, or, on the other hand, lying carelessly asleep on the plain, and lazily stretching out their limbs, the modelling of which is free and truthful.

Next to the lion, the Assyrian artist takes the greatest pleasure in representing the horse. In one scene it is the wild horse, starting and bounding as he is caught by the lasso of the hunters; in another it is the war-horse, dashing at full gallop towards the enemy, and ridden by a warrior who draws his bow or brandishes his lance; or again it is the draught-horse, harnessed to the royal chariot, trampling corpses under his feet, or drawing the heavy waggons in which the booty from the enemy's country is transported into Assyria. Such was the skill of the artist, that naturalists have been able to decide from the study of the bas-reliefs what breeds of horses were produced in Assyria. The dog, the goat and the sheep, the ibex and the wild boar, the bison and the wild ass, the deer and the gazelle, the camel and the dromedary, are also among the animals which frequently occur in the bas-reliefs designed to perpetuate the memory of particularly successful hunting

Fig. 82.—Slaves carrying a lion and birds. Bas-relief from Khorsabad (after Place).

expeditions, or of the capture of herds belonging to a vanquished people.   The artist took pleasure in placing them in the most fanciful attitudes, sometimes with the happiest effect.   It was also his delight to introduce in procession the figures of foreign animals, sent to the King of Assyria by tributary nations, such as the elephant, the ape, and the rhinoceros. But the rarity of such animals in Mesopotamia explains the peculiar clumsiness of the Assyrian sculptor in the reproduction of them.   Here are apes treated with an almost grotesque *naïveté*; they look like men disguised in the skins of animals, and trying to walk on all fours (fig. 83).

Fig. 83.—Envoy bringing apes as tribute (Bas-relief from Nimroud, British Museum).

Among birds we find the eagle, the vulture and the ger-falcon hovering heavily and ungracefully over the battlefields, though the anatomical details of these birds are sometimes executed with skill.* The ostrich, a sacred bird, appears on cylinders and among the embroidered designs on official robes.   Locusts, that plague of the whole East, figure in the character of offerings to the gods, and, no doubt, represent legions of evil spirits.   In the rivers eels, crabs, and fish are placed.   In the field, on the mountains, or on the

* Layard, *Monuments of Nineveh*, vol. i., pl. 26, and *passim*.

river-banks we find palms and trees of every species, onions, ears of corn, lotus-flowers, vines, marsh-plants. But if the scrupulous imitation of nature sometimes leaves nothing to be desired in these sculptured forms, ignorance of the laws of perspective has forced the artist to employ devices of childish simplicity. Thus, to indicate that trees grow on each side of a stream, he has placed them upright on the further bank, and stem downwards on the nearer.

In the same way, when he wishes, for instance, to show us what passes within the enclosure of a fortress (see fig. 57), he is reduced to display it on the ground with the bastions and battlements in profile around it, turned outward like the points of a coronet; at the same time he arranges all his scenes within this enclosure in divisions one above the other, without regard for the laws of proportion, and without even taking the trouble to contain himself, as he has done with regard to the enclosure, within the spaces marked out by radii starting from the centre. By a further neglect of perspective, in the representation of an ox or other horned animal, he places the horn in profile projecting forwards from the head.

Besides the bas-reliefs which were displayed upon the walls of the palace-chambers, there were secondary pieces of sculpture in which the originality of the Assyrian genius comes to light. A notable example is found in the decoration of the thresholds of the palaces, which were carved in such a way that they looked like rich carpets. One of the most remarkable of these is a large slab of gypsum found at Kouyunjik, (fig. 84), in which the lotus or tulip-flower is combined with rosettes, open daisies and geometrical designs most harmonious in effect; nothing more elegant in decorative sculpture has ever been conceived.

To sum up, Assyrian sculpture triumphs in the bas-relief, and in the patient and minute labour of orna-mental design. If the work of the Ninevite chisel is compared to that of the Greeks in the archaic period, down to the appearance of the Æginetan school, a surprising affinity will be observed between them. The stela of Aristion, that primitive Athenian bas-relief, known under the incorrect name of the *Warrior of Marathon*, looks, at first sight, as if it had been taken from the walls of Sargon's or Sennacherib's palace. At Khorsabad a cippus, ac-quired by Victor Place, is adorned with parallel

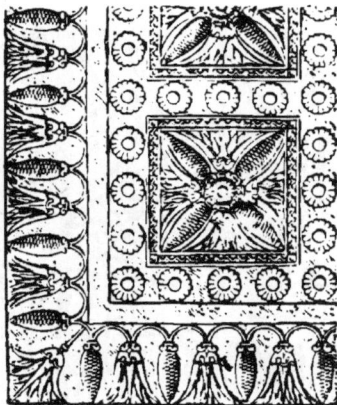

Fig. 84.—Fragment of threshold Kouyunjik (British Museum).

flutings terminating in a hemisphere of elegant palmettes ; it presents the appearance of a Greek stela.*

If we compare the sculpture of Kouyunjik, Nimroud, Khorsabad and Kalah Shergat with one another, we observe, beneath the general uniformity that we have indicated, differences important enough to enable us to characterise the progress of art during the three centuries before the fall of Nineveh, and not simply

* Perrot and Chipiez. *History of Art in Chaldæa and Assyria,* vol. i., p. 257.

the result of the varying talent of the artists. We
seem to be able to distinguish in Assyrian art, as we
learn to know it in the bas-reliefs, three periods or
three successive developments. Under Assur-nasir-pal
the figures are already bold and powerful, but thick-set,
and they appear in small numbers in the scenes represented ; their motions are sober, but full of truth.

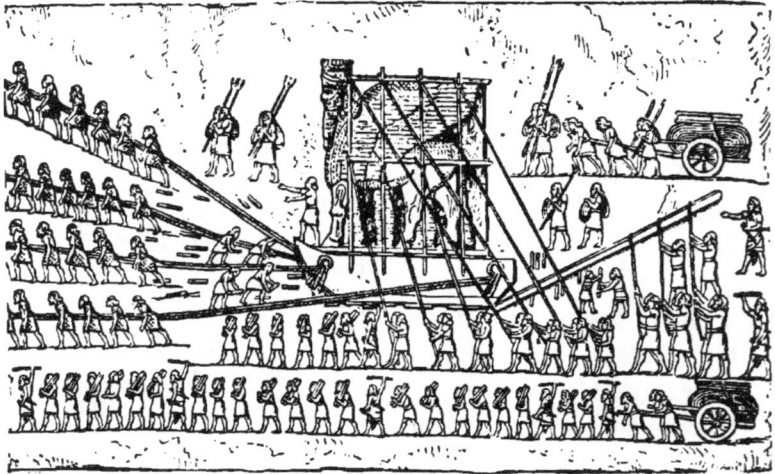

Fig. 85.—Slaves dragging a winged bull.   Bas-relief from Kouyunjik
(British Museum).

The artist has the singular habit, only observed in
Assyrian art, of covering a portion of his figures with
long inscriptions explaining the scenes which he intends
to portray (see fig. 83) ; we have already seen that the
Chaldæan statues of Gudea are covered with inscriptions, and Herodotus' statement* that the figures of
"Sesostris" in Ionia, doubtless the Hittite figures
described below, bore inscriptions across their breasts

* Herod. ii. 1c6.

is probably based on a confusion with the Assyrian
figures in Syria and elsewhere. Under Sargon and
Sennacherib, the sculptors became more experienced
and more ambitious. In their works the figures are far
more numerous, and concur more visibly in a common
action; they have more life and movement; the scenes
representing battles, hunting expeditions, the worship
of the gods, or slaves engaged in public works are more
varied; the gestures of the figures are more marked
and more energetic, the muscles of the legs and arms
more deeply outlined ; lastly, the human forms are no
longer covered with
inscriptions; these
are placed at the
side, as explanatory
legends.

In the time of
Assurbanipal, a more
natural art, and one
which conformed

Fig. 86.—Deer hunt. Bas-relief from
Khorsabad (after Place).

more to the true principles of sculpture in bas-relief,
came into being. Instead of giants, we find on the
contrary small figures forming a series of pictures,
containing the greatest variety of scene, and full of
freshness and action. This art reaches its apogee in
the figure of the lioness which we have cited (fig. 81).
It must be added that all the parts of the same bas-
relief are seldom sculptured by the same artist, and
that figures of very unequal merit are met with. The
master's chisel reserved for itself the principal personages, the royal train and the officers who surrounded
it ; the disciples worked at the secondary portions, the

8

corpses of the enemy, the processions of prisoners, the background of the landscape. Matters were not managed differently with regard to the sculptures of the Parthenon.

§ III. Painting and Enamelling.

The bricks which composed the structure of the walls in Chaldæan or Assyrian edifices were nowhere visible. Above the slabs sculptured in bas-relief and under the spring of the vaults a white stucco was applied, made of plaster and lime, like that still used by the Orientals to coat their houses; this custom explains the phrase "whited sepulchres" in the Gospels. It was doubtless on a plaster of this nature that the mysterious hand of which the Book of Daniel speaks traced out Belshazzar's sentence of condemnation on the night of the ill-famed banquet: the sacred writer says that the hand wrote "on the plaster of the wall." This stucco was often decorated with paintings in distemper, at any rate in the principal chambers, above the line of the bas-reliefs.

Modern explorers have collected some fragments of these frescoes or decorative paintings; at Warka, among the ruins of the temple called Wuswas, Loftus acquired some which belong to the remotest Chaldæan period. At Khorsabad, V. Place found on some pieces of stucco elegant rosettes formed by the application and juxtaposition of very decided colours: white, yellow, green, red, and black. One of the most remarkable examples of this painting is a border of bulls painted white on a yellow ground, their form being

relieved by a broad black outline (fig. 87). Above is
a row of blue battlements ; below festoons of many
colours. The effect is harmonious, though the tints
are flat, and in spite of the absence of all modelling in
the figures.*

The application of stucco of different colours is particularly conspicuous in the construction of the staged
towers, the terraces of which are, beginning from the
lowest, white, black, red, yellow, vermilion, silver and
gold. In the interior of the chambers, to avoid the
disagreeable con-
trast between the
uniform whiteness
of the stone bas-
reliefs and the
brilliancy of the
many-coloured
paintings, the
fashion was to
colour the figures
in the bas-reliefs

Fig. 87.—Painting on plaster, Nimroud
(after Layard).

themselves. Some traces of colouring may still be
recognised in the sculptures preserved in our museums,
and though it is true that they are being gradually
effaced, they were quite evident when the slabs were
disinterred. The beard, hair, weapons, and even
the face and costume of the figures were coloured
in a similar manner to the paintings on plaster, so
that this painted stucco seemed to be the continuation
of the bas-reliefs. There are, for instance, evident

* Perrot and Chipiez, *History of Art in Chaldœa and Assyria*,
voL ii., p. 294 ff.

traces of vermilion paint* on the figures of demons in the Assyrian basement of the British Museum. The Assyrians obeyed the same laws of æsthetics as the mediæval artists, who applied polychrome colouring to their marble or stone statues, to bring them into perfect harmony with the rich decoration which filled their cathedrals from the floor to the keystone of the vault.

Enamelled brick played the same part as painting in

Fig. 88.—Portion of an enamelled archivolt at Khorsabad
(after V. Place).

fresco, only it was more solid and was better able to resist the action of damp. In Chaldæa, where it rains oftener than in Assyria, greater use has been made of enamelled brick than in the latter country. The Ninevite artists scarcely ever employed this method of decoration, except round the principal doorways and to make an elegant border for the archivolt. The bricks of brilliant colours, which are conspicuous from a distance, are ornamented with floral designs and rosettes in exquisite taste. In Sargon's palace

* Cf. Fzekiel xxiii. 14.

V. Place found nearly all the bricks of the archivolt
of a door. Between two borders of white rosettes is
a broad frieze containing winged genii and symbolical
animals bearing the same attributes as the similar
figures in the bas-reliefs (fig. 88). On the lower plinth
of the chief door of the hareem there figured on
the enamelled bricks a lion, an eagle, a bull, and a
plough ; at the turn ·of the angle stood the king. At
Nimroud most re-
markable enamelled
fragments were also
discovered depicting
portions of soldiers,
weapons and chariots,
and even parts of
inscriptions. On a
single brick, found
by Layard, a king
is seen offering a
libation and attended
by two warriors
(fig. 89). But in

Fig. 89.—Enamelled brick, Nimroud (after
Layard).

general each figure was made up of a large number
of bricks, since the restricted dimensions of a baked
brick did not allow more than a part of the subject to
be placed upon it. The design was executed and the
vitrifiable colours applied before the baking ; the artist
had to apportion to each brick the different parts of
a figure in such a manner that when they were put
together there might be perfect agreement in the lines
which had to join ; the marks to indicate their position,
set on the backs of the tiles, made this operation, which

required great technical skill, much easier. At Babylon, where enamelled brick played a far greater part in the decoration of buildings than at Nineveh, the device was adopted, in order to replace coloured sculpture in stone, of stamping bricks with figures or parts of figures in relief. Imagine a slab of soft clay several square yards in size ; on the surface of this the whole picture was modelled in relief as it might have been carved on stone. When this operation was finished, the slab of clay was cut into rectangular pieces of the size of ordinary bricks. These pieces, provided with a mark to indicate their position, were then separately coated with colour and varnish, and afterwards baked. Subsequently they were joined together with bitumen, which formed a strong mortar, and in this work of reconstructing the design the workman was guided by the position-marks. This was the first origin of the mosaics in relief made by the Greeks and Romans. The Achæmenid palaces of Susa were decorated by the same methods, and Persian artists imitated the Babylonians in their execution of the great brick bas-reliefs with which the expedition conducted by M. Dieulafoy has enriched the Louvre.

Unfortunately only unimportant fragments of bricks modelled in relief have been, down to the present time, brought to Europe. Travellers pick up hundreds of fragments of flat enamelled bricks like those at Nineveh on every mound which covers the ruins of Chaldæa. Those which have been deposited in our museums represent floral designs, rosettes, genii, animals, and human figures. Only skilfully directed excavations could bring to light complete pictures and scenes analogous to those displayed upon the walls of the Ninevite and Susian palaces. Diodorus, following Ctesias, relates that at Babylon, on the walls of the palace built by Nebuchadnezzar, but which he attributes to Semiramis, there were scenes of every sort painted on brick. "Animals of every kind," he says, "were here to be seen, copied according to all the rules of art with regard both to form and colour. The whole represented the hunting of various animals, the dimensions of which exceeded four cubits. In the midst was Semiramis on horseback, hurling a javelin at a panther, and beside her, her husband Ninus striking with his lance a lion which he is attacking at close quarters." Berosus is no doubt speaking of enamelled bricks in his description of the paintings in the Temple of Bel, in which were seen "marvellous monsters of every sort presenting the greatest variety of forms." Lastly, the prophet Ezekiel, who lived at Babylon, says, speaking of Jerusalem: "she saw men pourtrayed upon the wall, the images of the Chaldæans pourtrayed with vermilion, girded with girdles upon their loins, exceeding in dyed attire upon their heads, all of them princes to look to, after the manner of the Babylonians of Chaldæa."

The art of enamelling brick, handed down by the Babylonians to the Persians of the Achæmenid period, long remained flourishing in the East. The decoration of the mosques of Broussa, Tabriz, and Ispahan, which excites the admiration of every traveller, is based on the same principles as that of the Ninevite, Babylonian, and Susian palaces. Only, instead of figures of living beings, which the Koran does not tolerate, the enamelled

tiles bear religious inscriptions in ornamental Cufic
characters, and elegant designs of flowers and trees.
Every one has had the opportunity of seeing specimens
from the workshops which were still flourishing in the
last century in Asia Minor, and the productions of
which adorn the palaces and the richest mosques of the
Mussulman world.   This art is directly derived from
the Chaldæo-Assyrians, and it is interesting to observe
that their successors, down to our own times, have not
made the smallest progress in it.

CHAPTER IV.

§ I. CERAMICS.

THE causes which impeded the development of pottery in primitive Chaldæa had the same unhappy influence on Assyrian pottery and on Chaldæan pottery in the age of Nebuchadnezzar. Though a few terra-cottas are fashioned with a certain elegance and present graceful features, their walls are always extremely thick, on account of the friable nature of the clay, and the types created by the modeller are totally wanting in variety. Botta found under the pavement of the courtyards at Khorsabad little cavities containing, besides cylinders and other amulets, terra-cotta statuettes of talismanic character, intended to conjure and drive away the infernal powers. " These statuettes," says M. Heuzey, "are designed with a remarkably sure hand, in grey clay, which is almost crude, and pitted with small holes, as if it had been mixed with chopped straw or hay, according to the process followed in the manufacture of bricks." * The example which we reproduce represents the hero Izdubar, so often drawn upon the bas-reliefs and

* L. Heuzey, *Les Figurines de terre cuite du Musée du Louvre*, p. 1.

cylinders as he is here, that is to say, with curled
beard and long hair in ringlets. His countenance is

expressive, and shows signs of
careful work. The same praise
must be given to the head of a
fantastic animal, also found at
Khorsabad (fig. 91); this head, in
whitish clay, is covered with a
glaze of a fine bluish green, resembling, and perhaps imitated
from, Egyptian pottery; a similar
figure of a monster roaring at
winged genii appears among the
bronze monuments; in both cases
the art is realistic, and has rendered
ugliness and ferocity with all the
force of ideal expression.

Fig. 90.—Izdubar. Terra-
cotta (Louvre).

The terra-cotta vases discovered
during the excavations in Assyria
no doubt denote a real progress

when compared with Chaldæan ceramics;
but they are still nothing but heavy amphoræ, with or without handles, with a more
or less elongated neck and a more or less
broadened body, and they could never be
compared to any but the most archaic
productions of Greece. They are sometimes
decorated with brown or yellowish paintings,
or with designs in relief, representing floral
scrolls, geometrical lines or diapers, but never

Fig. 91.—
Head of a
monster.
Terra-cotta
(Louvre).

with anything that reflects the beauty of the Ninevite
sculptures. Among them all there are no vases which

formed part of the luxuries of a refined civilisation, as the Greek vases did; neither in Assyria nor in Chaldæa have any clay vessels been discovered except vulgar jars and pots. This is, perhaps, the place to notice fragments of two small circular vases of steatite or soapstone discovered at Nimroud and Sherif Khan, near Kouyunjik. They are probably of the age of the Sargonids, and are dedicated to certain deities. The thin walls give these vessels almost the appearance of porcelain, of which Layard supposed them to be, and the figures carved upon them in relief, give them an artistic character which the Assyrians could never impart to their pottery. One of the fragments is engraved by Layard.*

Fig. 92.—Tablet with figure of boar in relief (British Museum).

At Babylon, whither the seat of government was transferred after the fall of Nineveh, the modellers seem to have made a great artistic effort. Mr. Rassam obtained from the ruins of the southern capital a small terra-cotta tablet, 1¾ in. by 2¾ in., on which the figure of a boar, such as lived among the reeds and marshes of Mesopotamia, is modelled in relief. The forms of the animal are here reproduced with all the excellence of the later Assyrian artists, by Azaru, of the tribe Esaggilai (doubtless connected with the great Chaldæan Temple), whose name inscribed on the back adds to the interest of the little work. Solid figurines have

* *Nineveh and Babylon*, p. 358.

been found in Chaldæa, like those in Assyria, moulded
on one side only in greenish clay, forming remarkable
examples of Babylonian art.   The chronological position
of these figurines is, however, difficult to determine,
but they seem to us to be, perhaps, contemporary with
Nebuchadnezzar.   They represent priests or gods,
standing upright in their long robes, with their hands

Fig. 93.—The
Divine Mother.
Terra-cotta
(Louvre).

Fig. 94. — Istar.
Terra-cotta
(Louvre).

clasped in the attitude of respect; women dressed in
fringed garments, carrying a vase upon their breast;
nude goddesses, standing upright, and suckling the
divine child.   One of these last (fig. 93) is, says
M. Heuzey, "A purely Asiatic type, the rather full
forms of which are modelled with charming truth and
rare delicacy; I do not fear to describe it as a little
wonder of its kind."*   Another and commoner ex-

* Heuzey, *op. cit.*, p. 2.

ample is the goddess Istar, nude and holding her hands against her breasts, adorned with bracelets and necklaces, with her hair elaborately dressed : this naturalism and immodest freedom in the representation of Istar form a contrast with the ordinary habit of Chaldæo-Assyrian art. This series of figurines is chronologically terminated by the statuettes of the Achæmenid or Parthian epoch, modelled of the same clay, but showing all the characteristics of decadence. The forms are less carefully studied ; sometimes Istar, the goddess of Erech, is represented in these figurines of terra-cotta or alabaster, half-reclining on a banqueting couch, like that described by Herodotus in the temple of Bel-Marduk at Babylon ; her head is often crowned with the crescent, her proper symbol, in the centre of which a garnet or other sparkling stone is set. In short, these coarse images of the voluptuous goddess condemn at once the art and the manners of the people who produced them.

§ II. Metals.

The art of working in metals, which was already so highly developed among the primitive Chaldæans, reached its apogee under the Sargonids. We find statuettes, bas-reliefs in repoussé, vases and utensils of every sort, weapons and ornaments, so that there is no use of the precious metals, or of iron and bronze, to which they were not put by the industry of Ninevite craftsmen. Among the ruins of Sargon's palace, objects of iron and bronze, such as hooks, rings, chains, pick-axes, hammers, plough-shares, weapons, fragments of chariots, and tools of all sorts, were picked up. From the strictly artistic point of view, we have already described the wooden pillars plated with overlapping scales of bronze, so as to imitate the bark of the palm tree.

The most important of the Assyrian monuments in bronze hitherto discovered is the famous decoration of the gates of the palace of Shalmaneser III. (857—822), at Balawat. It consists of metal bands, 9 in. broad, decorated in repoussé with reliefs representing the campaigns of Shalmaneser. They were fixed horizontally, at intervals, on wooden gates, which may have been quite 7 or 8 yards high ; the scenes are reproduced upon them with the same ease and the

Fig. 95.—Gates of Balawat.   Restoration.

same details as on the limestone slabs : battles, landscapes, trees, rivers and mountains are to be seen ; the figures, however, are treated more roughly, and the muscles are marked with less precision and delicacy. Each band (fig. 96) is divided into two compartments by a row of rosettes, imitating the heads of nails. " Taking them all in all," says M. Perrot, "these bronze reliefs are among the works which do most honour to Assyrian art." *

The perfection of the work in certain Assyrian bronze vessels makes these monuments real master-

Fig. 96.—Fragment of metal band of Balawat gates (British Museum).

pieces. Pateræ found at Nineveh, sometimes incrusted with gold and silver, present on their inner surface, in an exquisite style, concentric zones of rosettes and symmetrical festoons of figures engraved in outline or standing out in relief (fig. 97). Symbols are encountered

* *History of Art in Chaldæa and Assyria,* vol. ii., p. 217.

which have evidently been borrowed from Egypt, such

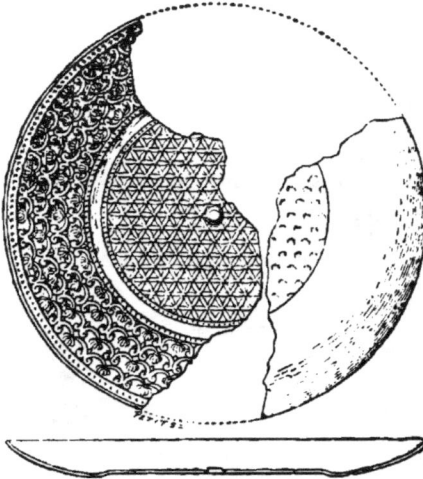

Fig. 97.—Bronze dish, Nimroud
(British Museum).

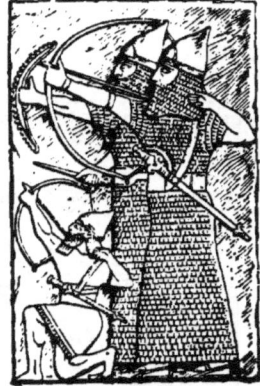

Fig. 98.—Assyrian archers.
(Bas-relief in British
Museum.)

as the winged scarabæus and the figures of Athor and

Fig. 99.—Various forms of the Assyrian helmet.

Bes. Similar in form, in the metal of which they are
composed, in the gold and silver incrustations, and

even in the choice of subjects, to the Phœnician vessels from Cyprus (figs. 233 and 234), the pateræ of Nineveh are not, for the most part, of Assyrian manufacture; they were brought thither by Phœnician commerce, and were probably fashioned in the workshops of Tyre or Sidon, where the artistic traditions of Egypt and Assyria were united. The glass found among the

Fig. 100.—Bronze lion (Louvre).

Assyrian ruins was also probably of Phœnician manufacture, as it will be seen in the chapter on Phœnician art. Much more exclusively Assyrian are the bronze seals which the bas-reliefs show us in the hands of priests or genii. We find among them lions' heads, flowers and elegant rosettes on the bottom, on the border, or at the point at which the handles are attached.

Fig. 101.—Bronze siren.

The equipment of an Assyrian soldier consists of a bow and arrows, a lance or javelin, a club, a sword, a dagger, a helmet, a coat of mail, and a buckler; the battering-rams which sap the walls had a metal carapace and head. Might it not be imagined that these Assyrian soldiers, wearing the conical helmet, and entirely covered, with the exception

9

of their arms, nose and eyes, with a long coat of iron
mail, were mediæval
knights ? The shape
of the Assyrian hel-
met varies according
to the time, and per-
haps also according
to   military   rank.
There is the helmet
formed of a conical
basin, without orna-

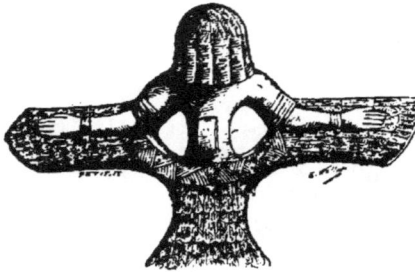

Fig. 102.—Bronze siren.

ment, the helmet provided with cheek-pieces, as among
the Greeks, the helmet deco-
rated with an elegant crest
bearing   an   aigrette   of
feathers   or   of   horsehair.
But the essential form is
always   that   of   a   hemispherical basin, covering the
head, but leaving the face
bare.   A   votive   shield,
preserved   at   the   British
Museum,   has,   like   those
represented   in   the   bas-
reliefs,   the   form   of   a   large
round disk, convex in its
central   part ;   this   metal
disk, 34 in. in diameter, is
decorated like the pateræ
with   a   central   rosette   and
several   concentric   zones

Fig. 103.—The demon of the
South-west wind. Bronze
(Louvre).

containing lions and bulls in relief.

The preceding examples prove the existence of a manufacture of metals which had reached a high degree of perfection, and was in possession of all the technical methods. Accordingly, we believe that the scanty number of statues or statuettes in bronze of human beings or of Assyrian deities must be attributed to an unfortunate chance. They must have been produced in large numbers, as in ancient Chaldæa, and a good proof of this is the large cow's head disinterred near Bagdad and preserved at the British Museum*; another example is the statuette of a lion found at Khorsabad (fig. 100); this has, doubtless, serious defects, such as a singular disproportion between the head and

Fig. 104.—Bronze plaque. De Clercq collection.

the body, between the fore legs and the hind legs; but what truth of expression in the muzzle with its gaping mouth, and in those powerful claws !

A statuette in M. de Vogüé's collection, found at Van, represents a sort of siren which seems to have

* Perrot and Chipiez, *History of Art*, vol. ii., p. 143.

acted as an ornament attached to a vessel or a piece of
furniture (figs. 101 and 102).   The oriental appearance
of the head, the hair in ringlets, the large eyes, the
bracelets upon the outstretched arms behind the wings,
and the artistically marked feathers, make of this little
monument one of the
most precious relics
of the art of working
in bronze among the
Assyrians. A similar
figure is preserved in
the British Museum,
and in this instance
the loose ring by
which the vessel was
held is still in place.

The Louvre pos-
sesses the figure of
a monster with four
wings which repre-
sents the demon of
the south-west wind,
as the cuneiform
inscription upon it

Fig. 105.—Bronze plaque. De Clercq
collection (other side).

teaches us (fig. 103).
Nothing can be im-
agined more hideous and more expressive than the head
with its glaring eyes, roaring throat, horned brows,
crooked fingers and fleshless body with lion's claws.
It leads us naturally to cite a bronze plaque from the
collection of M. de Clercq, in which M. Clermont-Ganneau
has recognised a representation of the Assyrian hell. One

side (fig. 104) is occupied by a monster with four wings and eagle's claws, looking over the top of the plaque; on the other side (fig. 105) the monster's head is seen, and under it scenes arranged in four rows: first the symbolical figures of the stars, then a procession of seven creatures dressed in long robes and having the

Fig. 106.—Standard in a
bas-relief from Khorsabad
(Louvre).

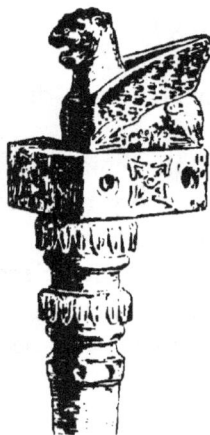

Fig. 107.—Foot of a
piece of furniture.
De Vogüé collection.

heads of various animals: these are the heavenly genii called Igigis. Below this we witness a funeral scene: two creatures with human bodies combined with the head and body of a fish, like the god Oannes, stand by a bed on which a corpse is laid out, swathed in its mummy-clothes; near them stand two monsters like the demons which appear in a battle scene belong-

ing to the campaigns of Assur-nasir-pal, and, of larger
size, on the walls of Assurbanipal's palace; they face
one another in the same attitude here as there, and
seem to be disputing or quarrelling. The lowest row
shows a stream of water in which are fish. In a boat
is a kneeling horse; on his back is a monster holding
serpents in his hands; lion-cubs are springing forwards
towards him; another monster stands on the brink
of the water; in the background are trees and fragments of different kinds, looking like the remains of
a banquet. There is some artistic merit in several
portions of this curious scene. The monster on the
other side is boldly designed, and his form is vigorous
and supple.

In the chiselling of a royal standard (fig. 106), the
artist really attained to the highest technical skill: the
bulls' heads and the lions' heads arranged along the
pole are masterpieces of taste, and might be proposed
as models at the present day. In the palaces fragments
of thrones have been found formed of bronze plating.
One of the most remarkable pieces, found at Van,
belongs to M. de Vogüé (fig. 107); the deep sculpture
in the claws of the crouching lion reminds the spectator
of a bronze statuette from Tello (fig. 26).

§ III. Wood and Ivory.

No people of antiquity carried as far as the Chaldæo-
Assyrians their taste for elegant furniture, which is as
delicately sculptured among them as the most precious
bronze utensils. We shall never know, doubtless,
except through the testimony of literature, what that

carved wood-work was, and what those ceilings of
cedar were, to which the prophets of Israel allude with
such jealous enthusiasm, and which the kings boast of
having had executed, speaking to us in their inscriptions
of palaces in which "the gates are of ebony, with
fittings of silver plating and polished iron, the pillars
of cypress-wood, the posts of cedar carved by skilful
craftsmen, and coated with plates of wrought metal."
But the bas-reliefs place before our eyes wooden
furniture in which the superiority of the Assyrian
genius is conspicuous, and which reveal to us a people
gorged with wealth, among whom luxury in furniture
holds an important place. The animal and vegetable
kingdoms are turned to profit by the craftsmen with
astonishing skill in the decoration of the tables, stools,
beds, tripods, umbrellas and fly-flaps. At every opportunity lions' heads and claws, goats, panthers and bulls
occur, fancifully arranged, but always in perfect harmony
and excellent taste ; flowers, festoons, undulating and
interlacing lines, rosettes and geometrical figures are
all found in endless variety and in perfect equilibrium ;
nowhere has such work been better done, neither in
Egypt nor in Greece.

The bas-relief (fig. 77), which represents Assurbanipal
drinking with one of his wives, shows us some of the
furniture of a royal palace. The prince reclines upon
a divan, the queen sitting upon a chair, with a stool
under her feet ; before them is a table. Are not the
sculptured couch, the table with its feet carved in the
form of lions' claws, and the chair, lavishly decorated
with sculpture and ivory ornaments, as rich and as
skilful in workmanship as any such objects to be found

in European drawing-rooms ? Another bas-relief (fig.
108) shows a tent erected in the open plain during a

Fig. 108.—Tent serving as the royal stable
(Bas-relief in British Museum).

military expedi-
tion; it is simply
the stables, as it
seems. Notice the
elegance of the
wooden pillars,
the shafts of which
are decorated with
geometrical de-
signs, and termi-
nate in floral or-
naments on which
slender kids,

ready to spring, are poised. Wood formed the framework of these chairs, coffers, and
shrines, but disappeared more
or less completely under the
bronze or gold plating, the incrustations of ivory, coloured glass,
lapis lazuli, and brilliant stones,
or, lastly, the embroidered rugs
and the carpets. In the camp
before Lachish, Sennacherib sits
upon a throne, the sides of
which are composed of three
rows of figures, raising their
arms to sustain the bars of the
chair.

Fig. 109.—Sennacherib's
throne. Bas-relief
(British Museum.)

Wood was the essential part of the structure of the
chariots, the wheels of which have spokes turned in the

lathe, and the body of which is of woven wicker-work, while the pole, describing a graceful curve, ends in an elegant horse's head or in the head of a deer, a bull, a lion or a swan.

The very weapons, lances, daggers and bows have shafts, hilts, and handles carved into figures of animals, crouching, sleeping, springing or folded in two,

Fig. 110.—Assyrian chariot (from a bas-relief).

similar to the figures drawn and carved by the mediæval decorators.

These objects, however, are not always of wood; oftenest, perhaps, they are of bone or ivory, as it is

Fig. 111.—Ivory plaque (British Museum).

proved by the ivory tablets and the toilette articles, such as combs and pins, which the excavations have brought to light.*

But side by side with these knick-knacks in the Ninevite style, there are others which, though found in Mesopotamia, seem to be of foreign origin. Witness to this is borne by an ivory plaque found at Nimroud, which was certainly part of the incrustation of a piece of furniture (fig. 111). The relief is clear, the work highly finished; the figure, which holds in its hand a large lotus-stalk, has woolly hair like an Ethiopian, and bears the Egyptian Uræus on its brow.

* Perrot and Chipiez, op. cit., vol. ii., p. 319 ff.

Another tablet from Nimroud represents the head of
a woman, whose hair is arranged in Egyptian fashion.
She is enclosed in a frame which resembles a window
with a balustrade, the capitals of which, original in
style, seem to have been coloured. An ivory statuette
of the goddess Istar, found at Nimroud, has the same
heavy coiffure in successive rolls, and resting upon the
shoulders; here we have again the Egyptian style with
an exaggerated naturalism proper only to the Phœnicians.
We may conclude that these ivories were fashioned,
like the bronze dishes, in the workshops of Phœnicia.
Thence caravans transported all these small objects
as far as Nineveh; we know that the merchants of
Tyre and Sidon had numerous stores in the very heart
of Mesopotamia. Phœnician commerce was the great
vehicle by which Egyptian and Assyrian art was carried
abroad.

§ IV. LEATHER AND STUFFS.

The art of embroidery and tapestry, which we have
seen so highly developed in primitive Chaldæa, and a
most remarkable example of which was furnished us
in the costume of Marduk-nadin-akhi, did not cease
to flourish during the whole existence of the Ninevite
empire, and was more prosperous than ever at Babylon
in the time of Nebuchadnezzar. Can robes of greater
richness be imagined than those worn by Assur-nasir-
pal, Sargon, Sennacherib, or Assurbanipal? Are there,
even at the present day, any embroideries or tapestries
of more wonderful delicacy or in more exquisite taste?
Assyrian stuffs are celebrated throughout the ancient

world for the beauty of their varied tints, and above all for the marvellous embroideries which the chisel of the Assyrian sculptor has so delicately reproduced? All this decoration, in which we find figures in adoration before the sacred tree or the symbol of the supreme deity, genii struggling with lions, fights between animals, the mystical pine-cone, flowers, and a hundred other varied designs elegantly and symmetrically arranged, reveals extraordinary manual skill. History, mythology, botany, and real or fanciful zoology are turned to profit with inimitable perfection, and we are forced to take

Fig. 112.—Assur-nasir-pal* offering a libation (Bas-relief in the British Museum).

everything literally that has been related by ancient authors about the tapestries which adorned the palace-chambers. In the banqueting-hall of Ahasuerus, king of Persia, there were, according to the

* Wrongly called Sennacherib by M. Babelon.

Book of Esther, white, green, and blue hangings,
fastened with cords of fine linen and purple to silver
rings and pillars of marble. In the description of a
picture portraying the adventures of Themistocles,
Philostratus the Elder also speaks of the various subjects embroidered by the Babylonians upon their stuffs,
and of the golden threads skilfully mingled with the
tissue; we have seen that the Babylonian stuff called

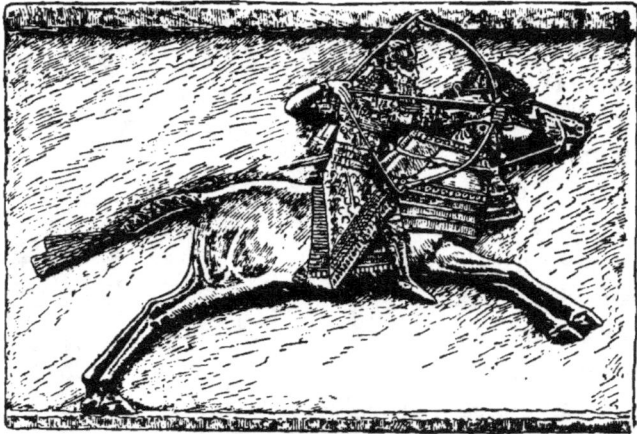

.Fig. 113.—Richly caparisoned horse and rider (Bas-relief in
the Louvre).

kaunakes, and characterised by rows of long fringes,
was still celebrated among the Persians and the Greeks.
Pliny, the natural historian, claims for the tapestry-
weavers of Babylon the honour of having been superior
to all their rivals in other countries in the art of har-
monising colours and representing figures. "In fact,"
says M. E. Müntz, "the words, Babylonian tapestries,
—*Babylonica peristromata,* recur constantly in the Latin

poets, who are never satisfied with praising them. Roman connoisseurs bought such hangings for their weight in gold. Metellus Scipio spent 800,000 sesterces in *triclinaria Babylonica.* Nero paid, for the same stuffs, an even higher price : 4,000,000 sesterces." *

Thus the East, which remains to our days the classical land of embroidery and tapestry, has only perpetuated the traditions bequeathed to her by Nineveh and Babylon when they ceased to exist.

The industries of saddle-making and working in leather, which are still so flourishing among the Turks, Persians, and Arabs, can be traced back, according to tradition, to the Assyrians who raised them to the dignity of an art. Notice the harness of the king's chariot horses. The leather straps, embroidered with red and yellow threads, form variegated trimmings. Sometimes a leather band, crossing the chest and fastened on the withers, is decorated with a double row of tassels, and finished off by bells. Another embroidered band descends from the top of the head, and sustains under the jaw a tassel formed of three tufts, one above the other, also adorned with bells. Above the head rises a superb plume with a triple crest. The head-piece is adorned with rosettes, and above the horse's eyes there is a band formed of over-lapping scales, joined to the head-stall by a double tassel. Everything, including even the strap which holds the bit, and that passed under the nostrils, is relieved by rosettes and brilliant trimmings, and probably also by metal disks, perhaps of gold and silver.

* E. Müntz, *La Tapisserie*, p. 22.

§ V. Ornaments and Cylindrical Seals.

The excavations in Chaldæa and Assyria have, down to this day, scarcely furnished us with any ornaments of gold or silver. However, we know from the inscriptions that these metals occupied the first rank, and were abundantly employed in the ornaments of the Ninevites and Babylonians. The tombs of primitive Chaldæa contained bronze bracelets and ear-rings of the simplest form. These are circular rings, sometimes thinner at the two ends, which are both pointed. At Khorsabad Botta found necklaces formed of precious stones pierced with holes, which were spheroidal in form

Fig. 114.—Assyrian deities carried in procession. Bas-relief (after Layard).

or elongated like olives ; these balls of marble, jasper, chalcedony, amethyst, lapis lazuli, were sometimes mixed with cylinders or other seals of conical shape. At Kouyunjik a necklace was discovered, formed of little golden balls alternating with little cylinders of the same metal. A bronze bracelet at the Louvre has lions' heads at the two extremities.

But we learn more from the bas-reliefs about the taste for ornament among the Assyrians, and about the goldsmiths' work at Nineveh and Babylon. Kings

and genii wear necklaces, ear-rings, diadems, and
bracelets.   Their forms are always elegant and present
great variety.   The diadems are circles, perhaps of
gold, broader in the middle, and generally decorated
with a rosette, in the centre of which a glittering gem
was doubtless conspicuous.   Deities carried in procession wear high tiaras also surmounted by a rosette,
the essential element of which is a precious stone.
Bracelets are worn above the elbow and on the fore-
arm ; these are circular disks, sometimes closed and
decorated with rosettes, at other times ending in two
lions', deers', rams', or serpents' heads ; some are
twisted two or three times round the arm.   Among
the ornaments which hang from the necklace, the
cross, of that form which we call the Maltese cross,
must be cited ; the same symbol, which reminds us of
the Egyptian *crux ansata*, is also found in the ear-rings
(fig. 63).

As for seal-engraving, its abundant examples do not
surpass in artistic merit the Chaldæan work which we
have already described.   Assyrian cylinders, that is
to say, those which were especially manufactured at
Nineveh, are distinguished from those of Babylon and
Chaldæa by a drier and more commercial style of work.*
Inscriptions are rarer, and engraved in Ninevite characters : the myths represented by the engravers are
the same as at Babylon, but the figures have a more
modern appearance : for instance, the winged bulls
with human heads, and the genii with eagle's beaks
and four wings, are copied from the bas-reliefs in the
palaces of Khorsabad, Nimroud and Kouyunjik.   The

---

* See especially J. Menant, *La Glyptique Orientale*, t. ii.

Assyrian cylinders of the archaic epoch present the
technical characteristics that we have already indicated
in Chaldæa : the joints of the limbs are rendered by

Fig. 115.—Archaic Assyrian cylinder
(after Menant).

means of a drill
producing small
hemispherical holes,
and the rest of the
body is executed
with another instru-
ment which hollowed
out parallel lines.
These peculiarities
are clearly distin-
guished on a fine cylinder which we give after M.
Menant (fig. 115): it represents three figures who seem
to sacrifice upon a tripod to the sun, the moon, and the
seven planets.

The cylinders of the Sargonid epoch prove a progress parallel to that of Chaldæan
glyptics ; the traces left by the
action of the saw and the drill
have disappeared to make room
for the modelling of the figures,
which sometimes reach a degree
of suppleness true to nature. We
will cite as examples a cylinder
of the De Clercq collection, representing two genii in adoration

Fig. 116.—Assyrian cylin-
der. De Clercq col-
lection (after Menant).

before the sacred tree (fig. 116), and a cylinder in the
British Museum (fig. 117) on which the god Rammanu
is seen, armed with a bow and arrows, standing upon
a crouching lion and receiving the homage of a pontiff.

The two cylinders are very fine : on the first, extreme exactness is to be noticed in the details of the costume, and great delicacy in the features of the two genii. On the second, on the contrary, the forms have a freer and easier pose, and the scene has more life; the palm is remarkable for truth ; the ibexes,

Fig. 117.—Assyrian cylinder. De Clercq collection (after Menant).

above all, are absolutely pure in design; the modelling of their thighs and flanks reminds us of the lions on the Chaldæan cylinder which we admired

Fig. 118.—Assyrian cylinder. De Clercq collection (after Menant).

before (see fig. 35); it also reminds us of the famous lioness among the sculptures of Assurbanipal's palace (fig. 81), which is probably contemporary with it. Assyrian glyptics has produced no-

thing more highly finished ; like sculpture on a larger scale, it excels in the rendering of animal forms.

CHAPTER V.

PERSIAN ART.

THE most ancient monuments of Persia date from no earlier period than the reign of Cyrus (B.C. 549—529). If any Persian art existed in the previous epoch, when the country was no more than a satrapy of the Median empire, its traces have not yet been found. Median art is scarcely known at all, except by a cylindrical seal at the British Museum, bearing a Medic inscription,

Fig. 119.—Median cylinder (after Menant).

upon which a rider is seen fighting with a lion: the rider's high tiara is characteristic, but the lion is copied from a Ninevite cylinder (fig. 119). No doubt this monument would not be enough by itself to prove that Median art was tributary to Assyrian art; but the description given us by Herodotus of the fortress of Ecbatana confirms the hypothesis. On the other hand, it is natural to suppose that the Persians, who were the vassals and consequently the political and religious heirs of the Medes, should have borrowed from the latter certain artistic traditions, if Median art had any originality of its own. Now, while a threefold foreign influence—that of the Chaldæo-Assyrians, the Egyptians, and the Ionic

Greeks, is conspicuous in Persian works of art, there is nothing that can be referred to Media.

The monuments of the Achæmenid dynasty are gathered together upon three principal sites, the ruins of which have been explored in a fairly complete manner : Susa, where the Achæmenids, including Darius and his successors, erected their palaces at the spot on which the old capital of Elam, destroyed by Assurbanipal, formerly stood ; Persepolis, the imposing remains of which form two groups, called at the present day Takht-i-Jemshid and Nakhsh-i-Rustam ; lastly, the pile of ruins at Meshed-Murgab and Madar-i-Soleiman, two Persian villages in the valley of the Polvar, on the road from Ispahan to Shiraz, where, without doubt, the ancient city of Pasargadæ must have been.

§ I. CIVIL ARCHITECTURE.

When Cyrus had his new capital, Pasargadæ, built in the valley of the Polvar, he had completed the destruction of the kingdom of Crœsus, finished the conquest of Asia Minor, and made himself master of Babylon. The precise date of the monuments of Meshed-Murgab is fixed by the cuneiform inscriptions, which, while they are all composed in honour of Cyrus, are written in three versions, Persian, Medic, and Assyrian, and consequently we cannot place them earlier than the conquest of Chaldæa in B.C. 538. In his victorious expeditions through regions remote from the table-land of Fars, his native country, such as Mesopotamia, Lydia, and the coasts of Asia Minor, Cyrus had the opportunity of observing monuments which must have astonished him by their architecture, and palaces which seemed to him far finer than those inhabited hitherto by his ancestors, princes of proverbial austerity and simplicity. He conceived the idea of constructing for himself a royal residence as sumptuous as those of Crœsus and Nabonidus, and of importing into the heart of Persia the architecture of Babylon and the Hellenic architecture of Asia Minor. His military successes assisted him wonderfully in this undertaking. The prisoners of war whom he captured at Babylon and in the Greek cities of Ionia became the workmen who built his palaces; and he allured the architects, whom he could not carry away by force, by loading them with wealth and honours. The successors of Cyrus continued, like him, to appeal to the artists of Greece, whose voluntary exile from their native country has often been remarked by historians. Pliny, for instance, cites a worker in bronze, Telephanes of Phocæa, who passed among his contemporaries as a worthy rival of Polycletus, Myron, and Pythagoras, and whom the kings of Persia, Darius and Xerxes, attracted to their court, where he exercised his craft during the greater part of his career.*

The structures begun by Cyrus at Pasargadæ, which were never finished on account of his death, which abruptly ended the work, receive their inspiration both from Greek and Assyrian art; there is nothing to be referred to the architectural types of Egypt, not yet invaded by the Persian conquerors. The palaces stand upon platforms like those of Nineveh and Babylon; but these substructures follow the Greek method of building.

* Heuzey, in the *Revue politique et littéraire*, 1886, p. 661.

The monument called by the modern Persians *Takht-i-Madar-i-Soleiman* ("throne of the mother of Solomon") is nothing more than the platform of Cyrus' palace (fig. 120). It is a structure built of large stones, in which mortar is replaced by iron clamps. The facings are seldom trimmed, but only rough hewn, and surrounded by a double moulding like rusticated stonework with marginal draftings. The courses are alternate rows of headers and stretchers. The nucleus of the structure is a mass of blocks arranged in horizontal layers, always level with

Fig. 120.—Platform of the palace of Cyrus (after Dieulafoy).

the facing courses. M. Dieulafoy* observes that the Lydians practised this method of building from the eighth century before our era. The Assyrians did not proceed in the same manner. At Khorsabad, for instance, no clamps bind the stones of the facing to one another; the wall is straight and absolutely vertical, while in the Takht-i-Madar-i-Soleiman the upper courses recede from one another like steps, in order to give greater thickness to the base. Over the greater part of the facing, position marks have been detected,

* *L'art antique de la Perse*, t. i., p. 8.

carved upon them by the stone-cutters, in order to know the place of each hewn stone. These marks are conventional signs, which do not belong, it is true, to any alphabet, but which—a matter worthy of remark—are the same as those discovered in Greek buildings.

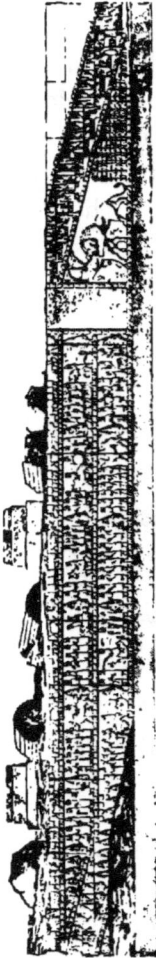

The palaces of Persepolis were erected by Darius and Xerxes only fifty years after those at Pasargadæ; but in this short interval Egypt had been conquered by Cambyses; and after that event the monuments of the Pharaohs were destined, for the same reason as those of Assyria and Asia Minor, to exercise a direct influence upon Persian art. The latter, however, could never fuse these heterogeneous elements together and assimilate them to its own character, but could only group them in a hybrid style. The buildings of Persepolis are still standing to a considerable extent, and its ruins, rising in the midst of a vast amphitheatre of grey marble rocks, are an object of enthusiastic admiration to all travellers. The palaces rest upon a platform built on the model of that of Takht-i-Madar-i-Soleiman. The outer coating of this basement is formed of carefully trimmed ashlar, and the blocks, fitted together without mortar, are fixed by iron clamps. Better preserved

Fig. 121.—Basement at Persepolis (after Flandin and Coste, *Perse ancienne*).

than the ruins of Pasargadæ, those of Persepolis enable
us to reconstruct more perfectly the principal forms of

Fig. 122.—Gate and windows of the palace of Darius (after Diculafoy).

Achæmenid architecture. The platform of the Persepolitan palaces was ascended by a flight of a hundred
and eleven steps, broad enough to be mounted by ten
men abreast ; a gently inclined roadway, formed on one

side of the platform, enabled carriages to reach the
summit : here we have precisely, except in point of
material and manner of construction, the platform of
the Assyrian palaces. The summit of the terrace was
crowned, as at Khorsabad, with a row of battlements.
The peculiarity of the artificial mound called Takht-i-
Jemshid by the Persians is that it is only an immense
basement supporting three other terraces of smaller
area upon it. These terraces are of unequal height, and
communicate with one another ; they are reached by
stone staircases. The grand staircase, leading to the
second platform, is adorned with a colonnade and flanked
by gigantic human-headed bulls, similar to those at
Nineveh. Upon the highest of these three platforms
were built four palaces, upon the walls of which the
names of Darius, Xerxes and Artaxerxes Ochus have
been found.

In the buildings at Persepolis and Susa, the doorways and window-frames take the form of a rectangular
parallelogram, and in their architectural decoration,
besides the traditional influence of Chaldæa and
Assyria, the new exotic element, that we have indicated
above, may be recognised ; it is the intrusion of
Pharaonic art. The doors, framed in three Græco-
Ionian architraves, projecting one beyond the other, are
surmounted, as well as the windows, by an Egyptian
ornament above a line of alternate ovals and disks.
In the thickness of the doorway sculptures in relief,
copied from those of the Chaldæo-Assyrian palaces,
show us the king in close combat with a lion or fantastic animal, or else the king sitting on his throne
rendering justice at his palace gate, or again the prince

solemnly advancing, surrounded by his officers and dressed in his ceremonial robes.

M. Dieulafoy* recognised that the greater number of the windows were condemned to lessen the air and light in the interior of the rooms ; these windows filled up by a thinner wall, formed, on the exterior, niches which broke the uniformity of the façade. Doors, windows, staircases and the pilasters arranged at the corners, are of white limestone or of grey porphyry with blue veins ; but the walls in which these architectural features occur are of baked brick coated with enamelled tiles.

The architecture of the Achæmenid palaces includes the

Fig. 123.-- Persepolitan capital (after Dieulafoy).

pier and the column as the supports of the structure. Among the ruins of Pasargadæ at present only three piers and one column, the height of which still exceeds 36 feet, are standing. But at Persepolis and at Susa, the Persepolitan capital, with all its elegance and

* L'art antique de la Perse, t. ii., p. 37.

originality, has been studied in all its varieties. It is found in every part, but notably in the great state saloon or *apadâna* of the palaces. It is thirteen times as high as its diameter at the base : its slender form reveals the imitation in stone of an original structure supported by light trunks of trees. The apadâna of the palace of Xerxes at Persepolis, situated on the middle platform, covered an area of nearly an acre and a quarter, and its roof was sustained by a hundred columns. Before the anterior façade rose a portico

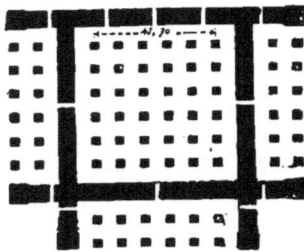

Fig. 124.—Plan of the *Apadâna* of Artaxerxes (after Dieulafoy).

guarded by two gigantic bulls with human heads, partly built into the structure like those in the Assyrian edifices. The apadâna of the palace of Artaxerxes at Susa (fig. 124) was of no less gigantic proportions, and had a double portico on three of its sides ; it covers an area of an acre and a half. The columns are not less than 18 feet 4 inches in diameter ; slightly conical in shape, they are composed of long cylindrical drums, placed end to end, the base and capital being separated from the shaft. Two varieties may be distinguished.* The simplest type is to be seen in the interior halls of the palace of Xerxes at Persepolis. The base is formed of two tori placed one above the other on a square pedestal ; the shaft is decorated all round with forty-eight flutings ; the capital includes a series of ornaments borrowed from the architecture of Egypt ; it is

* Dieulafoy, *op. cit.*, t. ii., p. 80.

developed in a succession of bells and inverted volutes, above which two bulls' heads are arranged, even with the intercolumniations ; this is the bicephalic capital, characteristic of the Achæmenid architecture, which has never been employed except in Persia.

Fig. 125.—Susian capital restored (Louvre).

Other columns differ, but only in the base, from that which we have just described ;. the double torus supporting the shaft is sometimes placed, not on a square pedestal, but on a cylindrical drum, decorated with twenty-four vertical lines and growing gradually broader in the lower part, so as to present the form of a much elon-

gated ogee or of a bell. At Susa, instead of lines, the
ornament of the base is sometimes formed of elegant
inverted foliage (fig. 126). The comparative study of
the Achæmenid column, together with the monuments
of Egypt and Greece, has led M. Dieulafoy to conclude
that the outlines of the Persepolitan column are
Egyptian, but that its structure is composed of Græco-
Ionian elements. These volutes, strings of ovals, and
tori at the base,
had already become
classical in the
Hellenic world long
before Cyrus, since
they are found every-
where, at Mycenæ,
Segesta and Selinus,
in Attica and in
Ionia : here again
we are forced to
recognise that the
architect, even when
he copies motives

Fig. 126.—Base of a column (after
Dieulafoy).

derived from Egypt or Assyria, is imbued with the
principles of Hellenic art.

Besides columns, the Persepolitan and Susian palaces
had pilasters placed at the extremities of the porticoes,
as continuations of the façades. In the façades of the
palace of Darius at Persepolis two square pilasters of
porphyry are seen, so perfectly preserved that in the
upper part they still have holes, cut to receive the
ends of the entablature. They would suffice to prove, if
any proof were wanting, that in these structures, the

columns, which are placed at long intervals and are tall
and slender, did not support stone but wooden architraves. These were enormous beams which formed a
line even with the tops of the columns, and, running
from capital to capital, and placed in grooves contrived
with this object, contributed to give homogeneity and
solidity to the structure. Upon these great beams the
rafters of the roof were arranged, and then a flat ceiling
supporting neither a terrace nor a second story.

It is important not to lose sight of the fact that the
palaces, the elements of which we have just described,

Fig. 127.—Façade of the *Apadana* of Artaxerxes
(restoration by M. Dieulafoy).

constitute an official kind of architecture implanted in
Persia by the " kings of kings " who were pleased with
the monuments that they had observed in Egypt,
Assyria, and Asia Minor. Springing from the caprice of
sovereigns, this foreign architecture never took root in
the country, and was not required by the nature of the
ground and the necessities of existence on the mountainous table-land of Persia ; it disappeared with the
Achæmenid dynasty. But by the side of this conventional architecture there was that created by the natives
of the country, because it had been imposed upon them

as a condition of life. As well as the people of Chaldæa and Assyria, the Persians must have known how to build vaulted houses, alone capable of protecting them from the rays of a too ardent sun ; they also built, at least in the cantons of Susiana, houses with terraces, supported by palm beams and trellis-work arranged over the rooms which were narrow like passages. Strabo tells us this while speaking of Susiana : " To protect the rooms from the excessive heat, the roofs are covered with two cubits' depth of earth ; the weight of this earth obliges the people to build all the houses long and narrow, because, although the beams must not be very long, nevertheless the rooms must be spacious ; otherwise the people would be stifled." Even at the present day, since the climatic conditions of the country have not changed, the method of building houses is the same as that practised by the ancient inhabitants of Iran. Travellers find houses, according to the wealth of the owner, surmounted by vaults, domes, and terraces, wonderfully suited to local requirements. It is, then, quite certain that the Iranians in the time of the Achæmenids knew the vault and the cupola as well as their neighbours on the banks of the Tigris.

But have the vaults and domes of Persia, more fortunate than those which rose above the Mesopotamian edifices, come down to us, at least in a few instances ? M. Dieulafoy believes so. The ruins held to be of the Sassanian epoch at Sarvistan, Firuzabad, and Ferashbad, would date, in his opinion, from the Achæmenid period. A certain reserve, however, is required, from the chronological point of view, in speaking of these monuments in which the traveller can still see brick cupolas supported

by pendentives,* these cupolas being 97 ft. high and 49 ft.
in diameter, semicircular vaults, pointed vaults nearly
similar to those of our Gothic churches of the thirteenth
century—in short, all the elements of Sassanian and
Byzantine architecture. On the other hand, the decoration of these buildings seems to have been remarkably
poor ; at Sarvistan the interior columns are heavy and
badly hewn, the cornice placed at the foot of the vaulting is composed of nothing but a serrated ornament ;
the interior walls must have been coated with red
paint ; the exterior walls were smooth, and even the
façade showed no decoration except groups of half-
columns buried in the masonry. Not the smallest
trace has been remarked among these ruins of bricks,
whether enamelled or bearing figures in relief, or of
those slabs imitating the wall sculptures of Assyria
which were such characteristic elements of Achæmenid
art. The same reflections are applicable to the monument of Firuzabad, the architectural decoration of which
has preserved, perhaps only by tradition, elements of
Persepolitan origin.

§ II. Sculpture.

In sculpture, even more than in architecture, the
triple influence, Chaldæo-Assyrian, Egyptian and
Græco-Ionian, which is dominant among the works
of the Achæmenids, is to be traced. Like the sculp-

* Pendentives are generally held to have been introduced into
architecture several centuries after our era, and to have first appeared
in a perfect form in the Church of St. Sophia at Constantinople, the
dome of which, as Procopius says (*De Ædificiis*, Bk. I., c. I.) seems to
hang by a golden chain from the sky.

tures of Ninevite palaces, those of Pasargadæ and
Persepolis are in low relief, the figures being always
placed in profile, and arranged for the purpose of
lining the lower portion of the walls. In the execution,
however, the chisel of a Greek artist is felt, or at
least of one who has studied under Greek masters.

Fig. 128.—Cyrus. Bas-relief
(after Dieulafoy).

M. L. Heuzey* reminds
us that an archaic
Greek school existed
in Thessaly, which was
remarkably flourishing,
and the productions
of which, such as the
bas-relief known under
the name of the Exalta-
tion of the Flower, were
closely analogous in the
details and the finish
of the work to the
Persepolitan and Susian
sculptures ; there are
the same draperies with
broad flat folds, and the
same methods of treat-
ment in the muscles of the face and limbs. The
most ancient Persian sculpture known is the famous
bas-relief in which the full-length portrait of Cyrus
himself has been preserved for us (fig. 128). Cyrus,
of Iranian origin, has a face like that of an European ;
he has nothing in common with Egyptian and Assyrian
faces ; the top of his head is bald or shaved, his beard

* *Revue politique et littéraire*, 1886, p. 661.

is slightly curled, his hair is short and matted. But everything else in this royal figure is of foreign importation. His head is crowned with a triple disk surrounded by Uræi, in the fashion of Egyptian deities; the king is furnished with wings, like the genii of Assyria and Chaldæa, and these wings, with rows of well-marked feathers, are like those of the Ninevite monsters. Even the border of the robe is decorated with a broad

Fig. 129.—Bas-relief at Persepolis (after Flandin and Coste).

Assyrian fringe; finally, the king holds in his right hand a statuette, the headdress of which is surmounted by the Egyptian Uræus.

After the portrait of Cyrus in chronological order

11

come the bas-reliefs of Persepolis. These are sometimes epi-
sodes in the
Chaldæo-
Assyrian epic
of Izdubar,
which, imi-
tated not
only in Persia
but also in
the Greek
world, gave
birth to the
legends of
Heracles and
Theseus, so
often repre-
sented on
archaic Greek
monuments.
In other bas-
reliefs the
court-officers
walk in pro-
cession with
the tributary
satraps, or
else (fig. 129)
the "king of
kings" him-

Fig. 130.—Bas-relief at Persepolis (after Flandin and Coste).

self, calm and impassive like a Colossus whom nothing
can terrify, plunges his dagger, without moving a muscle

of his face, into the heart of a lion, a bull or a fantastic animal, which rises erect upon its hind legs, ready to devour him. Do not the exaggerated muscles of the beast betray a servile copy of the Assyrian monsters? Elsewhere, on the wall which borders the staircase of the palace of Darius, a lion devours a bull (fig. 130); he bites him on the thigh, and furiously digs his powerful claws into his haunches. Though the lifelike attitude of the two animals strikes us, it reminds us, at the same time, of the Chaldæo-Assyrian cylinders in which a similar subject is reproduced.

Fig. 131.—Bas-relief from Persepolis (after Flandin and Coste).

Farther on, on the same wall of the staircase, servants appear to mount the stairs, with their hands loaded with presents of all kinds which they are about to offer to the "king of kings"; Assyrian sculptures contain analogous scenes. The same must be said of the bas-relief of the central door of Darius' palace, in which the prince is seen attended by two servants, one holding the umbrella and the other the fly-flap (see fig. 122); how many times this subject is repeated on the Ninevite walls, with the same naïve representation of the king, like a Greek hero, as of colossal stature in comparison with the

Fig. 132.—Bas-relief at Persepolis (after Flandin and Coste).

persons of his suite, in order to exhibit his superiority and strength! On one of the walls of the apadâna of Xerxes' palace, the prince sitting on a high throne, with a canopy above his head and his feet upon a footstool, is seen surrounded by his guards. He is receiving a personage of high rank, doubtless a satrap, who is bringing on his shoulder the tribute of his

province. In the compartments below rows of Persian
soldiers are drawn up in line, probably those that
composed the famous guard of the *Immortals*; they carry
lances, bows and quivers, and have swords at their
sides. The throne is of a truly Assyrian form. "The
canopy, made of woven stuff," says M. Dieulafoy,*

Fig. 133.—Bas-relief at Persepolis (after Flandin and Coste).

" is decorated with a very curious design. Each strip
is composed of two similar bands heavily embroidered.
A band covered with rosettes is followed by a band
adorned with bulls like those which decorate the
cornice of the royal tombs; in the centre appears the
winged emblem of Ahura-Mazda. The lower band
ends in a trimming covered with rosettes, and a thick

* *Op. cit.*, t. iii., p. 186.

fringe ; round patches adorn the angles. The position
of the winged emblems on the top give this piece of
drapery the appearance of an Egyptian tent, but the
procession of bulls, the trimmings, the fringes, and the
rich embroidery are of Assyrian origin."

The symbolic figure of Ormuzd, with his winged disk,
is a reproduction of the similar divine figure so often
seen hovering over the king and his soldiers on the

Fig. 134.—Portico at Persepolis (after Flandin and Coste).

Assyrian bas-reliefs. Scenes of most significant cruelty
also passed from Chaldæo-Assyrian sculpture into Persian
sculpture. On the bas-relief which Darius caused to
be carved upon the rock of Behistun, to recount his
exploits to distant posterity, the king is holding his bow
as Sennacherib does, and placing his foot on the breast
of a prisoner who holds out his hands in supplication,
while nine other kings stand bound with chains, with

their hands behind their backs and cords around their necks.*

Like the porticoes of Ninevite palaces, those of Persepolis are garnished with human-headed bulls; the latter have preserved the walking attitudes, the curled hair, and often even the high tiara decorated with rosettes and feathers, which characterise their elder brothers on the banks of the Tigris. Only, while the Assyrian bulls are sometimes placed even with the surface of the façade and facing one another in the doorway, the Persepolitan bulls, on the contrary, are always placed parallel on each side of the opening and look outwards, facing the terrace. Finally, in the sculpture of these gigantic monsters the Persian artist shows himself superior to the Assyrian artist: while preserving the animals in the same hieratic posture, he has had the skill to soften the modelling of the limbs, and to give to the wings a more elegant and graceful curve; the bulls have only four legs instead of five; their flanks are more supple and plumper; the horns, emblems of strength, which surround the head of the Ninevite monsters, are suppressed; the anatomical forms and the respective proportions of the different parts of the body are more closely studied; we have here Assyrian art interpreted by artists formed in the school of the Greeks.

§ III. Painting and Enamelling.

The art of enamelling brick, invented by the Chaldæans, did not perish with Babylon. The Achæmenids

* Lenormant and Babelon, *Hist. anc. de l'Orient*, t. vi., p. 18, f.

adopted it, and seem to have brought it to perfection;
the same is true, as it seems, of that ingenious and
delicate process which consisted of stamping scenes in
relief upon bricks, a number of which thus formed an
enamelled frieze, intended to replace the sculptured
slabs of Nineveh. It was at Susa that this system
of decoration seems to have reached its ideal perfection; at any rate, it is only among the ruins of this

Fig. 135.—The lion frieze; restoration by M. Dieulafoy (Louvre).

capital that we can study it in detail, thanks to the
discoveries of M. Dieulafoy, which add a new chapter to
the history of art. It has been possible to reconstruct
at the Louvre two entire friezes disinterred at Susa,
before the façade of the apadâna of the palace of
Artaxerxes Mnemon. That of the lions (fig. 135) is
composed of bricks in relief, 1 ft. 2 in. long by 7 in.
high and 9 in. thick. The lions, nine in number, are
each 11 ft. 3 in. long by 5 ft. 6 in. high. The ground,
on which the figures stand out, is a flat surface of a

turquoise-blue colour; the lions, which are, for the most part, of a greyish-white colour, have certain parts of their body, for instance the mane, of a watery greenish blue; and others, for instance the swell of the muscles, of a deep yellow. They are treated in the Assyrian manner, to such an extent that, if i were not for the relief, they would exactly resemble the enamelled lions on flat bricks at Khorsabad. As at Nineveh, the muscles are exaggerated, the head and forepart of the lion too small. The procession of wild beasts is framed in several lines of elegant symmetrical designs: rows of chevrons, of Egyptian palmettes, and of Assyrian daisies.

The frieze of the archers (fig. 136) represents a procession

Fig. 136.—Susian archer (Louvre).

of warriors in relief, like those on the marble slabs of Persepolis; this is the most wonderful specimen

of polychrome Persian enamelling. The materials of
which the composition is formed, instead of being, as
in the lion frieze, baked bricks in the form of elongated
parallelopipeds, are little squares, of which each side is
1 ft. 1 in. long, and 3 in. thick, made of artificial concrete, which combines the whiteness of plaster with the
resistance of limestone. The soldiers are represented
in profile and on the march. They carry on the left
shoulder a bow coloured yellow, and a quiver of reddish
brown. They hold in their hands a pike, the shaft of
which ends in a silver knob. Their tunics, the colour
of which alternates from one figure to another, is golden
yellow or white ; the shape of it is the same for all,—
narrow, open at the side, with very broad gathered
sleeves ; it falls to the ankles and shows a certain variety
of ornament ; the stuff is spangled sometimes with green
or blue daisies, sometimes with designs in the form of
lozenges; the border is embroidered. A greenish turban,
twisted into rolls, is placed on the head of these oriental
soldiers, who wear bracelets, ear-rings, and yellow or
sky-blue leather boots ; their beard and hair are dressed
in ringlets, in the Assyrian fashion. This is doubtless
the rich costume which provoked the declamations of
Greek rhetoricians against the effeminacy and cor-
ruption of the Persians. According to the testimony of
Herodotus (vii. 83), the twisted turban on the hair,
the golden ornaments, and the silver knob on the
javelin, were the distinctive marks of the thousand
knights and the ten thousand immortals who formed
the escort of the "king of kings." There can be no
doubt, then, that we are in presence of a group of this
famous troop of janissaries, whom the Achæmenid

monarchs recruited in great part from among the blacks
of India; a certain number of the figures on the frieze
acquired by M. Dieulafoy actually have a skin coloured
of a deep brown.

It is observed, from a technical point of view, that
all the figures of one frieze came out of the same
mould, and that they are exact repetitions one of

Fig. 137.—Polychrome decoration of the palace of Artaxerxes (Louvre).

another, though variously coloured. The vitreous
coat is transparent and iridescent, like the enamel on
porcelain; the gamut of the colours is poor: blue,
green, yellow, black, and white. These decided tints
must, on account of their brilliancy, have produced
a striking effect; and under the hot sun of Susiana,
the portico walls of Artaxerxes' palace sparkled more
marvellously than even the richly decorated tiles of

Mussulman mosques and palaces. The interior of the apadâna seems to have been simply coloured by means of a red monochrome stucco, almost completely concealed, however, by the rich carpets and embroidered draperies with which the walls of all the chambers were hung.

§ IV. RELIGIOUS AND SEPULCHRAL MONUMENTS.

Ormuzd (Ahura-Mazda), the great deity of the Persians, was not to have, according to the regulations in the Avesta, either temples or statues. The conception of the supreme and only God, perfect in all things, was too vast to suggest any shelter for him except the vault of heaven in which he dwelt. Herodotus did not fail to observe this characteristic of Mazdeism and this absence of temples among the Persians : " The custom of the Persians," he says, " is not to raise statues, temples and altars to the gods ; on the contrary, they treat those who do so as madmen : in my opinion, this is because they do not believe, like the Greeks, that the gods have a human form." However, Ormuzd is often represented on the monuments of the Achæmenid dynasty ; he has the form of a man crowned with the tiara and enclosed in a winged disk (fig. 141). This is exactly, except in the modifications brought about by the progress of art, the figure of the deity in the Assyrian monuments.* Thus this symbol, borrowed from Mesopotamia, is a transgression of the precepts

---

* The existence of a supreme god, Ilu, among the Assyrian deities is not proved, though assumed by M. Babelon, who supposes that the winged figure on the Assyrian bas-reliefs is Ilu.

of the Avesta, and an act of tolerance which only penetrated into the monumental sculpture of palaces and tombs, and into the glyptic art. The only symbol admitted by the Avesta is the all-purifying flame. Hence the cultus of the sacred fire and the fire-altars, called pyrea or *atesh-gahs*, erected in the open air on heights. The atesh-gahs are the only monuments which represent the religious architecture of the Persians. Their remains are numerous, but they do not present many features of archæological interest. Several of them are seen at a short distance from Nakhsh-i-Rustam which seem to be earlier than the time of Cyrus. On a platform reached on all sides by a few steps, an altar is erected in the form of a truncated pyramid, with four sides. At the corners small columns, attached to the structure, support semicir-

Fig. 138. The tower of Jur. Restoration by M. Dieulafoy.

cular arches, which sustain the stone slab on which the sacred fire was lighted.

After the conquest of Asia the Achæmenids generally gave to the fire-altars the form of Græco-Lycian chapels. In the sculptures of a royal tomb at Nakhsh-i-Rustam we see a king in adoration before Ormuzd, and a fire-altar, which has the form of a square block of masonry with projections in imitation of pilasters, supporting an entablature formed of three steps one above the other ;

the highest, larger than the other two, forms the platform on which the fire is lighted (fig. 141).*

The architectural influence of Assyria is manifest in
the construction of certain fire-altars.   Near Firuzabad are the ruins of Jur, particularly interesting on
account of the remains of an *atesh-gah* ninety-one feet
high, described by travellers, and apparently a copy of
the staged towers (*zikkurat*) of Chaldæa and Assyria,
a type of which, the most complete in existence, is here
handed down to us.   M. Dieulafoy remarks that the
atesh-gah at Jur resembles the minaret of the mosque of
Ibn Tûlûn, one of the oldest Mussulman edifices.   Thus
types of religious architecture invented by the Chaldæans
exercised their influence even on the modern art of the
East.†

The funeral rites imposed by the Avesta had another
consequence—that of creating a kind of architecture
unknown in any country besides Persia.   Human
corpses might neither be committed directly to the
ground, nor burnt, nor thrown into the river, for this
would have caused pollution to water, earth, and fire.
Cities of the dead had been established in remote and
deserted spots : these were tall round towers called
dakhmas, built of masonry, and showing no architectural
ornament even round the top.   These towers supported
a wooden trellis-work on which the corpses were laid ;
birds of prey came and tore these abandoned bodies to
pieces : they often carried off separate limbs to a
distance, where wild beasts devoured what was left of
them.   That which remained in the charnel-house was

---

* Coste and Flandin, *La Perse ancienne*, pl. 164.
† Dieulafoy, *L'art antique de la Perse*, t. iv., p. 79.

buried, but previously covered with wax to avoid all
direct contact with the ground. Herodotus has preserved a reminiscence of these distressing practices.
"The corpse of a Persian," he says, "is not buried
until it has been torn to pieces by dogs or birds of
prey. . . . The Persians cover the dead body with
wax, after which they inter it." There is still at the
present day in Persia a certain number of ruins of the
sepulchral towers of the Mazdeans, and one of the best
known is not far from Teheran.

But the dakhmas only served for popular burials;
for the Achæmenid kings, at any rate, broke the Maz-
dean law, which perhaps itself made in practice an
exception in favour of the royal family. The tombs of
the Achæmenid princes can be divided, from the architectural point of view, into two large classes, according
as they are or are not anterior to the conquest of
Egypt. The former are conceived according to the
style and plan of Græco-Ionian tombs, the latter
according to the Egyptian hypogæa.

In the valley of Polvar-Rud, two and a half miles to
the south of Takht-i-Madar-i-Soleiman, stands a small
rectangular edifice, the probable burying-place of Man-
dane, the mother of Cyrus; the Persians call it Gabr-i-
Madar-i-Soleiman, "tomb of the mother of Solomon"
(fig. 139). The archaic Greek character of this monument is striking. Constructed of large blocks in regular
courses, without mortar, the stones being cut and fitted
with the greatest exactness, it is provided with a
triangular pediment, the only one ever observed in a
monument of ancient Persia; it is reached by six steps
running all round the little building. The roof is formed

of flat slabs, sloping on each side according to the
inclination of the pediment. Round the roof is a
cornice composed of a reversed ogee enclosed within
two fillets, an architectural decoration found repeated
round the door, the double frame of which is copied
from that of the Greek buildings in the Ionian style.
The inner chamber measures scarcely six square yards.
Round Gabr-i-Madar-i-Soleiman was a courtyard surrounded by a portico; the chapel was not exactly in the
centre of the courtyard, but stood at the bottom of it, so
that an open space
was left in front.

Fig. 139.—The Gabr-i-Madar-i-Soleiman
(after Dieulafoy).

Not far from this
is the tomb of Cam-
byses the First, the
father of Cyrus. It
is so dilapidated that
only one façade is
almost intact; this is
enough, however, to
enable us to compare
it with another tomb at Nakhsh-i-Rustam in a good
state of preservation. Both of them were square
towers, constructed of fine and regular masonry, the
mortar being replaced by iron clamps. The tower,
solid at the base, contains in its upper part a chamber,
the ceiling of which is formed of large slabs fitted
together; a staircase built outside gave access to a
small door. The exterior façade is furnished on its four
sides with false windows; the idea has even been
adopted of building the back of these niches of black
basalt, in order to give them the appearance of true

apertures. The summit of the edifice is composed of a cornice adorned with a row of denticulations.

When to all these details we add the rustication of the stones and the position-marks found on the blocks, it will be recognised that the architect and workmen came from Asia Minor and copied in servile fashion the sepulchral structures of that country. The architectural form of these towers reminds us of the Lycian tombs at Telmessus, Antiphellus, Aperlæ, and Myra, and above all of the celebrated Harpy tomb at Xanthus.

The descriptions given by Strabo (x. 3, 7), and Arrian (vi. 29), following Aristobulus, of the tomb of Cyrus, enable us to assert that it was like the square

Fig. 140. --Tomb of Cambyses I. (Restoration by M. Dieulafoy).

towers of Meshed-Murgab and Nakhsh-i-Rustam : " The tomb stood in the middle of the king's gardens ; it was surrounded by trees, running water and soft turf. It was a square tower, low enough to be hidden under the thick trees which surrounded it. The base was solid and composed of large cubical blocks. In the upper part was the sepulchral chamber, covered with a stone roof. It was entered by a narrow door. Aristobulus saw in it a golden couch, a table with cups

I 2

for libations, a gilded tub for washing and bathing, and a quantity of garments and ornaments. There was a communication, by means of an inner staircase, with the chamber in which lived the priests who guarded the tomb." It is not permissible, then, to

Fig. 141.—Façade of tomb at Nakhsh-i-Rustam (after Flandin and Coste, *Perse ancienne*).

doubt that, in the time of Cyrus, the kings of Persia had tombs built like those of Lycia, and that the towers which we have described preserve for us specimens of them.

But after the conquest of Egypt, Darius, who, as we saw, admired the monuments in the valley of the Nile, resolved to have a sepulchral cave hewn for himself, in the form of a speos, in the side of the rock, and analogous to the sepulchral hypogæa of the Pharaohs. His successors acted like him. The caverns of Darius and the princes of his dynasty, which are to be seen in the rocks of Nakhsh-i-Rustam and Takht-i-Jemshid, near Persepolis, differ in all points from the tombs of Cambyses I. and Cyrus : while the latter are square towers of masonry, those of the second Achæmenid dynasty are cut out side by side in the vertical wall of the mountain, and the façade, like that of the hypogæa at Beni-Hassan, is decorated with bas-reliefs. To reach these chambers it was necessary in the time of the Achæmenids, as in our own day, to be hoisted by ropes to a level with the aperture. The exterior sculptures are interesting. A colonnade with bicephalic capitals supports an architrave, the frieze of which is adorned with a procession of lions and surmounted with bas-reliefs. Two rows of soldiers fully armed raise their hands to sustain a sort of platform, the borders of which are decorated with two symbolical figures of lions provided with bulls' horns. These Persian warriors remind the spectator of the Assyrian soldiers who form the decoration of Sennacherib's throne. On the platform stands Darius on a pedestal in steps, dressed in the *persis* described by Herodotus, crowned with the *cidaris*, resting the end of his bow on the ground and stretching out his hand. Opposite him is a lighted fire-altar and the image of Ormuzd. Round this bas-relief and serving as its frame stand the figures of the satraps who helped Darius to slay Gaumates. The door of the cave is opened in the central intercolumniation. The

interior of the chambers was as severe as pcssible ; the
roof is hewn into the form of a vault ; in obedience
to the law of Ormuzd there is no trace anywhere of
painting or inscription. The cavities for the sarcophagi are formed in the side walls, as in the
sepulchral caverns of Egypt, Palestine, and Phœnicia.

§ V. Engraved Gems and Ornaments.

The glyptic art and the jewellery of the Persians
maintain nobly and without any sign of decadence
the artistic traditions of Chaldæa and Assyria. Assurbanipal and Nebuchadnezzar, when they made expeditions into the most distant provinces of Persia,
Media, and Armenia, had spread through all these
countries the productions of Assyrian industry and the
taste for luxury and works of art; their artists recruited
their disciples there : like Alexander, they carried the
torch of civilisation everywhere by their arms, and
when the Achæmenids took up their residence at Susa
and Ecbatana, they found the inhabitants profoundly
impregnated with Chaldæo-Assyrian ideas and customs.
To as high a degree as the Babylonians, the Persians
love full dress and ornaments : each citizen of dis-
tinction has his cylinder or his seal hung from his neck ;
he is covered with bracelets, rings, necklaces ; his tiara
is decorated with pearls and sparkling stones ; his
tunic, delicately embroidered, is encrusted with gems.
In his house he displays a luxury in furniture which,
handed on to the Parthians, will astonish the Romans
and Byzantines : cups of gold and silver enriched with
crystal and coloured glass, and adorned with figures in

relief; chairs, couches and tables overlaid with silver, gold, and carved ivory. In short, everything begotten of the passion for luxury among the Chaldæans in the matter of tapestry, embroidery, and goldsmiths' work, is also found among the Persians.

Only, the Persians were not servile imitators; they could give an original turn to the productions of their industry, even when they copied the Assyrians. There is in their cylinders and their seals a dry and nervous execution which characterises them as distinctly as the bulls of Persepolis are distinguished from the Ninevite monsters. It goes without saying also that the inscriptions and the details of costume give an absolutely precise character to the classification of the productions of the

Fig. 142.—Cylinder of Darius (after J. Menant).

glyptic art under the Achæmenids. Here is, for instance, the cylinder of Darius, preserved at the British Museum. The whole scene is evidently copied from Assyrian seals, but the figure of the rampant lion and those of the horses are quite different in treatment from Ninevite art; the denticulated tiara of the prince, the disk of Ormuzd hovering in the air, and finally the inscription traced with mathematical regularity, complete the proofs of Persian origin in this fine cylinder.

As we remove ourselves chronologically from the origin of the art, more perceptible modifications are introduced into the *technique*, and new foreign influences are revealed in Persian work. A cylinder (fig. 143), which belongs to a Russian collector, represents a scene which might be supposed to be imitated from the bas-

Fig. 143.—Persian cylinder (after J. Menant).

relief at Behistun. Darius is here seen slaying with his lance a kneeling enemy, whose head-dress is Egyptian.

The special distinctions of the productions of the gem-engraver's art under the Achæmenid dynasty are the sobriety and exactness of the work and the conventional character of the figured scenes; besides this, in consequence of the influence of Egypt and Phœnicia, the fashion spreads more and more of substituting for cylinders

Fig. 144.—Persian seal. Conical.

Fig. 145.—Seal of Artaxerxes (Louvre).

Fig. 146.—Persian seal. Conical.

conical, rhomboidal or spherical stones, flattened on one side, in order to form a field for the engraving. On these cones of chalcedony or agate the most common subjects are: the "king of kings" standing or kneeling, crowned with the denticulated tiara or

cidaris, and drawing his bow—a type analogous to
that of the coins known under the name of Daries ; the
king stabbing a lion which stands erect before him ; a
pontiff before the fire-altar, adoring Ormuzd; sphinxes
and gryphons which remind us of the Assyrian *kirubu*.
An opal seal (fig. 145) obtained at Susa by M. Dieulafoy,
shows two sphinxes crowned with the tiara of Upper
Egypt in adoration before the winged disk of Ormuzd ;
in the centre, in a little medallion, is the portrait of the
Achæmenid prince, no doubt Artaxerxes Mnemon.
The delicate execution of the royal portrait is striking,
and the elegant forms of the sphinxes are no less
worthy of remark. As among the
Assyro-Chaldæans, it is in the
representation of animals—lions,
deer, antelopes, sphinxes, and
gryphons—that the genius of the
Persian engraver reveals its full
strength. The winged and horned
gryphon found on an engraved gem (fig. 147) is
significantly analogous to a small limestone bas-
relief in the De Luynes collection (fig. 148) which shows
shows in what fashion Persian art interpreted the
Assyrian *kirubu*, and the modifications which it required. The monster has the body and fore paws of a
lion ; his hind legs, armed with powerful claws, are
those of an eagle ; he has the ears of an ox and the
horns of a wild goat ; his eye, face, and half-open beak
belong to the falcon ; a bristling mane adorns a neck
proudly arched like that of a horse ; he has a lion's tail ;
his great wings with well-marked feathers resemble in
their development those of the Persepolitan bulls. We

Fig. 147.—Persian seal
(Cabinet des médailles).

know nothing in Persian art superior to this figure, the symbol of strength and power, in which so many discordant elements are combined with so fortunate a harmony.*   At Susa and Persepolis, as at Nineveh

Fig. 148.—De Luynes' bas-relief (Cabinet des médailles).

and Babylon, minor sculpture was not inferior to sculpture on a grand scale, and the style of the engraver sometimes produced as noble and as striking effects as the chisel of the statuary: the copy did not yield to the model.

* Compare Flandin and Coste, *Perse ancienne*, pl. 152.

CHAPTER VI.

THE HITTITES.[*]

THE name of Hittites (Khatti, Kheta) appears simultaneously in the Bible, the hieroglyphic documents, and the cuneiform texts.   It is given to populations of different origin who inhabited Syria from the Euphrates to the borders of Egypt, and also Cappadocia and the greater part of Asia Minor from the mountains of Armenia to the banks of the Halys and the Hermus. But the country which was particularly the centre of the Hittite dominions, and in which they established a homogeneous and lasting empire, is Northern Syria, that is to say, the territory which extends from the great bend of the Euphrates to the Orontes, and from the limits of the Aramæan oases of Palmyra and Damascus to the mountains of the Taurus.   On the Euphrates they built the fortress of Carchemish (Jerablus), which remained like a threatening challenge in the face of Nineveh until the day when, about the year B.C. 710, the Assyrians gained possession of it ; on the Orontes their chief towns were Kadesh and Hamath.   It is among the ruins of these cities or in the neighbouring country,

---

[*] See especially W. Wright, *The Empire of the Hittites*, 8vo, 2nd ed., London, 1886; Perrot and Chipiez, *Hist. de l'art dans l'antiquité*, t. iv., pp. 483 to 812 ; O. Hirschfeld, *Die Felsen-reliefs in Kleinasien und das Volk der Hittiter* (*Abhandlungen der Berliner Akademie*, 1886).

including Cilicia, a geographical appendage of Syria, and also among the sparsely scattered ruins of Cappadocia and Asia Minor, that the remains of Hittite civilisation have recently been discovered, and that the works of its peculiar art have been found which we are about to describe in a few words.

Fig. 149.—The lion of Marash (after Wright, pl. 27).

§ I. HITTITE MONUMENTS IN SYRIA.

The Hittite art of Syria is derived from Assyrian art; it has nothing original either in the conception of its forms or in its technical execution. To characterise it in one word, we might call it Assyrian art interpreted by barbarians. In all its manifestations it is inferior to its model, like the works of the barbarians who copied Greek and Roman art. In imitation of the Assyrians, the Hittites confined themselves almost exclusively to sculpture in bas-relief. At Marash, on the Pyramus in Cilicia, it is true, a fragmentary torso has been obtained; but this is almost the only example of a Hittite statue in the round that we can cite. This figure, of coarse workmanship, is dressed in a fringed cloak like that which is to be seen everywhere on the walls of Ninevite palaces.*

* Perrot and Chipiez, *op. cit.*, t. iv., p. 547.

The bulls and other winged monsters, placed at the
entrance of Assyrian and Persian palaces, which keep
the mean between statuary and the bas-relief, also find
their parallel among the Hittites.   There is at the
Imperial Museum at Constantinople a basalt lion, found
at Marash, the head and neck of which are completely
disengaged from the stone block; the fore paws are
even with the front surface of the
wall, and the body of the beast is
continued round the corner.   Thus
it is sculptured on two sides in
imitation of the Ninevite bulls, and
the extent of servility in the copy is
finally proved by an inscription in
Hittite hieroglyphs covering the fore
paws, in accordance with the singular
fashion observed at Nineveh.

Assyrian influence is even more
obviously conspicuous at Carchemish, a fact to which witness is
borne by two figures standing on a
crouching lion, which remind us of
the rock sculptures of Sennacherib
at Bavian and Malthaiyah.*   Is not
a pseudo-Assyrian style also to
be detected in this figure† (fig. 150) surmounted by

Fig. 150.—Stela from
Birejik (British Mu-
seum).

* Perrot and Chipiez, *op. cit.*, t. iv., p. 549.

† There is some doubt whether this figure is Hittite at all.   It may
be of Babylonian origin.   (See Perrot and Chipiez, *Hist.*, t. iv., 550 f.)
The boots are so slightly turned up at the points that they are more
like those worn by Babylonian kings than the characteristic boots of
the Hittites.   The stela was brought from the castle of Birejik, no
from the site of Carchemish, as M. Babelon states.

the winged disk, with his tunic open in front? However, his cylindrical tiara, his twisted hair, and the peculiar disks which he holds in his two hands, are features which the artist did not copy from Mesopotamia.

Like the Babylonian Istar, the Hittite Astarte is represented standing, in full face and entirely nude; she holds her breasts with the same indecent gesture, the first example of which belongs to the plastic art of Chaldæa. Nevertheless Astarte is

Fig. 151.—Fragments of sculpture from Carchemish
(from the *Graphic*, Dec. 1880).

winged and crowned with a conical tiara which are peculiarities of Hittite symbolism. The priestess performing adoration before her is veiled, like the figures of Assyrian women.

Sculptures in debased imitation of the Ninevite reliefs were ranged on a series of slabs in the Hittite palaces, as at Khorsabad or Kouyunjik. At Sinjerli, M. O. Puchstein found still in place, that is to say, lining the lower portion of the wall of an edifice, a complete set of bas-reliefs representing a deer hunt, a man struggling with a fantastic genius, and a train or prisoners of war.*　In another tell in the same region, three slabs placed end to end contain a scene from a lion hunt ; the king is in his chariot with his charioteer, and draws his bow.　Everything here—the form of the chariot, the harness of the horses, the costume of the prince covered with his coat of mail—betrays a copy of Ninevite sculpture.　Even the lion, the anatomical forms of which are learnedly re-produced, brings to our memory the hunting expeditions of Assur-banipal.　But at the same time the inferiority of the imitator is con-spicuous in the arrangement of the scene, which lacks life and movement : the lion allows the javelins to be thrust into his eye and haunches in the most benevo-lent manner.　What a difference from the vigour and litheness of the terrible beasts which bound roaring around the hunters, true sons of Nimrod !

Fig. 152.--Bas-relief at Rum-Qalah.　(*Gazette archéol.* 1883.)

When we leave the regions which lie near the Euphrates, the imitation of Assyria, though equally perceptible, is, perhaps, less servile and more free ; a larger number of original elements enter into the com-position of the scenes.　At Rum-Qalah a bas-relief represents a bearded personage, wearing a cap, and dressed in a long tunic, drawn apart as if in imitation of the form of the drooping wings of

* Perrot and Chipiez, *op. cit.*, t. iv., p. 534.

Assyrian genii. At his girdle he carries a dagger; in his left hand is a sort of lyre, in his right a palm-branch; the handle of a leathern bag is passed over his arm. The coarseness of the workmanship makes the imitation itself almost unrecognisable. On a basalt stela at Marash (fig. 153) two women, sitting on chairs with backs, are separated by a table similar to those that we have seen in Assyria; the costume of these women has also much analogy to the Ninevite garments; however, their high tiara, under their long veil, seems to be indigenous. The same characteristics of imperfect and coarse imitation are to be observed in other pieces of sculpture from the same place; the only features which are particularly original are the expression of the faces, the diadem, and the arrangement of the hair: the spectator feels that he is on the confines of a territory which is already coming under the direct influence of the Hellenic art of Asia Minor.*

Fig. 153.—Stela at Marash (after Hirschfeld).

According to these examples, two groups of clearly distinguished Hittite monuments may be established in Syria itself: those of Carchemish and the region of the Euphrates, which are colourless copies of Assyrian works; and those of western Syria and

* Perrot and Chipiez, *op. cit.*, t. iv., p. 559.

especially of Cilicia, which, though also derived from
Ninevite art, separate themselves from it to a greater
extent, are ruder, and contain elements at once more
original and more barbarous. As peculiar characteristics of the Hittites, we will point out the diadem, the
high cap of the women, to which a long veil is fitted,
and, above all, the shoes with turned-up points. These
shoes, worn by men and women, have been described
as the chief mark of the Hittite monuments ; however,
it must not be forgotten that these shoes are still worn,
in our own day, not only in Syria but throughout Asia
Minor, by the most various races.

§ II. Hittite Monuments in Cappadocia.

A canton of ancient Cappadocia, the Pteria of
Herodotus, on the Halys, where the first meeting
between Cyrus and Crœsus took place, contains a
considerable number of Hittite ruins which have been
particularly explored by MM. Perrot and Guillaume,
and form a group by themselves in the history of
oriental art. The village of Boghaz-Keui, the ancient
capital of the Pterians has still, besides its fortifications
3¾ miles in circumference, bas-reliefs carved upon
rocks which are called Iasili-Kaïa, "the inscribed
stone," and remains of buildings not completely in-
distinguishable. The royal palace, almost rased to
the level of the ground, is a parallelogram 136 ft. by
185 ft. In the blocks which compose the wall, holes
are observed for iron clamps, as in the Achæmenid
edifices ; as in the latter also, the stones are large but
irregular ; the upper portion of the wall was of brick-

work, as at Nineveh and Persepolis ; lastly, the palace
of Boghaz-Keui was built on an artificial terrace.   In
the arrangement of the rooms, details peculiar to
princely residences in all oriental countries, are to be
recognised. The principal
door forms an independent
structure, to be compared
to that of the palace at
Khorsabad : it is 58 ft.
high ; two lions' heads,
original in style, project on
each side of the aperture,
above monolithic door-
posts.

The palace of Euyuk,
as well as that of Boghaz-
Keui, presents striking
features of resemblance to
those of Nineveh ; its
terrace, 812 ft. square, still
rises to the height of 39 ft.
The corners are turned
towards the four cardinal
points.   The principal
doorway is 11 ft. broad,*
and on each side stand two
sphinxes, in place of the human-headed bulls.   Next
to these, all along the façade, was a series of bas-
reliefs, the arrangement of which was the same as
that upon the façades of Khorsabad and Kouyunjik ;

Fig. 154.—The sphinx of Euyuk
(from Perrot and Guillaume*).

* Perrot and Guillaume, *Exploration archéol. de la Galatie*, etc.,
pl. lxv.

only, the sphinx, which is not Assyrian, discloses
another foreign influence—that of Egypt. Cappadocian
art was able to interpret the Egyptian type, and, on
this occasion, did not limit itself to a dull copy. " In
Egypt," observes M. Perrot, " the sphinx, to whatever
variety of the type it belongs, is always represented in
the reclining posture, never standing as here : instead
of being treated as a bas-relief and placed in front
of the doorway, it is sculptured in the round and set
on both sides of the entrance, perpendicular to the
path, towards the axis of which it looks." * Besides,
in the sphinxes on the banks of the Nile, the extremities

Fig. 155.—Rock sculptures at Iasili-Kaïa
(after Perrot and Guillaume).

of the hair, on each side of the head, fall straight
without forming the curls which we see here. At
Euyuk, the Egyptian sphinx is treated in the Assyrian
style ; the place which it occupies on the sides of the
doorway, and the position of its paws, turn it into a sort
of compromise between Egypt and Assyria, which vied
with one another in this land of Cappadocia, in artistic
influence as in political preponderance.

This double tendency is also observed at Iasili-
Kaïa. Here a rectangular chamber has been found
31 ft. by 37½ ft., hewn in the rock on three sides ; the
walls are covered with bas-reliefs forming a plinth.

* Hist. de l'art dans l'antiquité, t. iv. p. 667.

13

Another smaller chamber and a corridor contain similar sculptures; the height of the figures varies from 4 ft. 6 in. to 2 ft. 3 in. Two processions of

Fig. 156.—Rock sculptures at Iasili-Kaïa
(after Perrot and Guillaume).

figures go round the larger chamber and meet one another: on the right, women dressed in long robes with trains, their hair falling upon their shoulders, wearing a round tiara like the women at Marash; on the left the men, with the conical cap assigned by

Fig. 157.—Rock sculptures at Iasili-Kaïa
(after Perrot and Guillaume).

Herodotus to the Cimmerians, and a short tunic reaching no lower than the knees in front, but longer behind. In each group the figures grow larger in proportion to their nearness to the centre. Many of them are not human beings, but winged genii, satyrs with goats' feet, dog-headed monsters. Nearly all hold in their hands sceptres, curved staves, two-edged hatchets; some stand upon quadrupeds. Two are seen perched upon a two-headed eagle ; another, accompanied by a kid, stands on the shoulders of two porters.

Close to the entrance of this vast hall, a separate relief represents a giant standing on two mountains. This personage holds in his right hand a shrine, and in his left hand has a sort of long staff, the lower end of which is curved like a crosier ; he wears a hemispherical skull-cap, and is dressed in a long robe open at the side. The shrine which this deity holds is provided with two Ionic columns supporting the winged disk ; beneath the disk is

Fig. 158.—Rock sculpture at Iasili-Kaïa (Perrot and Guillaume).

Fig. 159.—Rock sculpture of Iasili-Kaïa (after Perrot and Guillaume).

a figure between two bulls seen in full face. At some distance a group of two figures is observed. One of them, of colossal proportions, is found elsewhere standing upon a quadruped. Here, he wears a highly decorated conical tiara, and is armed with a sword and clothed in a short tunic. He stretches out his right hand as if to carry or to seize a child standing before him. The second figure, protected by the deity,

who passes his left arm round his neck and holds his
hand, is the same as he whom we noticed just before.

The sculptures which decorate the walls of the
vestibule in the palace of Euyuk have so great an
analogy to those of Iasili-Kaïa that it is impossible
not to recognise their common style and origin. We
observe among them a woman, seated upon a throne,
with her hair flowing down upon her shoulders,

Fig. 160.—Rock sculpture
of Iasili-Kaïa (after
Perrot and Guillaume).

Fig. 161.—Tomb of Gherdek-Kaïasi
(after Perrot and Guillaume).

decorated with a necklace and bracelets, who reminds
us of the Assyrian queen sharing the banquet of
Assurbanipal; she raises a goblet to her lips, and holds
a flower in her hand.

All these scenes are priestly and religious, and not,
as in Assyria, devoted to the glory of the king and
to the memory of his warlike exploits. They refer
to the worship of the god Mên or of the goddess Mâ
or Enio, the Cappadocian name of Anaïtis or Astarte,

whose rites Strabo describes as performed in the two towns of Comana.

To this Cappadocian civilisation, again, purely oriental and anterior to Greek influence as it is, the sculpture of tombs observed at Gherdek-Kaïasi, near Boghaz-Keui and Euyuk, must be referred. The principal of these caves hewn in the rock, like those of Phœnicia and Nakhsh-i-Rustam, has a façade adorned with a portico with three low colonnades, the style of which closely resembles the Greek Doric order (fig. 161). At the extremities of this portico are the doors of two chambers intended to contain sarcophagi. Both of them have windows opened in the wall of rock; the sepulchral couches are hewn in the wall like alcoves. There is something in these monuments which partakes of the character both of the Phrygian tombs and of those of Nakhsh-i-Rustam, and perhaps they are not anterior to the destruction of Pteria by Crœsus in B.C. 549.

To sum up: we must conclude, with M. Perrot, * that the monuments of Boghaz-Keui and Euyuk, witnesses of primitive Cappadocian civilisation, underwent Assyrian influence as well as those of Northern Syria. The palaces look like "a reduced copy of the great royal edifices on the banks of the Tigris and Euphrates." The winged figures, the monsters with eagles' and lions' heads, are Assyrian, and so are the deities borne on the backs of different quadrupeds, the flowers in the hands of the figures and the winged disk, the symbol of the deity. Various elements of the Cappadocian sculptures seem, upon no less evidence, to have

* Perrot and Chipiez, *op. cit.*, t. iv., p. 697.

been borrowed from Egypt, Persia, and even from
the Greeks of Asia Minor, but this is exceptional.
In any case there is nothing original and individual
in this Hittite art of Pteria, except the eagle with
two heads (fig. 162), which is evidently connected
with the most ancient Asiatic worship, and suggests
reminiscences of the Sirens; except also the long
curved *lituus*, the robe cut in the form of a chasuble,
the peaked tiara, the pointed shoes; details of dress
more interesting for the
history of costume than
for that of art.

Fig. 162.—Sculpture at Iasili-Kaïa.

The connection of the
sculptures of Pteria with
those of Hittite Syria is
quite clear; there are
the same hieroglyphs, the
same short tunic, the
same long robe, the same
shoes, the same peaked tiara, and the same round
skull-cap. The female garments are almost identical
at Marash and Iasili-Kaïa; the deities have similar
attributes; the lion and the bull are the animals
which both regions prefer to represent. We must
conclude that the same semi-barbarous race, powerless
to free itself, whether in art or politics, from the yoke
of Egypt and Assyria, inhabited both the slopes of the
Taurus; we will now examine how far this Hittite race
extended its branches towards the west, and what
monuments it left in Asia Minor beyond the Halys.

§ III. Hittite Monuments in Asia Minor.

To the north of the Taurus and beyond the Halys, the monuments belonging to Hittite civilisation are, as in Cappadocia, bas-reliefs carved on the sides of rocks or not.

At Kalaba, near Ancyra, in Galatia, M. Perrot dis-

Fig. 163.—Rock sculptures at Ghiaur-Kalesi
(after Perrot and Guillaume, pl. x.).

covered a large. slab (4 ft. 4 in. by 2 ft. 6 in.) on which is carved a lion, analogous in style to those which we have met in Syria or in Cappadocia.* A nine hours' journey south-west of Ancyra, among the ruins called Ghiaur-Kalesi, the same scholar found two large figures, cut this time on the side of the rock. These are warriors, like several of those at Boghaz-Keui; both

* Perrot and Chipiez, *op cit.*, t. iv., p. 713.

wear a conical helmet or tiara, to which a piece of stuff
is attached behind, which covers the nape of the neck;
they are clothed in a short tunic, drawn in at the waist
by a sash; their feet are shod with curved boots.

The sculpture at Ibriz, in Lycaonia, consists of an
inscription in Hittite hieroglyphs and two colossal
figures, one 19 ft. 9 in.
high, the other 11 ft.
9 in. A priest is
standing in adoration
before his deity. The
god holds in his left
hand an ear of corn,
and in his right hand
the branches of a vine
which grows from the
ground behind him.
His tiara is provided
with several pairs of
horns, and his beard
and hair are curled in
the Assyrian fashion.
The pontiff is tho-
roughly Assyrian in
appearance and cos-

Fig. 164.—Rock sculpture at Ibriz (from
Wright, *Empire of the Hittites*).

tume; his robe edged with fringes is decorated with
square or lozenge-shaped designs, which remind us
of the tunic of Marduk-nadin-akhi (fig. 22), and also
of the ornaments of the Phrygo-Hellenic tomb called
that of Midas.

The ruins of Eflatoun, in Lycaonia, scarcely consist
of anything more at the present day than the façade of

a ruined edifice; it is adorned with a bas-relief in which
the winged solar disk is to be distinguished, the symbol
of the deity in Egypt and in Assyria; below are two
other smaller disks; then come two rows of figures
with their arms raised above their head, as if to support
an entablature.

Hittite monuments grow more rare as we leave
Cilicia, Lycaonia, Cappadocia and Phrygia to penetrate
into more western
regions.   However,
fresh monuments are
met with every day
in Lydia and even on
the coast of Ionia,
accompanied by
hieroglyphs which do
not allow us to doubt
of the origin of the
people who carved
them on the rocks.
Herodotus attributed
to Sesostris two Hit-
tite bas-reliefs, near

Fig. 165.—Rock sculpture at Nymphio
(Revue arch., t. xiii, 1866).

Smyrna, which are to be seen at the present day.
One, at the village of Nymphio, on the side of a rock
which overhangs a branch of the river Hermus, rises
at least 162 ft. above the ravine.   In a niche, 8 ft.
high, a warrior is seen wearing the conical tiara and
clothed in a short tunic; he carries a lance and a
bow; he is shod with the pointed boots. The second
monument alluded to by Herodotus has been lately
discovered by M. Humann; it is less well preserved,

and represents an almost exactly similar warrior.* Besides traces of Hittite inscriptions, the style of these rock sculptures, the costume and attitude of the figures connect them inevitably with the bas-reliefs of Cilicia, Lycaonia, Cappadocia and Syria; there is the same indistinct outline and the same lack of modelling. Wherever the Hittite people went, they remained feeble imitators ; the works of art which they have left us can be referred to two or three types, copied from Assyrian and sometimes from Egyptian sculpture, but always much inferior to the model.

Less mediocre is the manufacture of models in serpentine which have come down to us, and which were employed by Hittite or Lydo-Phrygian goldsmiths in making metal ornaments or talismanic figures. The two most curious of these matrices are that which is preserved in the Cabinet de Médailles under the name of *Baphomet,* and another, found a few years ago near Thyatira in Mæonia.† The latter, which is 3½ in. high by 4½ in. broad and ½ in. thick, shows us a naked woman, with her hands upon her breasts like the Babylonian Istar ; next a man, perhaps Bel-Marduk, clothed in the Chaldæan robe with a series of fringes one above the other. Farther on there is a lion with a ring, intended to hang the ornament when it came out of the mould ; a sort of altar ; and, finally, the planetary symbols found on a large number of Assyrian monuments.

In the glyptic art, Hittite engravers surpassed themselves, and showed themselves worthy of their Ninevite masters. Far be it from us to treat with disdain the

* Perrot and Chipiez, *op. cit.,* t. iv., p. 750.
† S. Reinach, *Rev. Archéol.,* 1885 (3 se. t. v.), p. 54, ff.

seal-impressions on terra-cotta, the seals of precious stone and the cylinders, the inscriptions and figures upon which have only recently attracted the attention of archæologists. The silver seal, now lost, of the king Tarkudimme, bears a bilingual inscription in Hittite hieroglyphs and in Assyrian cuneiform. A cylinder at the Louvre, found at Aïdin, in Lydia, shows a scene of presentation to a deity (fig. 167). Three figures walk in the same direction, with their hand upon their mouth, carrying the curved sceptre which we noticed in the rock sculptures of Iasili-Kaïa; a large table, supported by two lions, is laden with offerings. Then comes an Assyrian genius with two faces, a deity sitting upon a throne, and some secondary figures. M. Heuzey * has observed that though the subject is almost entirely Assyrian, there is, nevertheless, a national element in it; this is the decorative part of the cylinder. The ornamental design occupies, indeed, a considerable place on the surface; it is composed of a double border of interlacing lines and symmetrical scrolls, which are never met with except in monuments of the Hittite glyptic art.

Fig. 166.—Boss of Tarkudimme (after Wright).

Fig. 167.—Hittite cylinder (Louvre).

* *Gazette archéol.*, 1887 (t. xiii. p. 60).

CHAPTER VII.

JEWISH ART.

PALESTINE, which unites Syria to Egypt, was inhabited by numerous Semitic and Canaanitish tribes which have left us very meagre remains of their art. Like that of the Hittites, this art drew its inspiration both from Assyria and Egypt, though it never did more than imperfectly imitate them. Pharaonic influence is, however, more deeply to be felt here than among the Hittites, since Palestine was nearer to the valley of the Nile. The most important inhabitants of this region were the Jews, and in spite of the poverty of our archæological documents, numerous scholars have, for three centuries, taken a special interest in the works of this people who played so extraordinary a part on the stage of the world. It must be added that almost all these researches have been concentrated upon the exploration of the Temple of Jerusalem and its furniture, which in fact were the highest effort of Jewish art ; and though the monuments themselves are no longer in our hands or before our eyes, there is not a single edifice in all oriental or classical antiquity of which we possess written descriptions so circumstantial and so numerous. A hundred restorations of the Temple, taking these as their basis, have been attempted ; the least complicated system, and that which has obtained the greatest scientific

credit, is that of M. de Vogüé. We will correct and
complete it by means of the more recent researches of
English explorers. Accordingly, all the art of Palestine
being concentrated in the Temple of Jerusalem and its
furniture, we shall only speak incidentally of the few
other ruins anterior to the Macedonian epoch that have
been remarked, whether in Judæa or among other
nations of southern Syria, and even among the Naba-
tæan Arabs.

§ I. The Temple of Jerusalem.

The city of Jerusalem occupies at the present day the
southern extremity of a plateau bounded on the east by
the Valley of Kedron, and on the west and south by
the Valley of Hinnom. This plateau is cut in two
from north to south by a ravine called the Tyropœon
Valley, so that it forms two hills—one on the east,
Mount Moriah, the southern extremity of which, called
Ophel, was Sion or the city of David ; the other on
the west, of much larger extent, to which the name
of Sion is improperly given at the present day, and to
which the city began to extend only under the kings of
Judah. When Solomon ascended the throne, Jerusalem
consisted only of Sion or the city of David—that is to
say, the narrow hill of Ophel, between the Kedron
and Tyropœon valleys. Mount Moriah, on the north,
was given up to cultivation, and a rich man of Jerusalem, Araunah, possessed some ground there, with
a threshing-floor on which camels and oxen trod out
the corn at the time of harvest. David had bought the
field of Araunah in order to build upon it the Temple of

the true God, and before beginning the construction he had erected an altar on the threshing-floor in order that sacrifice might at once be offered to Jehovah. The materials were collected in great part before the work began ; architects, workmen and artists recruited at

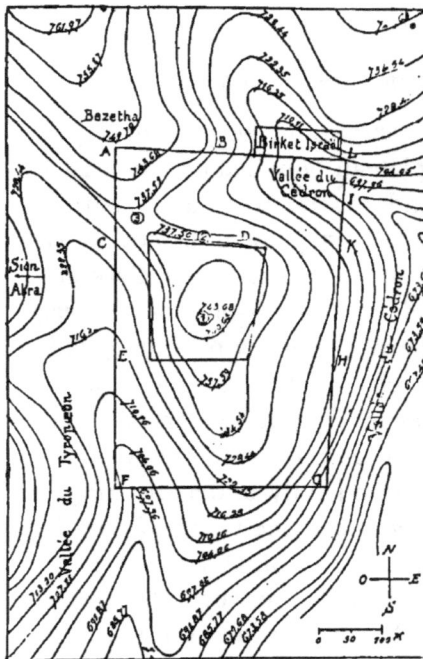

Fig. 168.—Site of the Temple on Mount Moriah.*

Tyre, thanks to the assistance of King Hiram, hastened to the spot, and the building began in the fourth year of Solomon's reign (B.C. 1013).

The summit of Mount Moriah, the centre of which formed the threshing-floor of Araunah, had to be levelled in order to serve as the site of the structure of the temple. In one place the hollows had to be filled, in another the ridges had to be cut away. The central crest was therefore surrounded by an immense quadrangular rockwork bounded by Cyclopean walls of the height of the truncated summit. These supporting walls, extraordinarily thick, formed of enormous blocks fastened

* From Wilson and Warren, *The Recovery of Jerusalem*, p. 298 (1871).

by iron clamps, were also embanked on the outside at the base, and all the empty spaces and interstices between the interior wall and the living rock were filled up with a nucleus of rockwork, so as to form on the upper part a square platform. A F G L is the threshing-floor thus surrounded. At the north-western angle—that is to say, A B C D—it was necessary not to construct a supporting rampart and fill up the declivity of the mount, but, on the contrary, to cut away the natural rock into the form of an angle, so that at this point the enclosure of the temple was bounded by a natural wall rising perpendicularly to the height of 26 ft. A trench dug by the English explorers at the north-eastern angle B L K proved that at this point, on the contrary, the artificial rockwork of the temple basement must have reached the colossal height of 123 feet. On the south, at E F G H, a labyrinth of vaults and corridors, supporting a mass of collected material, was contrived in the substructure, which at the south-eastern angle, at the point G, forms at the present day a terrace 45 ft. high ; and yet the accumulated rubbish causes the foot of the wall to be more than 65 ft. below the present surface of the ground ! By the system of levelling which we have described an irregular quadri-lateral was obtained, the eastern and southern sides of which are 1520 ft. and 1611 ft. long, and the northern and southern side 1017 ft. and 921 ft.

As Mount Moriah extended in a northern direction beyond the temple enclosure, the platform was on this side accessible to all comers. To remedy this incon-venience, and turn the new structure into an isolated citadel as well as a temple, a broad trench was hewn in the rock on the north-east, A B ; and on the north-west, B L, a gigantic moat called Birket-Israîl, which at the present day, though filled up to the extent of two-thirds, is still 104 ft. broad and 65 ft. deep. "Thus," concludes M. de Vogüé, "we have a large quadrilateral excavated on the north, supported on the south by vaulted sub-structures, and surrounded on three sides by terraces and on the fourth side by a broad moat. Such is the entirely homogeneous whole of the Haram esh-Sherif; such almost it has existed for long centuries, for successive destructions and rebuildings have little altered the primitive plan." *   We shall see directly, in the company of the same scholar, that this immense pedestal, the work of Solomon, was only modified and enlarged by Herod on one of its sides.

However, the platform thus prepared was not quite level with the natural crest of rock which crowns Moriah. The culminating point of this rock, called Sakhra, still rose 16 ft. above the terrace. Instead of sapping this peak of chalky limestone and removing it, it was taken as the level of a second platform above the first, but concentric with it and much smaller. This is the upper terrace which at the present day supports the domed building improperly called the Mosque of Omar, which would better be designated by its true name, *Kubbet es-Sakhra,* "Dome of the Rock." According to M. de Vogüé, the threshing-floor of Araunah, on which David set up the altar of Jehovah, was a little to the north of the Sakhra, where later the altar of burnt-offerings was placed.

After building the platform, Solomon occupied himself

* M. de Vogüé, *Le Temple de Jérusalem,* p. 3.

with the structure properly so called. The temple, or more plainly, the house of Jehovah, was to be enclosed in two concentric courts. Solomon had only time to finish the first court,—that which immediately surrounded the edifice, and then the eastern side of the second ; this was not completed till long after his death, in the reign of Manasseh. As soon as the interior building was ready, Solomon resolved to devote it to the worship of God, without waiting for the completion of the second court. He celebrated the solemn dedication of the temple only seven years after the laying of the first stone of the substructure. The Bible has bequeathed to us the description of the interior magnificence of this sanctuary, built and decorated by Phœnician workmen, and of the works of art collected within it by the most sumptuous of Jewish monarchs. The architecture and the interior ornaments were all Egyptian in style, like the Phœnician temples themselves. But nothing is left of the building of Solomon except the cisterns and the eastern side of the second court. This court is decorated with a portico, under which Solomon had the royal throne placed on which he sat when he was present at public ceremonies ; it was still called, even after Herod, the Porch of Solomon.

Under the kings of Judah there were numerous works of enlargement and restoration ; but all was destroyed in B.C. 588, when Jerusalem was taken by the Chaldæans. Nebuzar-adan, Nebuchadnezzar's lieutenant, caused the temple to be set on fire, and all was over with the legendary magnificence of the son of David.

Fifty-two years later the Jews who had been taken captive to Babylon were set free by Cyrus, and their leader Zerubbabel at once undertook to restore the temple of the true God. The work, hindered by the jealousy of the Samaritans, was not finished till b.c. 516. Sufficiently similar in plan to that of Solomon, the new temple was less beautiful and less grand in its proportions ; the old men wept when they remembered the former house. In the course of centuries the new temple underwent many modifications, at least in its exterior, although the original plan was not upset to any considerable extent. For instance, in the time of the Maccabees, the exterior enclosure was extended on the north, and at the north-eastern angle the fortress named *Baris* was built, which Herod altered in later times and which became the famous tower of Antonia. However, the temple of Zerubbabel lasted for nearly five centuries without being destroyed, and had the good fortune, rare in the ancient East, to pass through the period of Seleucid rule and the Roman conquest under Pompey, without being either pillaged or demolished. Herod, a man of Idumæan race, appointed king of the Jews by the Romans, conceived the project of making himself popular among his people by rebuilding the temple in all the splendour which Solomon had originally bestowed upon it. In the first place, he brought all his efforts to bear upon the enclosure, which he resolved to enlarge ; he doubled it, according to Josephus. Instead of four stadia in circumference it grew to six, preserving its former length on the smallest side, so that in fact it became geometrically double in area. This enlargement took place on the south, towards Ophel, so that the actual edifice of the temple, instead of standing in the middle of its peribolus, was removed to the north. The tower of Baris or Antonia continued to form the northern boundary. In the annexed figure, A B C D is the ancient peribolus, T the temple, and C D E F the square portion added by Herod.

"In order to carry out this plan," says M. de Vogüé, "Herod had the ancient terraces rased to the ground and rebuilt, as well as the colonnades which crowned them. Only he respected and enclosed the eastern colonnade called the Porch of Solomon and its fine supporting wall. This is the only part of the former temple that he seems to have preserved : all the rest was destroyed in order to be born again, restored to youth, and enlarged ; the inner sanctuary was demolished to its foundations."* The work undertaken by Herod began about the year B.C. 18. Ten thousand workmen were employed upon it under the direction of a thousand priests,

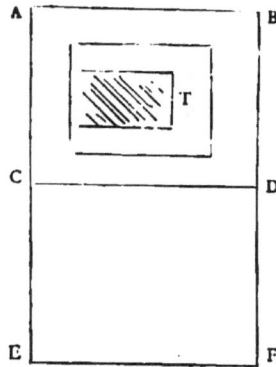

Fig. 169.

who alone might work with their hands in the Holy Place and the Holy of Holies. Eighteen months were enough to raise the inner building, but eight years were required to rebuild the court and the colonnades. The accessory structures were not finished till the year 64 after Christ, in the reign of Nero ; at this date the work was occupying eighteen thousand workmen.

The foregoing historical considerations compel us to conclude, with M. de Vogüé, that the Haram-esh-Sherif represents the very enclosure enlarged by

* M. de Vogüé, *Le Temple de Jérusalem*, pp. 21 and 22.

Herod. In fact, the southern side of the Haram is
919 ft. long, the circumference is 5,006 ft., which, with
the addition of 508 ft. for the projection formed by the
tower of Antonia, make 5,514 ft.—that is to say, six
times the length of the southern side. Besides, Herod
could not develop the enclosure on the north on account
of the tower of Baris and the gigantic moat *Birket-
Israïl*, which bounded it on that side, nor on the east
on account of the abrupt declivity which forms the
side of the valley of Kedron, nor on the west where
the Tyropœon valley is. The enlargement could
only take place on the south, and, moreover, as the
ground was sloping, it was necessary, in order to
remove the declivity, to proceed as Solomon had done:
that is to say, to construct an immense artificial platform, supported on three sides by high terraces. The
great substructures of the Haram esh-Sherif are the
remains of Herod's gigantic work. If since the time
of that prince the structure of the temple has been
several times overthrown from top to bottom and
continually rebuilt, these successive restorations have
not altered the original plan of the substructure; the
fragments of wall which remained in place served as
bases for the new edifices. The consequence of this
is that in these walls different layers of masonry are
perceived one above the other like geological strata, the
original Herodian courses being naturally the lowest.

The most ancient masonry visible, the lowest, is
formed of the largest blocks; the courses are from a
yard to two yards high; the length of the blocks varies
between $7\frac{1}{2}$ yds. and $2\frac{1}{2}$ ft. One block is to be observed
at the south-eastern angle which is 13 yards long.

Each layer recedes 2 in. from that beneath it; the stones, carefully trimmed, are laid without mortar. These large blocks are marginal-drafted—that is to say, each stone is, as it were, bounded by a groove which marks the courses and the joints. Besides the groove, each block is framed in a chiselled band smooth but not deep, which forms a second frame, carved within the groove round the surface of the hewn block. The lower masonry of the temple is, then, drafted and chiselled at the edge; besides, at intervals, the sur-face of the blocks is provided with projecting tenons, no doubt contrived to facilitate the plac-ing of them. The best preserved por-tion of this masonry is the Heit el

Fig 170. --The Jews' Wailing-place (after M. de Vogüé).

Maghreby, "the western wall," where the Jews come every Friday to weep over the destruction of Jerusalem and to await the Messiah; it is the Wailing-place. Recent English excavations, carried 107 ft. below the present surface of the ground, have proved that this masonry is to be found all round the enclosure of the Haram.

The system of construction immediately above the drafted blocks is characterised by Roman masonry formed of smooth stones without grooves, their outer surface being carefully fluted by means of a chisel with very fine teeth. The blocks, about a yard square, are laid with sharp-edged joints. This system is especially remarked on the western and southern sides. The following systems, in the order of their position one above the other, do not deserve to be described; they are relatively modern and belong to all epochs, but chiefly to the Saracenic period.

Not far from the Wailing-place, 39 ft. from the south-eastern corner, is the celebrated beginning of the bridge which united the temple to the city, crossing over the Tyropœon; it belongs to the first system of the substructure, and forms part of it. The English excavations have brought one of the piers to light; they have shown that the roadway of the bridge is 295 ft. long, and that the breadth of each arch amounts to 16 yards. While digging at the foot of the pier a pavement was discovered which no doubt represents the street which passed along there before Herod's epoch, or rather even before the destruction of the Temple by the Chaldæans. Some foundation is formed for this conjecture by the fact that when the English broke up this pavement and dug lower still they found the extrados of a vault: this was nothing less than the arch of another bridge of colossal masonry, which in the course of centuries had been buried under masses of rubbish: Herod, and perhaps Zerubbabel before him, built over the ruins without even trying to clear away the bridge. Who knows whether this arch, called *Robinson's arch*, from the excavator's name, is not the remains of a bridge erected by Solomon?

In the mass of substructure beneath the Haram, the existence of vaults and of a network of corridors of drafted masonry has been proved, and these must, from the character of the work, be contemporary with Herod. On the platform, two cisterns are seen which probably date from Solomon's time, if they are not even earlier, though it must be admitted that they have been subjected to successive restorations. One is under the rock Sakhra, the other in front of the mosque of El Aksa : the latter, especially, which is the largest, is a superb artificial grotto, upheld by pilasters contrived in the side of the rock. The descent into that under the rock Sakhra is by a flight of fifteen steps ; in the centre is a well which by means of a subterranean canal opens into the valley of Kedron, and was perhaps used by Araunah the Jebusite.

Fig. 171.—The western door. Present state (after M. de Vogüé).

The outer enclosure built by Herod was pierced by several gates giving access to the terrace, which are still partly preserved. They are subterranean with regard to the platform ; their threshold was of course on a level with the ground outside, and they opened on the staircases formed in the thickness of the terrace. At the present day, as the ground outside has been raised by rubbish of all kinds, Herod's doorways are filled up either entirely or partly. The *Western Gate* (fig. 171), near the Wailing-place, is at the present day buried to the extent of two-thirds. It is surmounted by a great monolithic lintel 16 ft. long, and its structure belongs to the Herodian system of masonry, but it has undergone subsequent alterations within.

The two most important of the ancient gates are on the southern side; they are called the *Double Gate* and

Fig. 172.—Interior View of the Double Gate.

the *Triple Gate*, on account of the number of their arches.

The two arched apertures of the Double Gate give access to a large vestibule, the vaulting of which is supported by an enormous central column; here the

hottest hours of the day might be passed in comfort.
From this vestibule there is an ascent to the upper
platform by two parallel flights of steps separated by a
row of pillars. There is nothing left of the time of
Herod but the two outer jambs of the door, the middle
pier, two monolithic lintels similar to those of the
Western Gate, and, lastly, the central column of the
vestibule. This column is squat, for it is only four
of its own diameters in height; it has no base. Its
capital, which broadens into the form of a basket, is
decorated with acanthus leaves in very low relief all
round.

The *Triple Gate*, also situated on the southern side
of the Haram, 67 yards from the Double Gate, is similar
to the latter, except that instead of two arches it has
three; besides this, a triple sloping corridor led to the
upper platform.

The *Golden Gate*,* opened in the eastern side of the
enclosure, was in its original form similar to the Double
Gate and the Triple Gate; and, like them, it is about
6½ yds. below the level of the platform to which it gave
access; nothing is left of the first structure except the two
monolithic jambs 10 ft. and 13½ ft. high, which seem to
be even earlier than Herod's building. On the north,
there was only one entrance, on a level with the platform, which communicated with the outside by a bridge
thrown across the great moat.

Now that we have arrived at the terrace we are
going to pass through the different parts of the

* This name is at present given to a building which has nothing
in common with this door of the Temple.--M. de Vogüé, *Le Temple de
Jérusalem*, p. 12, note.

buildings. They are commanded by the tower of
Antonia, which was built by the Asmonæan kings,
under the name of Baris, and enlarged and embellished
by Herod ; it occupied the north-eastern angle of the
structure. Its base was a scarped rock, the flanks of

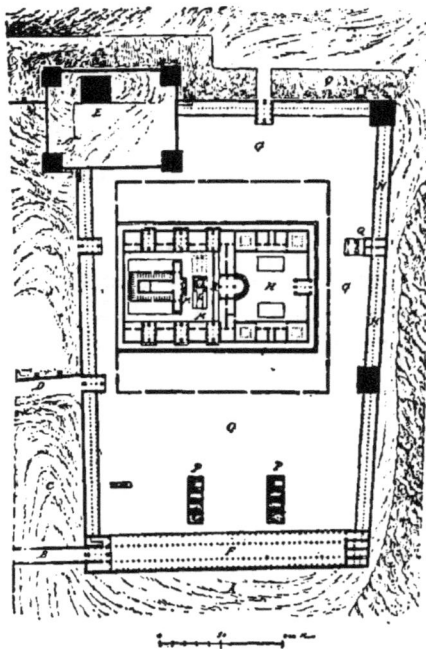

which had been cut
away by human
hands ; its outer wall
of enclosure was
three cubits thick.
An enormous trench
cut in the rock iso-
lated the fortress on
the north, and four
turrets flanked the
outer curtains at the
angles. Two flights
of steps led straight
down from the for-
tress into the outer
court of the Temple.

Fig. 173.—Plan of Herod's temple
(after M. de Vogüé).*

The great outer
court was on three of
its sides surrounded
by a double portico—
that is to say, by two

rows of columns of the Doric order, 25 cubits high ;
the roof, upheld by this double portico, which was

* A, Ophel.—B, Bridge.—c, Tyropœon.—D, Causeway.—E, Tower
of Baris or Antonia.—F, Portico.—G, Court of the Gentiles.—H, Court
of the women.—K, Court of Israel.—L, Altar of burnt-offerings.—M,
Court of the priests.—N, Solomon's porch.—o, Moat called *Birket Israil.*
PP, Double gate and triple gate.—Q, Golden gate.—R, Kedron valley.

30 cubits broad, rested upon the outer wall. Or the
south, instead of a portico there was a *basilica*, that is to
say, "a building with three naves of unequal height,
supported by columns." The aisles were 32 ft. broad
and 50 ft. high; the central nave was 48 ft. broad and
100 ft. high. There were 41 columns in each row,
which gave 754 ft. for the whole length of the basilica.
The central nave was supported by three rows of
Corinthian columns, and there were columns attached
to the side walls which corresponded to each row. The

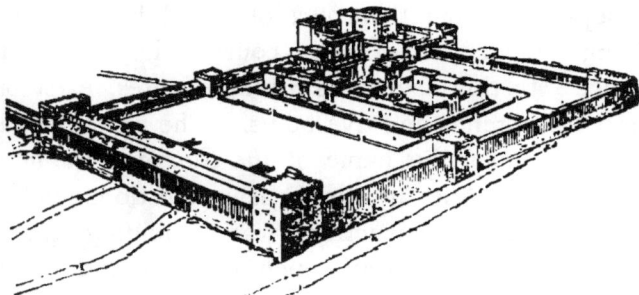

Fig. 174.—Bird's-eye view of Herod's Temple
(Restoration by M. de Vogüé).

building had a panelled ceiling of carved wood. The
basilica opened on the bridge which cut the valley of
the Tyropœon, and its axis was in a straight line with
the axis of the bridge.

Such was the court of the Gentiles, accessible to all
visitors. A barrier, only three cubits high, prevented
profane intruders from penetrating into the enclosure
reserved for the Israelites, which was contained within
that of the Gentiles. M. de Vogüé thinks that this
low wall of separation, on the southern side, must have
corresponded to the boundary of the outer enclosure of
the ancient temple of Solomon.

The enclosure reserved for the Israelites included
the *women's court* and the *men's court*, or that *of Israel.*
From the Gentiles' court access was obtained to the
women's court by a flight of fourteen steps. This court
had, at its four angles, square chambers which served
for the stores of the Temple, for the ablutions and other
pious exercises; there was also the Treasury chamber,
in which the specie was kept which was coined for the
exclusive use of the temple. Between these chambers
rose porticoes. On the inner side, the women's court
was separated from the court of Israel by a series of
buildings which opened on the court of Israel, and the
entrance into this court was by three gates, each provided with porches and five steps. The principal gate,
celebrated under the name of the *Gate of Nicanor*, on
account of its fine architectural proportions and the
richness of its construction, was a folding gate of
Corinthian bronze: twenty men were needed to open
and shut it; before it was a semicircular flight of
fifteen steps.

The court of Israel, reserved for the men who had
accomplished certain acts of purification, was 11 cubits
broad. The chambers which surrounded it on three
sides were used as appendages to Divine worship;
their façade was provided with porches. Each of them
was consecrated to a special service: the skins of
victims were salted and washed in them, musical
instruments, salt, the perpetual fire, and wood were
kept in them; the hall in which the Sanhedrim held
its sessions was one of them.

A step one cubit broad, which the priests alone might
cross, separated the court of Israel from the court of

the priests, and, in the middle of this court, the temple properly so called and the altar of burnt offerings stood. "The altar of burnt offerings was formed of three stages of rough-hewn stone, each stage a cubit less on all sides than that beneath it; the base formed a square of 32 cubits; the total height was 15 cubits high; the ascent was by an incline situated on the south, 30 cubits long; two smaller staircases led to the intermediate platform. On the upper surface the sacrificial fire burnt, and at the four corners were horns on which the blood was sprinkled and libations of wine and water were poured. A conduit situated at the southern corner of the altar received these liquids, and carried

Fig. 175. —The Altar of Burnt-offerings (Restoration).

them off into the subterranean drains, and thence into the valley of Kedron."* At the north of the altar of burnt offerings six rows of iron rings were seen fixed to the ground in order to fasten the animals to them; there were also eight small columns to which the victims were suspended that they might be cut to pieces and flayed, and eight tables upon which the flesh was placed.

The temple properly so-called, which stood 22 cubits to

* M. de Vogüé, Le Temple, p. 56.

the west of the altar of burnt offerings, was built on a
terrace six cubits high, mounted by a flight of twelve
steps.   There was thus a difference of 27½ ft. between
the level of the temple platform and the court of the
Gentiles.   As for the architectural arrangement of the
building, it was similar to that of Solomon.   The anterior
pylon was 100 cubits high and 20 deep; at each
extremity there were chambers in which the sacred
knives were kept, which were used for slaying the
victims.   The Holy Place or *Hekal*, and the Holy of
Holies or *Debir*, only separated by a veil, were both
60 cubits high, 30 broad, and together 65 cubits long
measured from outside.   " A series of thirty chambers
and three stories was attached to the sanctuary, as in
the ancient temple, for a length of 15 cubits, measured
without, and this gave to the sanctuary outside the
appearance of a basilica.   The whole edifice was roofed
with terraces, on which gilded points were fixed to
drive away the birds."*

The Jewish Temple was one of the grandest architectural works that the genius of the ancients produced.
The successive enclosures raised one above the other,
and crowned by the gigantic pylons of the sanctuary,
built of white marble, were the result of an inspiration
of genius that has never been realised except in this
instance, and all antiquity had but one voice to proclaim
its imposing majesty.   "When the rays of the rising
sun struck upon the metal plates which covered the
doors and roof of the sanctuary, when they illuminated
the gilding on the façade, and the gigantic golden vine
which spread its tendrils over the white marble of the

* M. de Vogüé, *Le Temple*, p. 37.

pronaos, the spectator's eyes were dazzled, and he was forced to turn them away, and the stranger who perceived the temple in the distance thought he saw a mountain covered with glittering snow."*

Such was the temple of the God of Abraham, Isaac and Jacob, restored by Herod, in which many of the scenes of the Gospels took place, and which was destined for so dramatic and mournful a fate. At once a public market, a house of prayer, and a fortress, it was condemned to be the tomb of Jewish nationality. Besieged and taken by the Romans, after a resistance unique in the annals of antiquity for its heroic desperation, it succumbed before the violence of Titus, and was profaned by Roman legionaries with torches and pickaxes in their hands. The echo of its fall, solemnly marked in the pages of human destiny, still resounds among us, for it was the overthrow of antiquity, and the irreparable destruction of the old civilisation of the East.

§ II. The Decoration and Furniture of the Temple.

The house of the Eternal was adorned with unheard-of spendour ; precious woods, gold, silver, ivory and gems—nothing was spared by this people, jealous for the honour of their God ; the accessories also of the worship of Jehovah, sacred vessels, knives, basins and utensils of every kind were works of art in which the chiseller and the metal-founder had each emulated the other's skill. But the artists who decorated the former

* M. de Vogüé, *Le Temple*, p. 58.

temple, let us not forget it, were Phœnicians. Now, the Phœnicians always confined themselves to the imitation of Egypt and Assyria; their technique has a hybrid character, which is, like Syria itself from a geographical point of view, a sort of compromise between Asia and Egypt. On these principles of criticism alone can we attempt to restore the decoration and furniture of Solomon's temple.

The veil hung between the Holy Place and the Holy of Holies, and concealing the latter from sight, was a large piece of silk, on which the skilful hand of Eastern embroideresses had represented the image of the world; the four colours which entered into its composition were the symbols of the elements: purple represented the sea, saffron fire, hyacinth air, byssus earth. The inner walls were panelled with carved planks of cedar. In the Holy Place these woodcarvings represented colocynths and open flowers; in the Holy of Holies, palm-trees and fantastic animals or cherubim were mixed with the flowers. This decoration was relieved by plates of gold fixed on the wood with nails of the same metal. The Ark of the Covenant, in the Holy of Holies, was sheltered under the wings of two immense cherubim of wood overlaid with plates of gold. The different parts of these monstrous figures were borrowed from the animal world, like those of the winged bulls in the Ninevite palaces. According to the Bible, the cherubim are winged and have bulls' feet; they draw Jehovah in his chariot or carry Him upon their back, like the Assyrian deities. Each cherub has at the same time a human face and a lion's face. They form a silent procession upon the cedar panels, the

leaves of the olive-wood doors, and the veil before the
Holy of Holies, alternating with palms and colocynths,
which, at Jerusalem, are substituted for the Egyptian
lotus.

In the Holy of Holies there were
two colossal statues of cherubs, 10
cubits high, overlaid with gold, which
guarded the Ark of the Covenant.
Each cherub had two gigantic wings,
one outspread and drooped over the
ark which it overshadowed, the other
symmetrically outspread in the opposite direction and raised towards

Fig. 176. — Egyptian
naos and cherubim
(M. de Vogüé, p. 33).

the ceiling.   M. de Vogüé ingeniously compares with
this description the Egyptian representations of two
figures with long wings, kneeling on each side of the
symbolic scarabæus or the solar disk supported by
uræi, which they cover with their wings.

Fig. 177.—Egyptian ark and naos
(from an Egyptian painting).

The Ark of the
Covenant itself re-
sembled those *naoi*
or *bari* which we see
carried by Egyptian
priests upon their
shoulders.   It was of
acacia-wood (*shittim*),
covered with plates of
gold both inside and

outside.   It was about 1¾ yards long, 2 ft. 8 in. broad
and high.   The lid was called the Throne of Jehovah.
The ark contained the two tables of stone upon which
the law of Sinai was engraved.

15

In the Holy Place was the altar of incense, on which
incense was burnt in honour of Jehovah; this was
probably a sort of tripod, surmounted by a bowl with

Fig. 178.— Egyptian
table of offerings
(M.de Vogüé, p.33).

a lighted brazier.   There was also the
table of shew-bread and the seven-
branched candlesticks.   The table, on
which twelve loaves were placed every
week, was undoubtedly analogous to
the tables of offerings to the gods
so often represented in Egyptian
bas-reliefs, with loaves piled upon
wine-pitchers; furniture of the same
kind also seems to be spoken of in the cuneiform
inscriptions of Nebuchadnezzer.   The bas-relief on the
Arch of Titus at Rome represents Jewish captives
carrying on their shoulders the furniture of their ruined
temple, and among this spoil figures
the table of shew-bread such as it
was in Herod's Temple, under the
form of a square cippus.

Fig. 179. — Seven-
branched candle-
stick(M.de Vogüé,
p. 33.)

The seven-branched candlesticks,
ten in number, had a peculiar form,
also revealed to us by the Arch of
Titus and some other monuments.
On the base with two steps a
central stem is fixed, to which six
branches are fitted, three on each
side, arranged in the shape of
a fan.   Each of the seven branches is adorned with
three flowers and a socket.   On the base, fantastic
animals are seen in relief.   Hiram-Abi, the famous
worker in metals from Tyre, in Solomon's pay, also

"made lamps and tongs of gold, and bowls and snuffers and basons and spoons and censers of pure gold,"* shovels and goblets of bronze. The candlesticks and other treasures of the Temple, carried away to Rome by Titus, were seized by Genseric during the sack of the city by the Vandals (A.D. 455). They were removed to Carthage, but, on the conquest of the Vandals by Belisarius, were taken in triumph to Constantinople. The Jews petitioned the Emperor Justinian to restore these treasures to the Holy City, to which they rightfully belonged, and he is said to have ordered that they should be sent to one of the Christian Churches in Jerusalem, but we hear no more of their fate in the pages of history.†

In the court of the priests, before the vestibule of the Temple, there were two separate bronze columns, reminding us of

Fig. 180.—Capital of the bronze columns. (Restoration by M. de Vogüe).

Egyptian obelisks, named Jachin and Boaz. The restoration of these two columns, marvels of Phœnician art, and invested in the eyes of the Jews with a talismanic power, has often been attempted. They were hollow, and their metal walls were $3\frac{1}{3}$ in. thick. "Their capital, 5 cubits high, had the form of fleur-de-lis, the lower part of which, swelling outwards, was covered with a reticulated ornament enclosed within

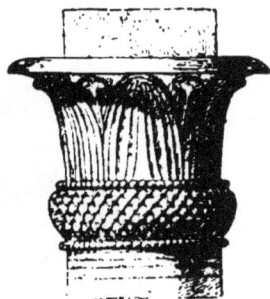

* I Kings vii. 49-50.
† Procopius, *De Bello Vandalico*, ii., chap. 9; Theophanes, *Chronographia*, p. 168, and Georg. Cedrenus, *Hist. Comp.*, p. 606 (Ed. Bonn, 1833).

two rows of pomegranates."* The total height of each column was 41 ft., the diameter of the shaft was 6 ft. 5⅓ in., the pomegranates, 200 in number, formed a double collar round each capital.

In the court of the priests, near the altar of burnt-offerings, which was itself covered with bronze, the famous *brazen sea* was placed, a great reservoir from which the priests drew water to purify themselves before the sacrifice. This bronze basin, which resembled the calyx of a tulip, was five cubits high

Fig. 181.—The brazen sea. (Restoration.)

(8 ft. 7 in.), and ten cubits (17 ft. 2 in.) in diameter; its exterior was decorated with two rows of colocynths in relief: the wall was 3⅓ ft. thick, as in the bronze columns; it contained at least 8,800 gallons. Instead of feet, the brazen sea was upheld by twelve bronze figures of oxen, in groups of three, which, in accordance with the proportion of the basin, must have been larger than life.

This gigantic basin was fixed and immovable; for

* M. de Vogüé, *Le Temple*, p. 34; Perrot and Chipiez, *op. cit.*, t. iv. p. 315 ff.

the purpose of drawing water, wheeled basins had been
constructed, ten in number, also of bronze, into which
the water intended for ceremonial purposes was poured.
Each had four wheels, like a chariot ; the wheels supported a square box, above which was placed the
cylindrical basin, large enough to contain from 150 to
170 gallons.   The walls of the receptacle and of the
box which supported it were decorated with palms,
colocynths, oxen and winged lions in relief.

Fig. 182.—Movable basin.   (Restoration.)

Such were the principal features of the temple
furniture ; smaller utensils, knives, pincers, tongs,
dishes, are scarcely known to us.   An exact idea of
them can, however, be formed by an examination of
the products of Egyptian and Assyrian industry,
especially of the dishes, vases, and utensils found
among the substructures of the Phœnician temples in
the island of Cyprus.
Various passages in the Bible enumerate the orna-

ments of the priests, such as the *ephod*, which, in
certain cases, signifies the liturgical vestment; in
others a sort of sacred casket, containing two talismanic cubes, called *urim* and *thummim*. The priestly
costume of Aaron is an embroidered garment in which
gems are set, according to the Book of Exodus. As
early as the period of Genesis, we see the children of
Israel making use of seals of precious stone, precisely
as their neighbours the Egyptians and Chaldæans
did. A certain number of gems carved in intaglio
have come down to us which bear names apparently Jewish: Shebaniah, Nathanyahu, Hananyahu,
Obadyahu. These seals for the most part only bear
the name of their possessor; they have neither ornament nor symbol.

§ III. CIVIL ARCHITECTURE.

The temple of Jerusalem, in which the national life
of the Jews was concentrated, was also, as we have
said, the summary of their art and industry. In vain
have many archæologists, during the last sixty years,
made efforts to discover in Palestine, or in the other
regions of southern Syria, and even in the heart of
Arabia, traces of an art which might have flourished
in these regions before the arrival of the Greeks and
Romans. Travellers have indeed observed at Ala-
Safat, at Jebel-Musa, in the land of Moab, on the Bahr-
el-Huleh in Galilee, near Hesban, and in many other
places, dolmens and upright stones, analogous to those
in Africa, in Brittany, and on Salisbury Plain, and
remains of walls of Cyclopean masonry, no doubt

built by those giants, the Rephaim and the Anakim, who, as the Bible tells us, were the first inhabitants of these regions. Certain circles of great blocks, like those of Minyeh and Deir Ghuzaleh in the land of Moab, may have marked the bounds of sacred enclosures, temples in the open air, that is to say, of those *bâmoth*, or "high places," of which the Scriptures so often speak. But these barbaric remains, like the borders of certain wells at which, perhaps, the flocks of the patriarchs slaked their thirst, have little interest for the history of art. No idea can be formed of civil architecture except by imaginary restorations. Solomon's palace, which communicated with the temple and was situated to the south, upon Ophel, was demolished and rebuilt twenty times with incessant modifications, until its final ruin. The principal building, standing in the middle of a spacious court, enclosed by supporting walls which bounded the hill like the temple-enclosure, was called the *House of Lebanon*, after the place whence the timber was brought of which it was partly constructed. It was 100 cubits long, 50 broad and 30 high ; its walls were built of large blocks ; forty-five cedar columns were counted in it, divided into three rows, and supporting architraves of the same sweet-smelling wood.* This edifice was used as an arsenal : like the monarchs of Nineveh, the kings of Judah had a magazine of weapons in their palace.

Behind were the royal apartments, consisting of a hall of columns, and another room panelled with cedar, called the *throne-room* ; in front of the former stood

* Perrot and Chipiez, *op. cit.*, t. iv., p. 463.

porch 50 cubits long by 30 broad. There were also
the *selamlik* and the *hareem*, arranged as in all oriental
palaces. The offices communicated with the city by
means of the *Horse Gate* ; the *Upper Gate* gave access
to the temple-enclosure. This is the extent of our
information upon the subject of Solomon's palace.

The palace of Hyrcanus, at Arak el-Emir, and
the fortifications of Jerusalem and of the Tower of
Antonia, are purely Græco-Roman, and do not come
within the sphere of our work. However, the English
explorers discovered by their soundings on the slope
of Ophel, above Kedron, a fortified wall which presents
several kinds of masonry one above the other ; the
lowest masonry is perhaps earlier than the rebuilding
of the ramparts by Nehemiah after the Babylonian
captivity : in this case it would date, if not from the
reigns of David and Solomon, at least from the time
of Jotham and Manasseh. The base of the quadrangular bastions is formed of very regular courses,
sometimes rusticated ; the blocks are 8 ft. long by
3 ft. 3 in. high ; the marginal draft is even found in
places. This tradition of bevelled masonry has been
already noticed in the Herodian substructure of the
Temple ; it is also to be seen in the wall of Hebron
(fig. 183).

In a country which generally lacks drinking water,
the building of cisterns is a matter of importance, and
this is the case in Judæa. One of the most remarkable works of this kind is that which carries the
waters of the Fountain of the Virgin to the Pool of
Siloam. In the tunnel an inscription has been found
which enables us to fix the date of the work about the

reign of King Hezekiah, and teaches us by what
methods this subterranean canal, 1,750 ft. long, was
successfully hewn in the rock.   Two bands of workmen
attacked the mountain on both sides at once, and the
miners, after numerous windings, which increased the
labour and the length of the tunnel, at last struck
"pick against pick," says the inscription, "and heard
one another shout" on each
side of the barrier.   Thus
the water was carried along
a passage not more than
2 ft. broad and of a height
which varies from 1 ft.
5½ in. to 14 ft. 7½ in.   But
bold as this work may
appear in the hands of
Jewish engineers, who
possessed neither compass
nor exact geometrical in-
struments, it teaches us
nothing from the point of
view of art, any more than

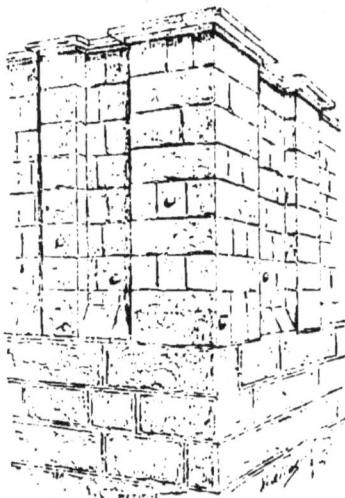

Fig. 183.—The tomb of Abraham
at Hebron (after Vogüé, p. 119).

the aqueducts hewn in the
rock which are found in other parts of Palestine.

§ IV. Tombs.

Palestine and the north-east of Arabia are covered
with sepulchral monuments, but there are few which
date from the pre-Hellenic epoch.   Abraham bought a
cave called Machpelah from the Hittites of Hebron for
400 shekels of silver, and was buried there, as well as

the other patriarchs of his race. The site of the cave is at the present day covered by a mosque, and in the crypt of this mosque the bodies of the patriarchs are supposed to lie. Now, the wall of the crypt, a superb

piece of masonry of imposing appearance, is incontestably contemporary with Herod; there is the same marginal draft that we have studied in the enclosure of the temple built by that prince. The tomb called Absalom's is also a small building not earlier than the time of the Seleucids, and if it preserves, like the Palestinian structures of the same epoch, a few architectural reminiscences of Phœnician art, it has columns, capitals, and mouldings which are entirely Greek. We need not, therefore,

Fig. 184.—Absalom's tomb (after F. de Saulcy, *Voyage autour de la Mer Morte*).

occupy ourselves with these monuments, or with the tomb of the Maccabees at Modin, or with the not less celebrated *hypogæa* known under the name of *Kebûr-el-Melûk*, or "Tombs of the Kings," *Tomb of Jehoshaphat*, of *Saint James*, with its Doric portico, or *Tomb of Zacharias*: sepulchral chambers which are visited by pilgrims in the neighbourhood of Jerusalem, and the date of which Saulcy has in vain tried to place even farther back than the Babylonian captivity. The tomb of Joshua, among the ruins known under the name of Khirbet-Tibneh, north-west of Jifneh (Gophna), does not seem to be more ancient.

In Arabia, at Medaïn Salih, several tombs have been observed hewn in the rock, the façade and inner arrangement of which are identical with those of the Palestinian caves. There are Greek columns, pediments and mouldings mixed with a few traditional motives, the original birthplace of which is in Assyria or on the banks of the Nile; cavities for sarcophagi are arranged around the chambers as in the Jewish tombs. The inscriptions obtained at Medaïn Salih prove that these burying-places were formed during the first eighty years of our era.

Fig. 185.—Sepulchral chamber at Medaïn Salih. (Doughty, *Doc. Epigr. du nord de l'Arabie.*)

However, at the village of Siloam, near Jerusalem, there is a tomb, known under the name of the *Egyptian Monolith*, which seems to be far earlier than all those of which we have spoken; there are some who would even assign it to the epoch of Solomon. This trapezoidal monolith, Egyptian in style, is 13 ft. high, and the platform measures 19 ft. 10 in. by 17 ft. 10 in. The door which looks westward gives access to a square ante-chamber which leads into a room 8 ft. long on each side. The ceiling of the chamber is slightly convex, like many Egyptian hypogæa; two large niches

are contrived in the walls.   Outside, the monument is
provided with an Egyptian cornice.   All tends to
demonstrate that this tomb is earlier than the Babylonian captivity, in spite of the architectural alterations
to which it has been subjected at a relatively modern
period.   Besides, to whatever date the sepulchral caves

Fig. 186.—The monolith of Siloam (after Saulcy, *Voyage autour
de la Mer Morte*).

of Palestine belong, they are all conceived in accordance
with the same traditional type, which is also that of
Phœnicia, and which we shall find at Carthage; there
is always a speos hewn in the rock, a façade with
Egyptian, Assyrian, or Greek ornaments, according to
the date, then a vestibule giving admission through
a low, narrow doorway into a sepulchral chamber.

From this chamber the visitor penetrates through one of several apertures into other rooms; and round these more or less numerous chambers the cavities for sarcophagi are cut. Thus the cave of Machpelah at Hebron

Fig. 187.—Tomb in the valley of Hinnom (after Saulcy).

must have been arranged as early as the time of Abraham, and in the same fashion, without doubt, the sepulchral cavern was formed in which the ashes of the kings of Jerusalem were deposited. The discovery of the hypogæum containing the sarcophagi of the princes of the house of David would doubtless be more important for epigraphy than for archæology properly so called. It would only confirm the verdict pronounced upon Jewish art: that it is entirely wanting in variety and originality in every instance except in the Temple of Jerusalem.

CHAPTER VIII.

PHŒNICIAN AND CYPRIOTE ART.

THE Phœnicians, established on the coast of northern Syria, were not simply the agents of commerce ; they also carried the art of the great Asiatic civilisations to all the coasts upon which they set up their factories, and among all the races with whom they formed relations of business. Their manufactured products have no more marked originality than those of the Jews and Canaanites : a mixture of Egyptian and Assyrian art is observed in them. These two powerful foreign factors, if they had been brought into action by an ingenious and enquiring people, would no doubt have begotten a new art which would have summed them up and absorbed them, by combining them with the peculiar inventions of the national genius : this was the case in Greece, for example. But the Phœnicians, exclusively occupied with business, were content to seek sometimes from Assyria and sometimes from Egypt the elements of a bastard industry, in which the exotic forms are so little disguised and so imperfectly fused that it is as easy as possible to detect them.

If ancient authors and epigraphic texts attest the importance of the Phœnician factories in Greece, Italy, Sicily, Gaul, Spain, and Africa, none of the great

nations of antiquity has left fewer material traces
than this of its industrial and artistic life.   In Syria,
Cyprus, Malta, and Carthage we have great trouble
in finding vestiges of the structures raised by the
Phœnician architects, or statues or ornaments which
can be attributed to the craftsmen of this nation : the
historian of art is obliged to glean in any direction
that he can the poor waifs and strays which he
considers, in spite of himself, as extremely precious,
but which he would often disdain if they came from
Assyria or Egypt.   Cyprus, partly inhabited by a
Hellenic population and thrown by nature like a bridge
between Asia and Greece, scarcely forms an exception
to this rule, although it offers by itself alone a larger
material for oriental archæology than all the other
Phœnician countries put together.

§ I. Temples.

Before the introduction of Egyptian and Assyrian
influence into Syria, the Semitic and Canaanitish races
of this country held the high places (*bâmoth*) in
veneration.   On the highest summit of the mountains,
in spots which recalled ancient memories, on peaks
that had been struck by lightning, stone altars were
raised and victims were immolated upon them ; the
surrounding forest became a sacred grove.   In the
same way our Celtic ancestors erected their dolmens.

Soon, under Egyptian influence, the Phœnicians
began to construct temples.   The *maabed* (temple) of
Amrith * is still an Egyptian temple on a small scale ;

* Renan, *Mission de Phénicie*, pl. 10

as in the latter, there is a *cella* or tabernacle of stone, within which the divine image was contained. It is composed of slabs erected on three sides. One side remained open, and was only closed by a curtain. The monolithic slab of the roof is adorned on its four edges with a light border with mouldings, and projects like eaves above the door ; in the interior it is cut in a semicircular form, so that it presents the appearance of a shallow vault. The rock which forms the base has been isolated from the mountain by sapping, and

Fig. 188.—Shrine at Ain el-Hayât (Renan, *Mission de Phénicie*).

h us the chapel, including this natural pedestal, reaches 22 feet in ·height. At the edge of the surrounding court were certain structures, doubtless a colonnade bordering the sacred enclosure ; but this has disappeared.

The *maabed* of Amrith is the most important remaining representative of the temples of Phœnicia. At Ain el-Hayât, however, two shrines have been discovered similar to that of Amrith ; one (fig. 188) tolerably well preserved, consists of a monolithic *cella*, resting on a substructure of large blocks ; the whole is 17½ ft. high. Above the door a row of Egyptian uræi is seen ; the ceiling within is perceptibly cut into the form of a vault on which two pairs of wings, surrounding the Egyptian solar disk, are sculptured in relief.

The famous temples of Melkarth at Tyre, and of Astarte at Sidon and at Gebal (Byblos), which excited the admiration of ancient travellers, are no longer known except in memory. The *maabed* of Amrith alone gives us some idea of their architectural arrangement; they consisted of courts, in the centre of which rose the shrine of the deity built upon a platform. The Phœnician and Canaanitish temple showed therefore a strong resemblance to the temple of Jerusalem and also to the great mosque of Mecca,—the only monument which perpetuates this architectural type among us.

Nothing but a few fragments is now left of the temples built by the Phœnicians in Cyprus. The great prosperity of this island under the Romans and in the middle ages is the direct cause of the destruction of the monuments of an earlier age. The superb cathedrals of Famagusta and Nicosia, the fine churches built under the Lusignan dynasty, the formidable ramparts constructed by the Venetians, rose at the expense of ancient buildings, the materials of which

Fig. 189. Coin of Paphos.

were turned to profit as stone-quarries. The celebrated sanctuary of Astarte at Paphos, for instance, is only known to us by the conventional representation of it upon coins belonging to the Roman period. We are able to distinguish in this figure a court surrounded by a balustrade, and beyond the court a structure which reminds us of the pylons of Egyptian temples: it is a gigantic gate between two towers, provided with a large aperture through which we perceive the sacred stone, flanked by two candelabra; above hover the star and crescent. The roof, on which doves are resting, was supported by columns forming a portico.

16

Tacitus, who relates the visit of Titus to the temple of Paphos, says that the goddess was represented in it under "the form of a circular block, rising in the form of a cone, gradually diminishing from the base to the summit." This description corresponds with the stone which the medals show us. According to the excavations carried on by P. di Cesnola on the site of the temple, the building was almost 220 ft. long by 164 ft. broad; the peribolus measured 688 ft. by 540 ft.; the principal gate, perhaps that which figures on the coin, had an aperture more than 16 ft. broad.

The temple of Golgoi (Athieno), the ruins of which were disinterred by Cesnola, was a rectangular building constructed of bricks dried in the sun; the substructure alone was of stone. On the north and on the east were doors with wooden frames. Within, wooden pillars, surmounted by stone capitals, supported the roof, formed of pieces of wood placed close together, on which mats and reeds were arranged with a thick layer of beaten earth. The exterior of the temple, coated with white rough-cast, must have been of a most modest appearance. The interior, on the contrary, was laden with the richest ornaments. In the middle of the enclosure a tall cone of grey stone was found, a yard high, which must have been the sacred stone of the goddess, and reminds us of the image at Paphos described by Tacitus. Round the mystic cone, a whole population of stone statues painted in brilliant colours, set in a line along the walls or ranged in files in the centre of the building, formed, as at Tello, the dumb train of worshippers of the goddess. Votive offerings were hung on the walls above a row of bas-reliefs, analogous to those of the Assyrian palaces. Stone lamps in the form of shrines, fastened to the walls, lighted up this curious scene.

In the temple of Curium, Cesnola ascertained the existence of a crypt to which a staircase gave access; it was composed of four subterranean chambers cut in the form of apses in the rock and communicating with one another by doors and a passage. These chambers are about 22½ ft. long on each side, and 13 ft. high; it was here that the famous treasure of Curium was found, consisting of the plate of the temple, and of votive offerings made to the deity.

The recent excavations which we have shortly described, though they have scarcely brought more than substructures to light, yet enable us to describe the Cypriote temples with some exactness. While those of Phœnicia are built on heights, reminding us of the primitive high-places, the sanctuaries of Cyprus are generally in the plain, in the midst of fertile fields, like the temples of Egypt. The shrine of the deity was under the open sky like the Greek temples; around, and at a greater or less distance, rose a gallery covered with a roof supported within by colonnades forming a portico, and without resting upon the wall of enclosure.

A Phœnician inscription of the fourth century before Christ relates the erection of several temples to various deities, notably to the god Sadambaal and to the goddess Astarte in the island of Gaulos (Gozo). The remains of these sanctuaries are still in existence: they are called the *Giganteja*, or "Giant's dwelling," and consist of two neighbouring enclosures not communicating with one another. Constructed of irregular masonry, formed of enormous blocks, they are parallel, and their gates open on the same façade ; though one is larger than the other they both follow the same interior arrangement. Each is composed of two oval or elliptical chambers next to one another, and communicating by a narrow passage ; the farther chamber contains also a semicircular apse. The great temple is 119 feet long from the entrance to the bottom of the apse ; its greatest breadth is 75 feet. The area is uncovered ; in one of these enclosures a conical stone has been discovered analogous to those in the temples of Phœnicia and Cyprus.

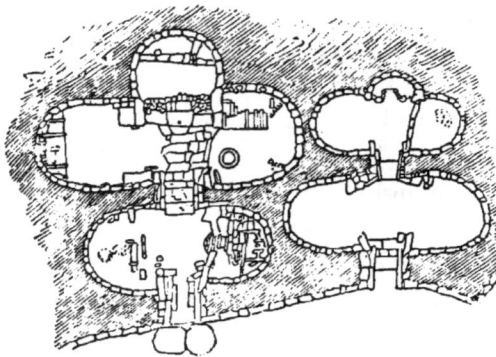

Fig. 190.—Plan of the Giganteja. (*Nouv. Annales de l'Institut arch. de Rome*, 1832, pl. ii.)

At Malta, ruins of temples have been discovered constructed on the same principles as the Giganteja of Gozo. The *Hagiar Kim*, " stones of adoration," near the village of Casat Crendi, presents identical architectural features, with the enormous blocks of its irregular masonry. The plan, however, is a little more complicated : it is a series of seven ellipsoid chambers built next to one another.

Not a single stone is left above ground of the temples raised by the Phœnicians in Sicily, Sardinia, Spain, and even Carthage.   The famous sanctuary of Astarte, which stood on the scarped peak which overlooks Eryx, in Sicily, has perished ; so has the temple of Baal-Hammon at Marsala (Lilybæum) and the Sardo-Phœnician sanctuaries of Baal-Samaim, Astarte, Eshmun, and Baal-Hammon indicated by the Punic inscriptions discovered at Sulci.   The temple of Melkarth, at Gades, so much resorted to in the time of Strabo has left no traces.   It is in vain that the name of the powerful city of Carthage and of the illustrious men whom she brought forth excite our enthusiastic curiosity ; to no purpose has the site upon which she was built become French soil : the Romans respected nothing in the city of their most formidable enemies.   The destruction which followed Scipio's conquest, in the

Fig. 191.—Roman wall at Byrsa (Boulé, *Fouilles à Carthage*).

year 146 before our era, was systematic, and extended to the very foundation of the walls.   What did escape was altered and transformed for the profit of the Roman colony which rose upon the Punic ruins, and which was itself upon two occasions the object of a savage demolition.   There is, therefore, nothing Phœnician to be expected from the archæological excavations at Carthage from the architectural point of view ; except mutilated inscriptions, almost all that is discovered is Roman, Christian, or Byzantine.   The

Chapel of Saint Louis, near which Boulé undertook his
excavations, stands on the site of the famous temple
of Eshmun in the middle of the acropolis of Byrsa;
on the neighbouring hill was the temple of Tanit,
whom the Romans called *Virgo cælestis*; between
Byrsa and the harbour, beside the forum, in the neighbourhood of which I carried on some excavations with
M. S. Reinach in 1884, rose the temple of Baal-Hammon.
To these topographical indications the memorials of the
sanctuaries of Hannibal's city are limited.   ·

§ II.   CIVIL ARCHITECTURE.

If hardly anything is left of the Phœnician temples
on all the shores of the Mediterranean, it must be
admitted that the state of the case is almost the same
with regard to civil monuments.   The position of the
formidable ramparts of Tyre, which held conquerors of
cities like Sargon, Nebuchadnezzar, and Alexander so
long in check, can with difficulty be recognised at a
single point: it is probably marked by a submarine wall
of enormous blocks, bonded with a concrete in which
lime is mixed with crushed bricks; these walls, according to Arrian, were 147 ft. high.

The enclosure of Banias (Balaneum), between
Tortosa and Latakieh, is still partly standing; but is
it of Phœnician or of Pelasgic origin?   It extends to
a length of about 1,970 ft.; the wall, pierced by three
gates, from 26 ft. to 32½ ft. broad, is built of blocks of
grey limestone of irregular form, which are neither
trimmed nor cemented.   It is from 16 ft. to 26 ft. thick,
and, in places, is still as much as 32½ ft. high.   Broken

lines, recesses and projections seem to announce the approaching appearance of bastions and towers in the art of fortification. The Pelasgic walls of Eubœa, Tiryns and Sipylus present analogous features.

What remains of the substructures of the walls of Aradus, Berytus, and Sidon, indicates the employment of large and fine blocks irregularly laid. In the Carthaginian ramparts of Eryx, in Sicily, the stones bear Phœnician letters which acted as position marks for the masons, but this fortified enclosure does not date from an earlier period than the fourth century, and the Punic architects must have imitated their neighbours the Greeks. The walls of Carthage, which roused the astonishment of the ancients, were from six to seven leagues in circumference; they consisted, at least at certain points, of three concentric walls, arranged in steps in consequence of the declivity of the ground. Nothing is left of them except a sort of talus at intervals, which serves as the boundary of cultivated fields. Constructed of hewn stone, they were, according to the statements of ancient writers, 77 ft. high and 34 ft. thick; the towers were still higher and stronger.

Since temples and ramparts have always been constructed in the most solid form, and that most capable of resisting the attacks of time and of men, if very little of these is left there is a much stronger reason why hardly anything should remain of civil monuments and private houses. In the soft limestone of the Phœnician coast the primitive inhabitants hewed out their dwellings like Troglodytes. In later times, by the aid of civilisation, the tombs alone were opened in the sides of the mountains, and the living cut out enormous blocks of stone with their picks, in which they hewed doors and chambers. At Amrith there is a monolithic house cut in this fashion, which M. Renan considers as the type of the genus. It is 98 ft. square and 71 ft. high; the walls are 2 ft. 7 in. thick; in the interior three chambers are divided by thin partitions contrived during the hollowing of the rock. Sometimes only the lower part of the walls have been hewn in the rock, which thus only forms a monolithic plinth one or several yards high, and completed to the roof by light masonry.

At Cyprus traces of structures which could be attributed to the period of Phœnician dominion are sought in vain. The only monuments which give some idea of the civil architecture of this famous island are

Fig. 192.—Terra-cotta house. (Louvre.)

models of houses in terra-cotta, found at Dali and preserved at the Louvre ($7\frac{3}{4}$ in. high). The most remarkable of these little buildings has a door guarded by a sphinx. At the two windows appear the heads of women; on each side of the door, columns with capitals in the form of lotus-flowers support a projecting roof. But of what architectural value can such a toy, modelled in so coarse a manner, be?

The poverty of monuments is even more absolute in the case of Carthage and the western basin of the Mediterranean. What travellers who visit the site of the old city admire above everything are the unheard-of efforts made by the ancients to catch the water from the sky and store it in vast covered basins, or else to bring water from springs at great distances. Nowhere throughout the East, where there has always been the greatest anxiety to provide water—not at Jerusalem, where the Siloam aqueduct was tunnelled, nor at Tyre, where the aqueduct was dug which brought the waters of Ras el-Ain into the city—are such grand traces left of the works undertaken with this useful object. Only the gigantic viaduct which goes for several leagues to bring the waters of Mount Zaghouan to Carthage, does not date, as it is at the present day, from an earlier period than the reign of Hadrian; and the same must be said of those immense vaulted cisterns, near Byrsa, in which a whole Arab village lodges at the present day, and in which tourists take drives : it has never been possible to say exactly how much is anterior to the period at which the Roman colony was founded. The Carthaginians, two hundred years before our era, certainly knew the vault and the dome, the natural and primordial elements of oriental architecture, as well as the Romans. The walls, vaults, and domes of the cisterns of Carthage are of a mediocre stone, furnished by the quarries of Zaghouan : small irregular blocks are buried in a very thick mortar of lime, so excellent that it unites with the stone and gives to the whole structure the homogeneous character of one single immense block. The Byzantine ruins which cover the plain of Carthage are built with equally bad materials and an equally good cement.

We must now enquire whether any trace remains of the constructions which the Phœnicians must have

undertaken in order to establish or maintain those
ports on the Mediterranean coasts in which their
vessels found a sure refuge.   These works must have
shown the most characteristic side of the art of
building among this nation of merchants.   However,
they have perished almost entirely like the rest, or else
they are still buried under the sand.   Tyre and Sidon
had two harbours, of which only the site is now to be

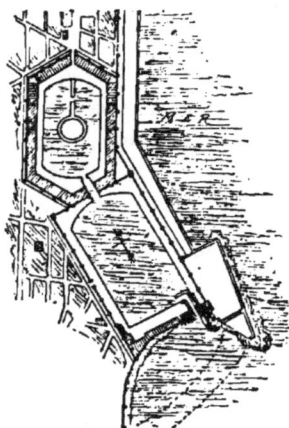

distinguished.   The two harbours at Carthage, the commercial harbour and the cothon
or military harbour, are still
there, but three-quarters of
them are covered with sand,
and they no longer contain
more than a pool of shallow
water.   Lengthy and costly
excavations, of which those
undertaken at Utica may give
some idea, could alone tell us
what they formerly were.   At
present we can only confirm
the exactness of Appian's de-

Fig. 193.—Plan of the harbours at Carthage (after
Daux, *Emporia phéniciens*).

scription when he says : "The harbours of Carthage
were constructed in such a way that ships passed
from one into the other ; on the side of the sea
they had only one entrance, 70 ft. broad, which was
closed by iron chains.   The first harbour, intended for
merchant vessels, was furnished with numerous and
various mooring-cables.   In the middle of the second
there was an island ; round this island, as on all the
edges of the basin, were large quays.   The quays pre-

sented a series of docks which could contain a hundred
and twenty vessels.   Above the docks, storehouses had
been constructed for the rigging.   Before each dock
rose two columns of the Ionic order, which gave to
the circuit of the harbour and the island the appearance of a portico.   In the island a pavilion had been
built for the admiral, from which trumpet-signals
sounded, and orders were transmitted by the herald,
and in which the admiral kept his look-out.   The
island was situated near the mouth ; its surface had
a perceptible elevation above the plane of the water,
so that the admiral might see all that passed on the
sea without those who were coming from the open
being able to distinguish what was being done within
the harbour.   Even the merchants who found shelter
in the first basin could not see the arsenals in the
second ; a double wall separated them from it, and a
special entrance gave them admission into the town
without having to pass through the military harbour."
Go at the present day to Carthage, and you will
observe with astonishment the modest extent of these
two reservoirs, which formed the harbour of the great
African city.   They are parallel to the sea, from which
a narrow strip of land separates them ; the admiral's
island is still in the centre of the cothon, which is
circular in form, and communicates by a narrow canal
with the merchant harbour ; the latter forms a large
rectangle, and opens into the Mediterranean by a mouth
a few yards wide.   The Carthaginian vessels were
scarcely larger than our fishing-smacks.   The jetty
which sheltered them on their entrance into the harbour
of Carthage has left a trace marked by large blocks,

which at certain points reach the level of the sea. The two harbours of Utica were not more spacious: one was only 328 ft. by 108 ft., the other 780 ft. by 327 ft.

Of all the Phœnician towns, that which has preserved the most remarkable remains of its ancient jetty is Thapsus (Dimas), on the eastern coast of Tunis. The mole which, though dilapidated, still rises 8 ft.

Fig. 194.—Jetty of Thapsus. (Restoration by Daux, *Emporia phéniciens.*)

above the waves, is 850 ft. long, and its breadth is 35 ft. The peculiarity of its construction is that it is pierced by a series of small passages, arranged in three rows: their object was to deaden the violence of the shock of the waves, by allowing them to pass through the openings. Here again it is uncertain whether we are looking at a work exclusively Phœnician, Roman, or Byzantine.

§ III. Tombs.

The most important of the monuments discovered in Phœnicia are the tombs. Nearly all are hewn in the rock, and are, as in Judæa and Arabia, great caves in which the sarcophagi of an entire family were deposited. The necropolis of Marath (Amrith), explored by M. Renan, furnished specimens of tombs which seem to be the most ancient, the most spacious, and hewn with the greatest skill. The descent into them is by a shaft, as in Egypt, and notches are cut in the wall of the rock into which the hands and

Fig. 195.—Tomb at Amrith. Plan (after Renan).

Fig. 196.—Tomb at Amrith. Section (after Renan).

feet must be inserted ; but in the more recent tombs a flight of steps is substituted for the shaft. At the bottom a low door is found on two sides, leading into a larger or smaller number of rectangular chambers. These rooms communicate with one another by means of passages in which a few steps are generally found, so that the most distant chambers are at a lower level than the others. Sometimes there are even two stories of chambers ; in the partition of rock which forms the intermediate ceiling a shaft is pierced by which they are entered from above. The sarcophagi are ranged round the walls, or placed in niches or cavities for coffins, hollowed out on the sides : once filled, these

niches were closed by a large slab, on which an
inscription might be written in
honour of the dead. The necropoles of Tyre· and Adlun present
the same types of sepulchral caves.

Now, may we ask, what was the
outer aspect of a Phœnician necropolis in which the tombs were thus
hidden under the ground ? Often,
especially when the tombs were
those of rich men, a stela or cippus
of small size appeared above them,
and marked the position of the cave and the opening
of the shaft. Tombstones of this kind, either mono-

Fig. 197.—Sepulchral
chamber at Amrith
(after Renan).

liths or constructed of
masonry, are scattered
over the plain of Amrith;
they are called on the
spot *meghazil* (in the
singular, *mighzal*) ; one
of them (fig. 198) is
described by M. Renan
as " a master-piece of
proportion, elegance,
and majesty " : it is 32½
ft. high, and consists
of a base from which
four lions project, two
cylindrical drums placed

Fig. 198.—Mighzal at Amrith (Restoration by M. Renan).

one above the other and decorated with denticulated
sculpture, and, finally, a small hemispherical dome
carved in the block.

A sepulchral monument at Amrith, the Burj el-Bezzâk, is entirely distinguished from caves and

Fig. 199.—The Burj el-Bezzâk. Section (after Renan).

Fig. 200.—Chamber of the Burj el-Bezzâk (after Renan).

structures of the form which we have just described ; it rises above the ground, like an ordinary house, and is built, without mortar, of regular masonry, with blocks 16 ft. long. It terminated formerly in a pyramidal roof, and its full height was $52\frac{1}{2}$ ft. In the interior, there are only two chambers one above the other, each communicating with the outside by a narrow aperture. Round the walls of these chambers there were numerous niches for coffins, separated one from another by partitions.

Fig. 201.—The Burj el-Bezzâk. Restoration. (Renan, *Mission de Phénicie*.)

The necropolis of Sidon, which is more considerable than that of Amrith, presents the same peculiarities : the caves are constructed in the same manner ; only at the present day no *meghazil* are any longer to be seen near the orifice of the shaft. In the poorest caves the corpses were laid upon the ground or deposited in graves; in other sepulchres cavities for coffins are hewn out all

Fig. 202.—Section of a tomb at Saïda (after Renan).

round the chambers; in the richest, finally, the bodies were placed in sarcophagi buried in the floor of the chamber. The hypogæa of Gebal differ from the type observed at Sidon, Tyre, and Amrith, by the peculiarity that the descent into them is neither by a shaft nor by a staircase; the aperture is formed in the vertical side of the mountain, and is sometimes surmounted by a pediment and a few decorative mouldings (fig. 203).

Of all the sarcophagi found in the Phœnician necropoles, perhaps not one can be attributed to an earlier date than the reign of Cyrus. The simplest are

Fig. 203.—Entrance of a tomb at Gebal (after Renan).

large monolithic troughs, provided with a convex or
triangular lid.   Some of them are decorated with
garlands, foliage, and chaplets ; the corners of the lid
are sometimes provided with acroteria.   The only ones
which have a real artistic interest are the sarcophagi
in the form of human figures, or rather of mummy-
cases, the head of the dead person, and sometimes the
arms also, being carved in relief on the lid.   These
sepulchral urns were coloured in imitation of the
wooden sarcophagi of the Egyptians, which they copy

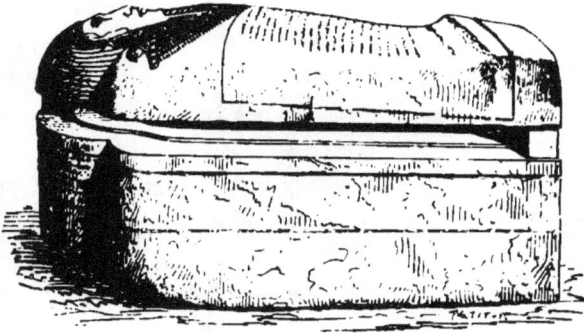

Fig. 204.—The sarcophagus of Eshmunazar.   (Louvre.)

in their form; while the carved work of the faces shows
us that Assyrian influence was dominant in Phœnicia
long after the disappearance of Nineveh.   The sarcophagi of Tabnit and Eshmunazar, which only date
from the year B.C. 350, disclose to us a remarkable
peculiarity in the means adopted by the Phœnicians,
merchants and navigators before all things, in order to
furnish the tombs of their dead with stone coffins.
These peculiar monuments, of black amphibolite, issue
from the Egyptian quarries of Hammamat near Cosseir,
and they originally contained Egyptian mummies.

17

Phœnician sailors stole them or bought them for money ; the ashes which they contained were thrown to the four winds, the hieroglyphic inscriptions and the Egyptian scenes, carved or painted upon the plaster which covered the stone, were entirely or partly removed and replaced by the epitaphs of Tabnit and Eshmunazar. A considerable number of Phœnician sarcophagi are thus borrowed coffins, and by no means the work of indigenous artists.

Sarcophagi in the form of the human figure have

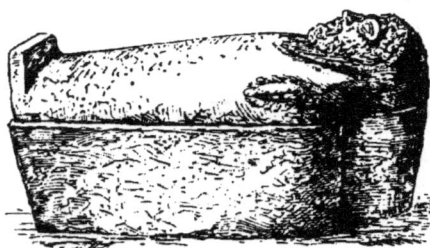

Fig. 205.—Sarcophagus in human form. (Louvre.)

been discovered in nearly all the countries in which the Phœnicians established their factories, in Cyprus, Sicily, and Malta, and they everywhere present the same characteristics : only the head of the dead man is in relief. At Saïda, a sarcophagus was found in which the arms are carved beside the body ; the sleeve of the garment ends above the elbow, and the left hand holds an alabastron. In the museum at Palermo a sarcophagus is preserved which came from Solus, the lid of which has the form of a true reclining statue like a mediæval tomb : it is a woman clothed in a long peplos over a short tunic, the sleeves of which end at the shoulder ; the left hand also holds a vase for perfume.* Besides

* See Perrot and Chipiez, *History of Art in Phœnicia and its Dependencies*, vol. i., p. 193 [Eng. Ed.].

stone sarcophagi, leaden and terra-cotta troughs have been found in the necropoles of the Syrian coast, and also coffins of cedar-wood, decorated with metal ornaments, generally bronze lions' heads.

The sepulchral chambers of Phœnicia contain mortuary furniture not without interest. It consists of *alabastra* of glass, terra-cotta and alabaster, standing against the wall ; and of idols in terra-cotta, representing Baal-Hammon sitting between two rams, the god Bes, of Egyptian origin, the god Pygmæus, Astarte sitting or standing with a dove in her hand, and, lastly, terra-cotta chariots holding one or two figures, with two or four horses harnessed to them. Besides these objects of Phœnician manufacture, amulets and statuettes, imported from Egypt, are found. The body of the deceased was enveloped in bands ; the mouth and eyes were often covered with gold leaf, and rich men often placed a complete mask, formed of gold leaf, in which all the features of the face are marked : it is thus seen to what an extent Egyptian habits were implanted in Phœnicia. Lamps, amphoræ, amulets and ornaments are also found in the tombs of the Syrian coast. Women were buried with their necklaces, their rings, their bracelets, their ear-rings, their metal mirror, their pyxes for cosmetics and perfumes, and their toilet articles. Rings, provided with engraved stones which served as seals, are also found ; nowhere, except in Cyprus, have weapons been discovered in the tombs of this nation of merchants.

In the Cypriote necropolis at Dali (Idalion) there are often at the side of the corpses pieces of pottery with geometrical decorations, bronze weapons, gold ornaments, metal dishes with figures engraved on the inner side, statuettes of Astarte, of warriors, of chariots and of riders similar to those on the Phœnician coast.

Fig. 206.—Tomb at Amathus (after Cesnola, *Cyprus*).

Among the tombs at Amathus which are Phœnician and date from the fourth century, there are some constructed of fine regular masonry, with a door framed in a fillet, and a flat roof, or one with a double slope like those of our houses. These tombs sometimes contain several chambers, along the walls of which the sarcophagi were set in a row, sometimes in the human form, sometimes with a triangular lid.

The Phœnician tombs found in Malta, in Sicily and in Sardinia, present the same arrangement as those on the coasts of Syria and Cyprus : the descent into the cave is by a sunken shaft or by a flight of steps, and the chambers resemble those that we have described. At Caralis and at Tharras pyramidal cippi have been found *in situ*, above ground, which marked the position of the

Fig. 207.—Sepulchral chamber at Amathus (after Cesnola, *Cyprus*).

burial-places, as we have already seen in Phœnicia : in these tombs the furniture is imported from Egypt, Etruria and Asia.

The necropolis of Mehdia, on the eastern coast of

Tunis, contains tombs, the descent into which is by
shafts as at Aradus.   The tombs of Thina (Thenæ)
near Sfax, those of Carthage on the hill near the town
called Jebel Kawi, have all been violated in antiquity
or by the Arabs.   Constructed on an uniform plan, they
consist of a rectangular chamber, the descent into which
is by a flight of steps.   All round this room, the orifices
of the coffin-niches are seen like the mouths of ovens.
The staircase may have as many as ten steps; the
chamber is 6½ ft. high, from 19½ ft. to 21 ft. long, and
9½ ft. broad.   The walls are coated with a white stucco
which sometimes was ad-
orned with figures in relief;
the   fragmentary   subjects
which I was able to detect
seemed to me to be Greek
and perhaps Roman in style.

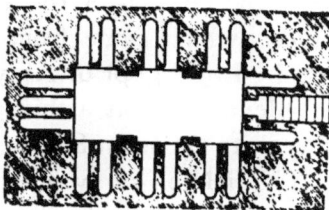

Fig. 208.—Plan of a tomb at
Carthage (Boulé, *Fouilles
à Carthage*).

To sum up, the Phœnician
tomb represented only two
types: the erect tomb above
ground, and the subterranean tomb.   The first was
monolithic, or built like a house; the second was either
on a level with its entrance in the side of the rock, or
else it was reached from above by means of a shaft or a
staircase.   Both contained a greater or smaller number
of chambers according to the number of corpses to be
buried in it.   These bodies were, save in rare exceptions,
placed in sarcophagi sometimes deposited in cavities contrived in the wall of the chamber, sometimes in ditches
hewn out in the floor, sometimes simply deposited along
the walls.   The mortuary furniture varied according
to the wealth of the families; it included, together with

amulets and figures of deities, all the toilet articles and
ornaments used by the deceased during his earthly
existence.

§ IV. Phœnician Sculpture.

Phœnicia, it must not be forgotten, was by turns
subjected to the yoke of the Egyptians and Assyrians,
who introduced into it, with their garrisons, their art,
their customs, their industries and all that characterised
the peculiar genius of their civilisation. The conquerors
were the masters of the Phœnician artists, and the few
objects which came from the hands of the latter were
inspired by Egypt or Assyria ; it is only from the time
of Alexander that a third element, Greek art, begins to
reveal its action in Syria.

The field of study offered by Phœnician sculpture is
remarkably limited : it consists of the bas-reliefs of
certain sarcophagi, of votive stelæ and of meagre fragments of stone statues. The sarcophagi in human
form, of which we have already spoken, though not
of an earlier date than the Hellenic epoch, show us
very clearly the Egyptian and Assyrian influences at
work in Syria. If the form of the troughs is Egyptian,
if the finest of them have actually been imported from
Egypt, the sculptures with which they are decorated
are altogether Assyrian. The symmetrically undulating
curls of the beard are like those of the Ninevite colossi;
only it is to be observed that the artist can handle his
chisel like a Greek. From the time of the Seleucids, the
physiognomy of these heads which stand out in high
relief on the lid of the sepulchral trough, grows more

and more Hellenic, and is modified in accordance with Greek models; so that if a chronological classification of all these monuments is undertaken, the most ancient would be those in which Egyptian and Assyrian influence is most marked; the most recent are those in which the Greek style finally prevailed.

In the rare fragments of buildings anterior to the Macedonian epoch, observed in Phœnicia, the elements of decorative sculpture are borrowed from Egypt and Assyria: nowhere has an original motive of indigenous inspiration been found. The gate of a structure described by M. Renan at Umm el-Awamid has a lintel on which two small figures of Egyptian appearance are sculptured in adoration before the winged disk supported by uræi.* The Phœnicians

Fig. 209.—Phœnician slab at Amrith (after Renan).

imported this solar globe, even more ancient in Egypt than in Assyria, into every coast. It is found in Cyprus, Malta, Sardinia and Carthage, where it is carved on the votive stelæ of Tanit and Baal-Hammon. The sphinx is also one of the principal elements of Phœnician sculptures: not only its form, but even its posture, is copied from the sphinxes of the Egyptian temples; it reclines on a pedestal, and has upon its head the pshent and the uræus; but it has more than the Pharaonic sphinx—

* Renan, *Mission de Phénicie*, p. 411.

namely, wings borrowed from the Assyrian and Persian genii. Other fragments of architecture show us the motives of their decoration,—rosettes, palmettes, guilloches and denticulated designs of Assyria.

Astarte, on the stela of the king of Gebal, Jehaw-melek, has the costume, attitude, and attributes of the Egyptian Isis, while the king, standing before her, resembles the Ninevite monarchs in adoration before their favourite deities, or Darius and Xerxes on the bas-reliefs of Persepolis. A stela at Amrith represents a deity standing on a lion, an Assyrian subject already reproduced in Hittite bas-reliefs; a still greater similarity is seen in the lion's cub held by the figure as by the hero Izdubar, and the energetic modelling of his limbs bears witness that the artist was educated at the school of Nineveh. And yet the god's head-dress, and the winged disk placed above his head, are Egyptian in form.*

The study of sculpture in the round leads to the same conclusions. The Phœnician *patœci*, images of the god *Pumai* (a word from which *Pygmy* and *Pygmalion* are derived), were only copies of the Egyptian gods Bes or the embryo Ptah: this type of ugliness united to strength was carved in wood at the bows of the ships, in order to terrify the enemy. While statues found in Phœnicia are clothed with the Egyptian shenti, lions forming the doorposts at Umm el-Awamid are only half sculptured in the round: the head, fore-quarters and front paws are the only parts carved. Nothing could more directly recall the lions of the Assyrian palaces.

* Perrot and Chipiez, *History of Art in Phœnicia*, vol. ii., p. 12.

If the Chaldæans, as early as the time of Gudea, were accustomed to erect in their temples statues of kings, of pontiffs, or even of private individuals, whose image thus remained always present before the eyes of the deity, the Phœnicians took care not to renounce this habit. M. Renan relates that in an underground chamber near the maabed of Amrith a considerable number of fragments of white limestone statues was discovered; they were also found at Cyprus (fig. 210). These statues are iconic in character; they are portraits of the " masters of the sacrifices," as the Phœnician texts call the devotees who had themselves represented in the very act of accomplishing their vows, in order that the deity might not forget them. The archaic statues lately found on the Acropolis at Athens seem also to have, if not the same iconic character, at any rate the same symbolic meaning.

Fig. 210.—Cypriote statue (New York Museum).

Carthage, which was a city of warriors as well as of merchants, had despoiled all the towns that she had conquered of their artistic wealth, in order to adorn her temples and palaces. This systematic

depredation was so great a scandal in antiquity that
when Scipio took possession of Rome's haughty rival,
he invited the inhabitants of the Sicilian towns to come
and point out their artistic property, and resume their
ownership of it; all that was not reclaimed was carried
away to Rome, and a nation of statues was seen passing
along in procession behind the triumphal car.   Besides
these Græco-Roman works, the fruit of pillage, which

Fig. 211.—Votive stela
from Carthage. (*Corpus inscript. Semitic.*)

adorned the public places of Carthage, there were those which
were the work of the Greek artists
whom Carthage was pleased to
summon to her bosom ; there were
also those of Carthaginian craftsmen educated at the school of the
Greeks : these last alone interest us
here, and the scanty specimens
which exist of them confirm us in
the opinion that the Carthaginians
were not more artistic than the
Phœnicians.

These monuments consist almost
exclusively of votive stelæ anterior
to the taking of Carthage by the Romans in B.C. 146·
These boundary stones, from 11¾ in. to 19½ in. long
by about 5¾ in. broad, were intended to be fixed in
the ground, and therefore the lower part is still in
the rough ; the upper part, trimmed on its four sides,
is particularly well smoothed on one of its larger
faces ; on this side alone is found a votive inscription
addressed to the goddess Tanit, the Punic Astarte,
and to Baal-Hammon. Above the inscription various

symbols are represented in engraved lines, rarely in
relief.   The stela terminates in an imitation of a gabled
roof, often provided with two acroteria.   The decoration of these Punic stelæ is, however, still Greek,
as is proved by the design of the acroteria, ovals,
triglyphs, volutes, pediments, and even Ionic columns
which figure in it.   The symbols, carved in the most
barbarous fashion by workmen who could not claim the
title of artists, are borrowed
from the Punic religion and
from the fauna and flora of
Africa.   The commonest is the
open hand, raised towards the
sky and generally set at the
point of the gable; the Arab
still paints it in black on the
white lime with which he plasters
his house : it averts the evil
eye.   We find also the Egyptian
uræus ; the solar disk with the
crescent, a symbol of Tanit ;
the ram, the symbol of Baal-
Hammon ;   the caduceus, the

Fig. 212. – Stela from Lilybæum.   (*Corpus in-
script.   Semit.*)

horse, the elephant, the bull, the rabbit, fish, the palm,
the rudder, the anchor, the hatchet, the lotus-flower,
vases of various shapes, ships and fruit.   We also meet
with the Divine Mother holding her child in her arms ;
a young child standing or crouching with an apple in
its hand ; or a funeral banquet, as on Greek stelæ.

The great female deity of the Carthaginian Pantheon,
Tanit, is found not only under the form of a human
figure, but very often under that of a symbol difficult to

describe. It is a sort of triangular mannikin (fig. 212), the traditional and degenerate representation of a sacred stone; this triangle is furnished with protuberances in its upper part, and resembles to some extent a man clothed in a long robe, who straddles his legs and raises his outstretched arms to heaven: this sacred cone with arms corresponds well enough to the description by Tacitus of the Paphian Aphrodite. The supreme Trinity, consisting of Baal-Hammon, Tanit and Eshmun, is also frequently symbolised by three cippi of unequal height, placed side by side, and joined on a common base. This symbol is also represented on the stelæ at Hadrumetum and Lilybæum; the cippi are broader at the base than at the summit, and the middle one is surmounted by the solar disk and the reversed crescent. Sometimes a fire-altar served by a pontiff burns at the feet of this symbolical figure (fig. 212).

Fig. 213.—Stela of Hadrumetum. (*Gazette arch.*, 1884, pl. vii.)

One of the most interesting Punic stelæ that can be cited was found at Hadrumetum (fig. 213). An image of two columns is seen upon it, supporting a complicated entablature. The base of the columns is very elegant, and resembles a large vase from which acanthus leaves emerge; from the middle of this tuft of leaves a fluted stem rises, the upper part of which is fashioned like a woman's bust. This woman is seen in full face, and holds her hands clasped upon her breast, which is also adorned with the round disk and the crescent; she has a similar disk upon her head. In the entablature a row of lotus-flowers, a winged disk supported by two uræi, and a row of uræi seen in full face and with heads erect are distinguished; everything in this monument is oriental, or, rather, Egyptian. Even in Sardinia and the Balearic Islands the votive stelæ of Tanit and Baal-Hammon enable us to follow the track of the preponderating influence of Egyptian art in Carthaginian symbolism.

§ V. Cypriote Sculpture.

If the very vestiges of Cypriote architecture have disappeared, it is not so with the works of the sculptor. The quarter of a century which has just passed has seen disinterred as if by enchantment from the bowels of the great eastern island, and then transported into the chief museums of Constantinople, Paris, London, Berlin, and especially New York, hundreds of stone statues and thousands of terra-cotta figurines of strange appearance, with picturesque head-dresses and with foolishly-smiling visages, which form a group apart in the history of art, since they are neither purely Asiatic nor purely Greek. Save in rare exceptions, the monuments of Cypriote sculpture were not imported from abroad; they are the work of that mixed race of Greeks and Asiatics, which, by means of the Phœnician ships, was in constant relation with Syria, Egypt, and Asia Minor.

The productions of Cypriote sculpture which seem to be the most ancient remind us of the figures

in the Assyrian bas-reliefs; the costume is the same:
a conical cap, a curled beard, a long tunic, and a
short cloak passed over the shoulder.   However,
there are essential differences : the muscles are far
from being expressed with the same vigour; no figure
wears that long beard like a regular screw, which is so
characteristic of Ninevite sculpture.   We feel that the
Cypriote artist works at a distance
from a model which he only sees
with the eye of memory, or else
that he imitates at second-hand,
and is compelled to interpret a
Phœnician work which is itself only
an interpretation of an Assyrian
prototype.   The   most   ancient
statues discovered in the temple
of Golgoi may date back from the
epoch at which the Assyrian con-
queror Sargon erected at Citium
(Larnaca) the triumphant stela on
which he relates that his vessels
have vanquished Cyprus.   They

Fig. 214.—Colossal head
from Athieno. (New
York Museum.)

are of all sizes.   There is a colossal
head 2 ft. 9½ in. high (fig. 214).   It
wears a conical helmet ; the eyes are prominent, the nose
is straight and regular, the mouth small but full-lipped,
the cheek-bones projecting ; the beard is composed of
long parallel tresses slightly curled at the end.   This
fine head, more than half oriental, may be considered
as the type of its kind.

After the overthrow of the Sargonid dynasty, Cyprus
was given up to Egyptian influence, which reigned

there during the period which extends from the fall of Nineveh, at the end of the seventh century B.C., to the Achæmenid dynasty.   But here again the imitation is only partial, and not as servile as in Phœnicia.   We find Egyptian fashion modified in Cyprus by the taste of a foreign race.   The figures are half-nude instead of being entirely draped ; they have no garment except the shenti, tied round the waist and adorned with uræi ; the bust is bare ; the arms are bare, but adorned with bracelets and held close to the body; the head-dress is the Egyptian *pshent* scarcely modified ; the hair, cut straight and falling in compact masses behind the beardless head, reminds us of the *Klaft.**

During the same period, but especially under the Persian dominion, we witness the interpenetration of the two influences—that of Egypt and that of Assyria —in Cypriote art : it is the marriage of the two styles, the union of the two streams.   In the statues at Athieno, for instance, the head is Assyrian in the features of the face, the curled beard and the head-dress formed of a peaked cap, but all the rest is Egyptian : the nude torso, the necklace, the shenti round the waist quaintly loaded ·with ornaments, the symbolical meaning of which the artist no longer understands.   A striking example of this hybrid style is the famous colossus of Amathus, which is 13 ft. 11½ in. high and 6½ ft. broad across the shoulders. He is a Hercules who offers a mixture of the athletic proportions of the Assyrian Izdubar, with the type of ugliness symbolized in the god Bes.   He has short

* See Perrot and Chipiez, *History of Art in Phœnicia, etc.,* vol. ii., p. 123.

horns, a low forehead, large ears ; his hair and beard
are treated in the Assyrian manner ; he has a lion's
skin round his waist ; in his two powerful hands,
pressed against his breast, he holds the hind paws of

Fig. 215.—The colossus of Amathus. (*Gazette arch.*, 1879,
pl. xxi.)

a lioness. Is he not the
giant Izdubar, whom Assy-
rian artists so often took
pleasure in representing?
On the other hand, his tat-
tooed arms, his hairy skin,
his lion's skin fastened round
his body, his bestial and
Silenus-like face, his legs
like the paws of a wild beast,
are all copied from those
figures of the god Bes, which
the excavations in the Nile
valley bring to light by
hundreds. At the same
time the artist handles his
chisel as a Greek might.
The limbs are plump and
rounded : no more of those
exaggerated muscles which
characterise Assyrian art ;
nothing Eastern in the in-
significant features of the
face. We have already, in certain points, the Hellenic
Heracles, with whom the Cypriote god is soon to be
confounded.

In fact, the third element which comes into
Cypriote sculpture is the Greek element, with all its

methods, as the colonies on the coast of Asia Minor understood them as early as the sixth century.   In the year B.C. 500 Cyprus made an alliance with the cities of Ionia; and Cimon's expedition in B.C. 450 determined the definite preponderance of Hellenic civilisation in that island.   The statues in which Greek inspiration is recognised have something original which distinguished them at first sight (fig. 210).   The physiognomy recalls that forced smile which has been called the *Æginetan smile*; the heads are freed from those conical head-dresses so dear to oriental art, which Greek art repudiated in order to replace them by a diadem or a high crown ; the hair is no longer in ringlets and scarcely forms a row of flat curls to frame the forehead ; the play of the drapery is quite different from that which comes from Nineveh, and reveals a good taste which is quite charming.   In short, the Cypriote monuments, which correspond to this descrip-tion, only form a branch of Greek

Fig. 216.—The priest with the dove. (New York Museum.)

archaic art, and we must no longer treat of them in a book devoted to the East.   Let us only cite, as an example, the famous statue of the priest with the dove, which seems to date from the Græco-Persian period.   It is a colossal statue 8 ft. high, representing a man holding in his hands a cup and a pigeon.   His head-dress consists of a hemispherical cap which ter-

minates in the head of an animal; three tresses of
hair, a characteristic sign of Greek archaism, fall
symmetrically from the back of his head on the front
of each shoulder. The rows of curls in the beard
which covers his mouth and chin are visibly imitated
from the Assyrian fashion of dressing the hair. The
fringes and draperies of the garment still remind us,
indeed, as well as the square form of the shoulders and
breast, of the statues of Tello; but how much more
ample and harmoniously arranged they are! We have
here Greek taste still imprisoned in the hieratic formula bequeathed to it by the East.

Fig. 217.—Bas-relief of Heracles and Eurytion. (*Colonna-Ceccaldi, Monum. antiques de Cypre*, pl. v.)

To the same Græcizing art belong all those iconic statues from the temples of Golgoi and Amathus, which, instead of the
peaked cap or of the pshent, wear on their heads
garlands of foliage or of narcissus, more or less high·
and more or less rich, but infinite in their variety.
Like the statues found in Phœnicia to which we
alluded above, they are portraits of priests, priest-
esses, or other personages who offer to the god for
perpetuity the object which they hold in their hand: a
flower, a fruit, a branch, a patera, a pyx, an alabastron,
a bull's head or a pigeon.

Few bas-reliefs have been noticed in Cyprus. However, a colossal statue of Heracles in the Græcizing

style, found at Golgoi, had a pedestal decorated with a most remarkable bas-relief, reminding us of those in the Ninevite palaces. The ground is painted red to make the figures stand out; the relief is low and flat, the anatomical details of the figures are carefully studied and exaggerated in the Assyrian manner. The scene represents Heracles driving away the herds of Geryon, a subject which seems to be of Tyrian origin. Heracles, nude, with the lion's skin on his back, was probably holding his bow, which has disappeared as well as his head; like the giant Izdubar, he is of colossal stature;

Fig. 218.—Sarcophagus from Amathus. (New York Museum.)

before him is the dog Orthros, with three heads, already pierced by an arrow shot at him by Heracles; Eurytion flees with his herds; his beard and hair are treated in the Assyrian manner. He carries a whole tree, with which he was no doubt lashing his oxen; this tree is treated like those that figure on the walls of Nineveh.

Certain Cypriote sarcophagi are also decorated with Greek subjects, treated in the oriental manner: the birth of Chrysaor, who issues from the neck of Medusa, for instance, is seen; banqueting scenes and bull or boar hunts are found. A picture represented on the principal side of a sarcophagus from Amathus (fig. 218) is copied in servile fashion from the sculptures of Assyria and Egypt; there are rows of pearls, lotus-flowers and daisies; a climbing plant is even to be remarked here like the sacred tree on the Ninevite bas-reliefs. One of the figures holds the Asiatic umbrella, and the tassels of the horses are Assyrian. However, the figures of the cortège are Greek in style, attitude and costume. On the smaller sides are two oriental subjects: at one end four figures of Astarte in full face, of the type reproduced in profusion in Chaldæa and Phœnicia; at the other four figures of the god Pygmæus, who is made up, as we have seen, of Bes and Izdubar together.

In two words, Cypriote sculpture, fruitful as it is, lacks variety, like Egyptian sculpture and Assyrian sculpture, its two mistresses. It lives only by borrowing, and has invented nothing. What characterises the stone statues which it produced is immobility and hieratic stiffness, together with finish in the details and decoration. They have no features which proceed from a realistic study of nature. It has been remarked that these statues, intended to be set in rows along the inner walls of the temples, are scarcely at all modelled behind, and are flattened as if they had been carved out of slabs of insufficient thickness; moreover, though broad in the chest, they are narrow in the hips and feet; the legs are pressed closely together, so that they have to some degree the appearance of reversed cones. Cypriote art has no originality except in the Hellenic element, which it assimilates; the Cypriote artist is a Greek who has served his apprenticeship among the Orientals.

§ VI. Phœnician and Cypriote Ceramics.

The triple influence that we have remarked in Phœnician and Cypriote sculpture is observed no less clearly in pottery. In the seventh century Assyria carried on the artistic education of Phœnicia; then it was Egypt till the end of the sixth; finally Greece enters into the lists in her turn, bringing her peculiar genius which, especially in Cyprus, joins hands with its two elder brothers.

The Phœnicians, then, learnt first of all from the Assyrians and Egyptians how to model clay, and to fashion of it figures and vases of every form.

In the list of terra-cottas from Phœnicia which depend upon Ninevite art, and which were found at Amrith

Fig. 219.—Phœnician chariot in terra-cotta. (Louvre.)

(Marathus), chariots holding four warriors and drawn by two or four horses hold the first rank. The figures, generally bearded, and wearing the conical cap, present in their features the purest Semitic type, like certain Babylonian terra-cottas; the harness of the horses shows the minute detail of the Ninevite equipages. Besides these chariots, figurines have been obtained from the Phœnician necropoles, which represent Astarte, nude, standing upright, carrying her hand to her breast, or else sitting and clothed in a long robe

down to her feet without folds ; she often wears a high
calathos of Asiatic origin, which has
been observed on the head of captives
in the Assyrian bas-reliefs.

Fig. 220.—Pygmy in
terra-cotta. (Louvre.)

We know that ceramics was never
highly developed in Assyria and
Chaldæa; accordingly, as soon as
Egyptian influence could show itself
in the political sphere in Phœnicia,
the pseudo-Egyptian style was not
slow to replace the pseudo-Assyrian
style in ceramics. The figurines of
the new school, fashioned like the
preceding ones in orange-red clay,
represent women standing or sitting,
sometimes suckling a child, holding a fan, a pigeon, or
the lunar disk. The Phœnicians even learned from the
Egyptians to coat their statuettes
with green or blue enamel,
analogous to that which is called
Egyptian faïence, so that it is
sometimes difficult to say whether
the enamelled statuettes found in
the tombs of Phœnicia are imported from Egypt or are works of
native industry. In their course
of servile imitation Phœnician
craftsmen have reproduced even
the hieroglyphic characters, which
they distorted because they did
not understand the sense of them.

Fig. 221.—Pygmy in
terra-cotta. (Louvre.)

The type most frequently copied by the Phœnicians

is the grotesque god ·Bes or the embryo god Ptah, whom they turned into the god Pygmæus, called Patæcus by Herodotus. This large-headed and bandy-legged dwarf, of repulsive obesity, the type of deformity and ugliness, is met with everywhere in Phœnician pottery.

Fig. 222. — Terra-cotta head from sarcophagus. (Louvre.)

The pseudo-Hellenic or Græcizing style has furnished numerous terra-cotta monuments in Phœnicia, as is attested by the large head found in the necropolis of Amrith, which is nothing less than part of the lid of a sarcophagus in human form. The head is vulgar, and has neither an Egyptian nor an Assyrian appearance; it was inspired by Greek art, but to some extent followed oriental tradition. Among the Phœnician statuettes which may be referred to Greek archaic art there are figurines of Aphrodite standing upright, clothed in a long tunic, the folds of which the goddess grasps in one hand, while she holds a pigeon in the other. Tresses of hair fall over the breast on each side of the head. On other occasions the costume of these women is composed of a long robe and a mantle fastened by a brooch on the shoulder; they hold their arms close to the sides of the body.

Fig.223.—Astarte. Phœnician terra-cotta. (Louvre.)

The clay of Cyprus lends itself better than that of
Phœnicia to moulding and to baking, therefore in very
early times it could be utilised for this
purpose ; and a considerable number of its
productions take us back to a very primitive
stage of art. The most ancient of the
Cypriote figurines follow oriental and
Asiatic traditions. They represent Astarte,
the goddess of fecundity ; they are modelled
with the thumb, with lines traced with a
point, and bands of black or red for all
their ornament. " The head is almost
formless," says M. Perrot;* "a curved,
beak-like nose, a pair of large round eyes,
and monstrous ears may be distinguished,

Fig. 224.—
Terra-cotta
from Cyprus.
(Louvre.)

each of the latter pierced with two holes at the place
of attachment of the heavy elaborate earrings worn by
Phœnician and Babylonian women. The arms are bent
round horizontally, so that the hands lie
either on the chest or the stomach. . . .
The extreme width of the hips seems to
give a promise of maternity. The scratches
on the clay may be meant to represent
a loin-cloth. The legs are held tightly
closed ; they taper rapidly downwards,
and end in feet scarcely large enough
to give stability." To the same period
belong those vases in the form of animals
or human heads, those strange statuettes
of foot-soldiers, of riders covered with speckled armour,
and of war-chariots, which one might suppose to be

Fig. 225.—Cypri-
ote terra-cotta.
(Louvre.)

* Perrot and Chipiez, *History of Art in Phœnicia, etc.*, vol. ii., p. 148 f.

modelled by children. Cypriote figurines are so numerous, however, that they can be arranged in a scale so as to mark without gaps the gradual stages in the progress of the art.

In Cyprus the grotesque god Pygmæus, whom we noticed in Phœnicia, is often met with, and he offers the same characteristics here as on the coast. We have always the mixture of the pseudo-Egyptian and pseudo-Assyrian styles combined in different degrees with the archaic Greek style.

Fig. 226. Cypriote terra-cotta. (Louvre.)

We will cite, following M. Heuzey, some statuettes of women with their hair dressed in Egyptian fashion, and marked by

Fig. 227.— Cypriote terra-cotta. (Louvre.)

the gesture of the divine mother, holding her hand to her breast, and by the gesture of the goddess of generation (fig. 227); this last, which reminds us of the Aphrodite of Cnidos, is not found in purely oriental art. Here we catch in the very act the fusion of Asiatic traditions with Hellenic ideas. Such was the skill of Cypriote artists in pottery that they manufactured terra-cotta statues of life-size; in this case they have all the characteristics that we noticed in statuary.

Phœnician vessels carried far away into the whole basin of the Mediterranean the products of Phœnician, Rhodian, and Cypriote pottery. At Corinth, for instance, a small aryballus in the form of a helmeted head, of pseudo-Egyptian style and of

Phœnician workmanship, was found. The helmet covers the whole head, except the eyes, nose, and

Fig. 228.—Mask from Carthage. (Louvre.)

mouth. There is an Egyptian cartouche containing the name of the king Uahabra (Apries), B.C. 599—569.

On the site of Carthage, a large mask in terra-cotta coloured reddish-brown was disinterred, which recalls at once the mask of Amrith and the lids of the Egyptian sarcophagi in human form (fig. 228). The hair is dressed in Egyptian fashion, the ears pierced to receive rings, and the cheeks marked with a groove at the natural limit of the beard. The modelling alone is rather Assyrian, and shows signs of Asiatic softness. In the excavations near the harbours I obtained one of the most remarkable examples of Punic pottery that can be cited (fig. 229). The cheerful smile of this head of Astarte gives it a strong family likeness to the head of Tanit on Carthaginian coins, and even to the archaic heads of Athena on the most ancient tetradrachms of Athens.

Fig. 229.—Terra-cotta mask from Carthage. (Cabinet des Médailles.)

The terra-cottas found at Tharras and at Sulci in Sardinia, present the same types and the same hybrid character as those of all Phœnician countries. Even the Chaldæan goddess has been observed among them, nude, in full face, holding her hands to her breast, and sometimes disguised in an Egyptian head-dress; figures of Pygmies, and of Astarte sitting on a throne, holding a pigeon or a lunar disk, have also been found.

Thus, from one end of the Mediterranean to the other, wherever the Phœnicians established their factories, they carried with them their hybrid art, in which the fusion of the elements is not sufficiently marked to prevent those that are borrowed from being recognised. The dissection and analysis of each of the products of Phœnician art, both in the terra-cottas and in sculpture, enable us to restore to Assyria, Egypt, and Greece what belongs to each of them ; this work done, nothing is left which is the property of the Phœnicians except the execution.

§ VII. Phœnician Glass.

According to Pliny's testimony the invention of glass has long been attributed to the Phœnicians. The following is a translation of his account : " In that part of Syria which is called Phœnicia, and which lies next to Judæa, a marsh named Cendevia exists at the foot of Mount Carmel. It is regarded as the source of the river Belus (Nahr-Halu), which, after a course of five miles, falls into the Mediterranean not far from the colony of Ptolemais. The waters of this river flow slowly; they are deep, muddy and unhealthy, but religious rites have made them sacred. The Belus only deposits sand at its mouth ; and this sand, formerly unfit for any use, becomes white and pure as soon as the waves of the sea have rolled and washed it. The bank measures at the most five hundred paces, and yet for many centuries this small space has sufficed for the manufacture of glass.   It is related that nitre-merchants, alighting on this shore, were about to prepare their meal, when they perceived that there were no stones to support the pots.   They ran in all directions without finding any, and then in despair they took the blocks of nitre with which the vessels were laden and made an impromptu furnace.   But scarcely was the fire lighted, when the salt melting mixed with the sand, and streams of a transparent liquid, unknown till then, were seen to flow.   Such was the origin of glass." *

It is easy enough to recognise the kernel of historical truth contained in the fable echoed by Pliny.   The Phœnician merchants having lighted their fire by chance in the cavity of a rock which concentrated the heat, obtained a commencement of vitrification of nitric salt : in this no doubt the invention of the Phœnicians consisted.   They had discovered white transparent glass, while before them the Egyptians and the Assyrians only knew an opaque glass produced by the combustion of certain plants.

Opaque glass, or rather glass paste, seems to be of Egyptian origin.   The vitreous substance serves as a varnish to terra-cotta from the time of the first dynasty, and it is found thus employed on the posts of the sepulchral door of the step-pyramid at Sakkara.   In later times it is applied as a glaze to scarabæi, sepulchral figurines, and paintings.   Soon it was perceived that this material had consistency enough to be used by itself: "From that time," says M. Frœhner, "the

* Pliny, *Hist. Nat.*, xxxvi. 67.

manufacture of what we call glass-ware, that is to say, of small ornaments, beads, armlets, and figurines of opaque glass, isochrome, or of several colours, was invented; it did not stop here, and commerce spread its products everywhere." * The invention of glass-blowing soon followed: the oldest coloured glass vase known bears the name of Thothmes III. (Eighteenth Dynasty). White glass appears in Egypt much later; bottles of trans-parent glass, preserved at the British Museum, are of the Twenty-sixth Dynasty.

In Chaldæa and Assyria, the progress must have been the same as in Egypt; the vitreous substance was employed at first as varnish on bricks, statuettes and vases; then opaque glass and finally transparent glass were arrived at gradually, perhaps under the in-fluence of Egypt.

Fig. 230. — Transparent glass vase bearing name of Sargon. (British Museum.)

Assyrian objects of vitreous paste, such as rings, necklace-beads, small vases, are not rare in our museums; but transparent white glass seems to have been imported from Phœnicia, and never used to more than a limited extent in Mesopotamia. The celebrated transparent glass vase of Sargon (B.C. 722—705) at the British Museum is well known: in spite of its cuneiform inscription, it is Phœnician in style and matter, so that we are obliged to suppose that it was executed in the workshops of Sidon at the time when Sargon was master of the country. " This

* W. Frœhner, *La Verrerie Antique, Coll. Charvet*, p. 10.

vase," says M. Frœhner, "is the prototype of the
unguent-flasks of which we have so many specimens
in alabaster (*alabastra*) of Egyptian and Phœnician
manufacture. Very heavy in form, and consequently
of a very archaic style, it resembles a purse ; its walls
are thick, and two square appendages form the handles.
The technical process followed in its manufacture is
no less primitive, for it was not blown ; the workman
took a piece of cooled glass ; then with a lathe he
rounded the body and hollowed out the interior, exactly
as if he were working in alabaster. To put it in its
true place, we must remember that the Phœnicians were
the first to produce white glass of this purity of tone."

But before chance taught them to utilise the fine
sand on the banks of the Belus and to manufacture
from it that fine transparent glass so much vaunted
by ancient authors, the Phœnicians had borrowed from
their neighbours the Egyptians and Assyrians the
art of employing vitrifiable matter as enamel. At
Rhodes, Salzmann discovered enamelled vases of
Phœnician origin ; the geographer Scylax informs us,
on the other hand, that Phœnician merchants exported
objects of vitreous paste, that is to say, amulets and
necklace beads, even beyond the pillars of Hercules.
The necropoles of Cyprus have furnished some glasses
with thick walls, slightly transparent, which were certainly manufactured in the workshops of Tyre or Sidon.
M. G. Rey brought from Phœnicia to the Louvre an
idol of vitreous paste in the form of a cone placed
between two quadrupeds ; but the most interesting
Phœnician monument in vitreous paste that we can
cite is the necklace from Tharras in Sardinia. It is

formed of forty beads, two cylinders, four bulls' heads, and a large grotesque mask of Pygmæus (Louvre).

From the foregoing facts, it results that though the Phœnicians had for many ages a monopoly of the glass-manufacture, they cannot be considered as its inventors. They only made admirable use of the material placed by nature in their hands. The wonderful properties of the sand of the Belus are vaunted not only by Pliny but by Josephus and Tacitus. The glass manufactured by the Phœnicians was purer and clearer than that of Egypt, and consequently more sought after; not only alabastra and amphoriskoi, worthy of mediæval Venetian artists, issued from their workshops, but also false gems of coloured vitreous paste, imitating precious stones so as to be mistaken for them; hence the prosperity and reputation of

Fig. 231.—Phœnician glass. (Louvre.)

the manufactures of Tyre and Sidon. Lucian says of the complexion of a beautiful young girl that it is more diaphanous than the glass of Sidon.*

This last city was the centre of the Phœnician glass manufacture from the remotest antiquity to the Roman period; but remains of ancient furnaces, glass fragments of various colours, and scoriæ, have been found at Tyre, which attest the existence there also of important glass-works.

* *Amores*, ch. xxvi.

A fine glass flask, moulded and decorated with fruit, found at Jerusalem, has been attributed to the age of the independence of Judæa; but it may well be not earlier than the Græco-Roman period, like the ornaments of vitreous paste found in the tombs of the kings by Saulcy. These objects, as well as flakes of greenish glass, found in Palestine, probably came from the workshops of Hebron or Aleppo, which are in activity to the present day, and produce before our eyes vases which imitate the ancient specimens to perfection.

Fig. 232.—Glass vase from Jerusalem. (Louvre.)

The glass-workers of Tyre and Sidon signed their works at the Græco-Roman period, like their colleagues the potters. Those of Sidon added the name of the workshop to their own; the Greek or Latin stamp placed in relief on the thumb-rest or handles had the double advantage of giving the name of the manufacturer and of presenting a rough surface, which made it easier to hold the vase. The best known of the Sidonian glass-workers, Artas, lived in the first century of our era; the productions of his workshops are found with his mark in all the countries bordering upon the Mediterranean.

§ VIII. BRONZES AND ORNAMENTS.

One of the most original sides of Phœnician art consists of the manufacture of bronze, silver or gold dishes, on which various subjects in Assyro-Egyptian style are chiselled, engraved, or even hammered in *repoussé*. The skill of the Tyrian and Sidonian artists in this branch of art was celebrated from the highest antiquity. Solomon appeals to them for the furniture of Jehovah's Temple ; in Homer, Achilles offers as a prize for the races, in the games organised for the funeral of Patroclus, " a crater of chiselled silver, holding six measures, and without rival on earth for beauty : skilful Sidonian craftsmen made it ; " elsewhere the poet speaks of a silver crater, the work of Hephaistos, which a king of Sidon gives to Menelaus. The Phœnician dishes found at Nimroud (fig. 92), in Cyprus, and at some points of the Mediterranean coasts, are specimens of those goldsmiths' works

Fig. 233.—Patera from Palestrina. (Kircher Museum, Rome.)

which astonished Homer's Greeks. They are paterae without feet, shallow and hemispherical, such as those seen in the hands of the Assyrians in the bas-reliefs of Nineveh. The figures which decorate them are on the inner surface, and arranged in concentric zones. Engraved or hammered in *repoussé*, these subjects seem sometimes to represent, not trivial figures nor images of deities, but, on the contrary, genre pictures, and scenes like those in the Egyptian paintings. Thus the subject which decorates the silver-gilt patera (fig. 233) dis-

19

covered in 1876 at Palestrina, the ancient Præneste, in Latium, has been ingeniously explained by M. Clermont-Ganneau.* In the concentric zone bordered by a long serpent a small drama is developed in relief in a series of successive phases; it might be called "A Hunting Day, or Piety Rewarded. An oriental play in two acts and nine tableaux." We see: (1) the hero leaving his house in his war-chariot; (2) he alights to shoot a deer; (3) capture of the deer; (4) halt in a wood after the hunt; the horses are unharnessed; (5) preparations for the meal, in which the deer is to be eaten; (6) an ape attacks the hero, who, fortunately, is protected by a winged deity; (7) the ape is pursued and thrown down by the horses; (8) the hunter kills the savage beast; (9) triumphal entry into the house. The interpretation would be complete if a mythical name could be given to the hero of the drama.

Fig. 234.—Dish from Dali.   (Louvre.)

Hunting scenes of the same kind, but not so easy to explain, decorate a silver dish from Cære in Etruria, of the same manufacture as the pateræ of Phœnicia, or Cyprus. On one of the silver dishes from Dali

* *L'imagerie phénicienne et la mythologie iconologique chez les Grecs*, part i., 1880.

(Idalion) possessed by the Louvre, there is a lion hunt ; on the patera from Amathus there is the siege of a fortress.

The treasury of Curium furnished Cesnola with a large number of these pateræ in silver or electrum, on which appeared engraved subjects of the same inspiration and the same style : figures with four wings, struggling with a lion ; Astarte with her hand upon her breast, beside hideous patæci, Isis-Hathor, Egyptian sphinxes and sparrow-hawks ; hunts, battles, religious sacrifices. Everywhere on these monuments, which, as the Homeric poems show us, were so greatly sought for by the Greeks of the heroic age, and imported by Sidonian merchants, we find copies of the usual designs on the Egyptian and Assyrian monuments, an unconscious mixture of hybrid scenes, which have nothing original except this quaint amalgam itself, even more striking here than in

Fig. 235.—Handle of a bronze crater. (New York Museum.)

the other manifestations of Phœnician and Cypriote art. If we had a larger number of these curious dishes, we should find, no doubt, that the motives are little varied, often repeated, even in subjects as interesting as the Hunting Day, and that the effort of imagination here made by the Phœnician artist has been little inventive. Fortunately for the reputation

of Phœnician and Cypriote goldsmiths, other monuments show that their metallurgy was not limited to
these interesting pateræ.   Thus, for instance, Cesnola
brought from his excavations in Cyprus a fragment of

a large bronze crater, the
handles of which are decorated in the most original
fashion.   We here find
lions standing on their
hind legs holding œno-
choæ, and clothed in
fishes' scales, like the god
Anu in Assyro-Chaldæan
symbolism.

In Cypriote furniture
and ornaments we ob-
serve the same charac-
teristics of a hybrid art.
There are little silver
vases chiselled in the
Assyrian style with rare
elegance, handles of
sceptres, and other pre-
cious utensils like those
of Nineveh.   Certain
ornaments, intended for

Fig. 236.—Phœnician gold ornament.

women's head-dresses, are of exquisite workmanship;
so are the ear-rings, the necklaces of gold, gems
and glass; with figures of lions, rams, deer, masks
with curled beards in the Assyrian fashion, heads
of Isis-Hathor and lotus-flowers.   Some of these
necklaces and bracelets end in lions' or serpents' heads,

and form models which Greek artists needed only to copy, for they are masterpieces in their kind. We have seen that the Ninevite excavations brought to light ivory tablets carved by Phœnician artists, and imported into Mesopotamia by commerce: plaques of the same style have been obtained from Phœnicia itself: they were ornaments of precious caskets. These products of Phœnician industry were imported into all the coasts of the Mediterranean ; and, at Palestrina, in Latium, an ivory tablet was found, on which a vessel manned by rowers is engraved, similar to those in the Egyptian paintings. Ostrich-eggs, found

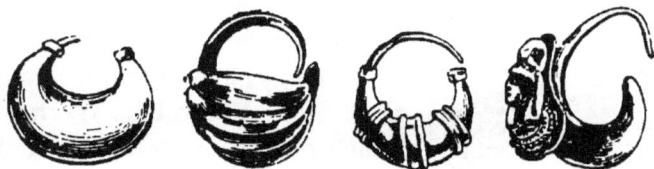

Fig. 237.—Phœnician ear-rings.

in Etruria, arranged to serve as vases, are adorned with engraved figures, the Phœnician character of which could scarcely be disputed : there are zones of warriors on foot, on horseback, and in their war-chariots ; files of animals, fights of lions with bulls in semi-Egyptian style ; the frame of these scenes is borrowed from Assyria ; the whole is relieved by iridescent colours.*

If we had in Phœnicia bas-reliefs like those of Assyria, and paintings like those of Egypt, we should be able to give some account of those brilliant stuffs of dyed purple, described by classical antiquity with so much enthusiasm. It was to the Tyrian god, Mel-

* See Perrot and Chipiez, *History of Art in Phœnicia, etc.* vol. ii. p. 404 f.

karth, that tradition assigned the invention of this dye, obtained, as it is well known, from the juice of a marine shell, the *murex*, which is found especially on the coast of Phœnicia. We can only affirm, according to literary testimony, that the workshops of Tyre and Sidon produced stuffs in abundance, the colour of which, as the ancients remarked, instead of being altered and deteriorated by a bright light, was only rendered more vivid and brilliant by it.

§ IX. ENGRAVED GEMS.

The glyptic art, through the multiplicity of its productions, is one of the principal elements of Phœnician

Fig. 238.—Cylinder in the De Clercq collection (after Menant).

archæology, and teaches us more than the miserable fragments which remain of pottery or sculpture. Here, more clearly than in the other branches of art, we find imitation of Egypt and Assyria taken for granted, as a witness of the poverty of invention of the Phœnician intellect. Two cylinders exist in the De Clercq collection which bear a cuneiform inscription by the side of Egyptian figures. That which we give as an example (fig. 238), after M. Menant,* is the seal of "Annipi, son of Addume the Sidonian." Thus the owner of the cylinder is a Phœnician ; he has inscribed his name in Assyrian beside the god Set,† Reseph, the

* Menant, *La Glyptique orientale*, t. ii.

† The figure representing the god Set has not a hawk's head, as M. Babelon states, following M. Menant. Here, as always, Set has the head of a nondescript animal, somewhat resembling an ass!

warrior god, and Horus with the hawk's head. The style of the inscription, like that of the figures, betrays, however, the unskilful hand of the Sidonian imitator.

We possess, on the other hand, cylinders on which the figures are purely Assyrian, while the inscription is in Phœnician or Aramaic characters. This one at the British Museum is the "seal of Akadban, son of Gebrod the eunuch, worshipper of Hadad" (fig. 239). The style of the figures and the details of the costume are so clearly Assyrian that this monument discloses to us the plagiaristic method to which the idle imagination of the Phœnicians had recourse. These mer-chants found it sim-pler and speedier to appropriate Assyrian or Persian cylinders, satisfied with having

Fig. 239.—Cylinder at the British Museum (after Menant).

their names engraved upon them.   They did not blush to wear during their life the ornaments of other nations, until their ashes should rest in sarcophagi stolen from the Egyptians.

However, in Cyprus, they tried to engrave cylinders for themselves.   The recent excavations have dis-interred a large quantity of them, and, by the side of cylinders brought from the continent by commerce, some have been found which were certainly manu-factured in the island.   But what astonishes us in these monuments is their extreme barbarism; the design is most summary, the figures are scarcely sketched, and the chisel has only made rough scratches on the jasper, the hæmatite, or the chalcedony. And even the figures of men or animals, the trees and the geometrical ornaments with which the Cypriote cylinders are covered, are copied by unskilful workmen from the productions of the Assyro-Persian or Egyptian glyptic art.

After all, Phœnician cylinders are rare enough. Practical before everything, the merchants of Tyre and Carthage preferred flat seals of multiple form to cylinders, the use of which was difficult; they manufactured scarabæi, scarabœoids, ellipsoids, cones, octagonal conoids, these last especially in the Aramæo-Persian period, and lastly bezels for rings. Among the numerous gems which have come down to us, and which must be attributed either to the Phœnicians themselves or to the Aramæan populations of Syria, some have still preserved their mounting: a ring in the form of a horse-shoe enabled the owner to turn the stone on its axis and to hang it from a necklace. The inscription of one or two lines, when it exists, gives the name of the owner, his father's name, and sometimes his quality. The subjects, naturally more limited than those of the cylinders, are always of Egyptian, Persian, or Assyro-Chaldæan inspiration. There are, for instance, the winged and radiated disk, deer, lions, bulls, sphinxes, gryphons, the divine bust in a winged disk, a pontiff sacrificing at an altar, or in adoration before the pyreum. The Louvre possesses a scarabæoid of red agate acquired in Mesopotamia by M. de Sarzec; a god is seen upon it, holding a serpent in each hand, like the Egyptian Horus; he has four wings, and bears on his head the solar disk supported by two horns.

The name, Baalnathan, indicates that its owner was probably an Ammonite or a Moabite. It may be admitted, with M. de Vogüé,* that among the Phœnician, Aramæan and Jewish intagli, those in which Egyptian influence appears exclusive are the most ancient, that is to say, anterior to the Assyrian rule in Syria.

Fig. 240.— Scarabæoid seal.

From the seventh century B.C. the action of Assyria appears in the Aramæo-Phœnician glyptic art, sometimes allied to the Egyptian influence, sometimes exclusive as on a scarabæus in the museum at Vienna, bearing the name of Akhotmelek, wife of Josuah, on which a deity is seen sitting on a throne and receiving a libation from a standing pontiff (fig. 240). A fine scarabæus in green jasper at the British Museum (fig. 241), with the name, in Phœnician characters, of *Hodo, the scribe*, shows a

Fig. 241.—Scarabœoid seal (after Menant).

principal scene inspired by an Assyrian cylinder, while on the field the Egyptian *crux ansata* figures, and the scarabæoidal form of the gem is certainly of Pharaonic origin.

In this hybrid coupling of Egyptian to Assyrian art the least trained observer can discern what belongs to each of the two constituent elements. The position of the outstretched wings, one raised, the other lowered, before and not behind the figures, the uræi, the pshent, the shenti, the hawk-headed gods, the lotus-flower, the sphinx, and the *crux ansata*, properly belong to Egypt. The long-fringed robe of

* *Revue archéol.* t. xxvii. 1868, p. 432 ff.

the priests, the curled hair and beard, the cylindrical
tiara, the fire-altar, the sacred tree, and the lions are,
besides other features, the property of Assyria and
Chaldæa. The writing alone is Aramaic or Phœnician.
At the Achæmenid epoch, seals are found in Phœnicia,
the workmanship of which shows signs of Persian
influence; sometimes even the legend, although
Aramæan, gives us a Persian name.

From the fourth century B.C., lastly, the glyptic art,
following the same laws as the other branches of art,
is rapidly invaded by the Greek genius. Engraved
stones with Cypriote or Phœnician legends show
subjects incontestably interpreted by Greek artists, even
when the incidents are oriental; at last we find Greek
subjects, so that the oriental influence is only shown by
the legend, which still remains Phœnician. We are
then arrived at the age of Alexander, and the ancient
civilisations of the East have ceased to live.

INDEX.

Nebuchadnezzar (*contd.*),—
builds Tower of the Seven Lights, 73.
restores E-saggil, 78.
restores E-zida, 78.
builds walls of Babylon, 80.
Nebuzar-adan, 209.
Necropolis,—
at Mugheir, 14, 20, 21, 38.
at Warka, 38.
at Marath, 253-5.
at Sidon, 255, 256.
at Dali, 259.
at Amathus, 260.
at Mehdia, 260.
at Thina, 261.
at Tyre, 254.
at Adlun, 254.
at Gebal, 256.
at Caralis, 260.
at Tharras, 260.
at Jebel Kawi, 261.
Nehemiah, 232.
Nejef, 50.
Nero, 141, 211.
Nicanor, Gate of, 220.
Nimroud, 51, 52, 61, 62, 72, 111.
Nin Girsu, 10.
Nineveh,—
walls of, 6.
vaulting at, 13.
extent of, 81.
Ninus, 119.
Nymphio, 201.

Oannes, 2.
Onyx, 44.
Ophel, hill of, 205, 210, 231, 232.
Orientation of Chaldæan buildings, 8.
of Assyrian buildings, 67.
Ornaments, 142, 143.
Oppert, 46, 79, 81.
Ourdeys, 82.
Ovoid gems, 45.

Painted bricks,—
Chaldæan, 19.
Assyrian, 74, 116-20.
Persian, 167-72.
Painting,—
on façades of Chaldæan palaces, 18, 19.
on stucco in Assyrian palaces, 56, 114, 115.
on Assyrian bas-reliefs, 115, 116.
on Assyrian vases, 122.
on walls of Persian buildings, 159, 172.
in Cypriote pottery, 280.
Palace,—
of Gudea at Tello, 8-22.
of Sargon at Khorsabad, 66-72.
of Cyrus at Madar-i-Soleiman, 148-50.
of Darius at Nakhsh-i-Rustam, 150.
of Xerxes, 150-8.
of Artaxerxes, 157.
of Solomon, 231.
Palestrina, 290, 293.
Palm-wood, use of, in roofing houses, 15, 60, 158.
pillars of, 63.
Paphos, 241, 242.
Parthians, 12, 56.
Partitions of rooms, 13, 54, 55.
Pasargadæ, 147, 148, 150, 151, 160.
Passages, vaulted, at Tello, 14.
Patæci, 264.
Pateræ, 127, 128, 289, 290.
Patesi, 8, 46, 81.
Pausanias, on size of Babylon, 79.
Pediments, 76, 77, 175, 235, 256, 267.
Pendentives, 159 (note).
Perrot,—
on Assyrian voussoirs, 58, 59.
on gates of Balawat, 126, 127.

Seals (*contd.*),—
  Median, 146.
  Persian, 180-3.
  Hittite, 203.
  Jewish, 230.
  Phœnician, 294-8.
Selamlik, 16.
Seleucids, 210, 234.
Semiramis, 76, 80, 119.
Senkereh, 2, 21.
Sennacherib, 60, 66, 67, 72, 92, 93, 103, 113, 139 (note).
Sepharvaim, 2, 42.
Sepulchral architecture in Assyria, 50.
  towers in Persia, 175.
Seraglio, 16, 69.
Sesostris, 112, 201.
Set, the god, 294.
Sewage, disposal of, 20.
Shalmaneser III., 72, 89, 126.
"Sharur," 6.
Shatt el-Hai, 3.
"Shenti," 264.
Shew-bread, 226.
Sidon, 247, 250, 255, 289.
Siloam, 232, 235.
Silver, use of, in Chaldæa and Assyria, 21.
Sin, the god, 16.
Sinjerli, 188.
Sippara, 2.
Sirens, bronze, 129-30.
Sirpurla, 3.
Sivan, 4.
Smith, G., 72.
Sockets for pivot of door, 17, 18.
Solomon, 205, 206, 208, 209, 210, 211, 215, 219, 221, 224, 232, 235.
  palace of, 231-2.
  porch of, 209, 211.
Solus, 258.
Sophia, church of Saint, 56, 159 (note).
Sphinxes,—
  Persian, 183.

Sphinxes (*contd.*),—
  Hittite, 192, 193.
  Phœnician, 263.
Stables, 17, 69, 70, 136.
Staged towers, 15, 16, 72-6, 174.
Staircases, 8, 67, 151, 152.
Standard, Assyrian, 133, 134.
State saloon in Chaldæan palace, 17.
Statues,—
  from Tello, 26-30.
  of Assur-nasir-pal, 86.
  caryatid, 86, 87.
  iconic, in Cyprus, 265.
  captured by Scipio at Carthage, 266.
  colossal, in Cyprus, 270-72.
  of priest with dove, 273.
Statuettes,—
  bronze, from Chaldæa, 35-8.
  of Canephoros, 36, 37.
  kneeling, with cone, 36.
  of figure standing upon lion, 37, 38.
  terra-cotta, from Warka, 40.
  alabaster, from Chaldæa, 42.
  terra-cotta, from Khorsabad, 121, 122.
  of Izdubar, 122.
  of Istar, 123-25.
  terra-cotta from Phœnicia and Cyprus, 277-82.
  of Divine Mother, 124, 281.
Steatite, 43, 123.
Stela,—
  the "Vulture Stela," 24-6.
  of Samsi-Rammanu, 88.
  of Assurbanipal, as Canephoros, 89.
  Hittite, from Birejik, 187.
  votive, from Carthage, 266.
Stone,—
  want of, in Mesopotamia, 4.
  staircase of, at Abu Shahrein, 8.
  scanty use of, in Assyria, 50, 65.

THE END.

www.ingramcontent.com/pod-product-compliance
Lightning Source LLC
Chambersburg PA
CBHW021124270326
41929CB00009B/1036